Thank you so much, Amelia! I really hope you enjoy t[illegible] are ☆ SUPER Cool. ☆

ARTIFICE

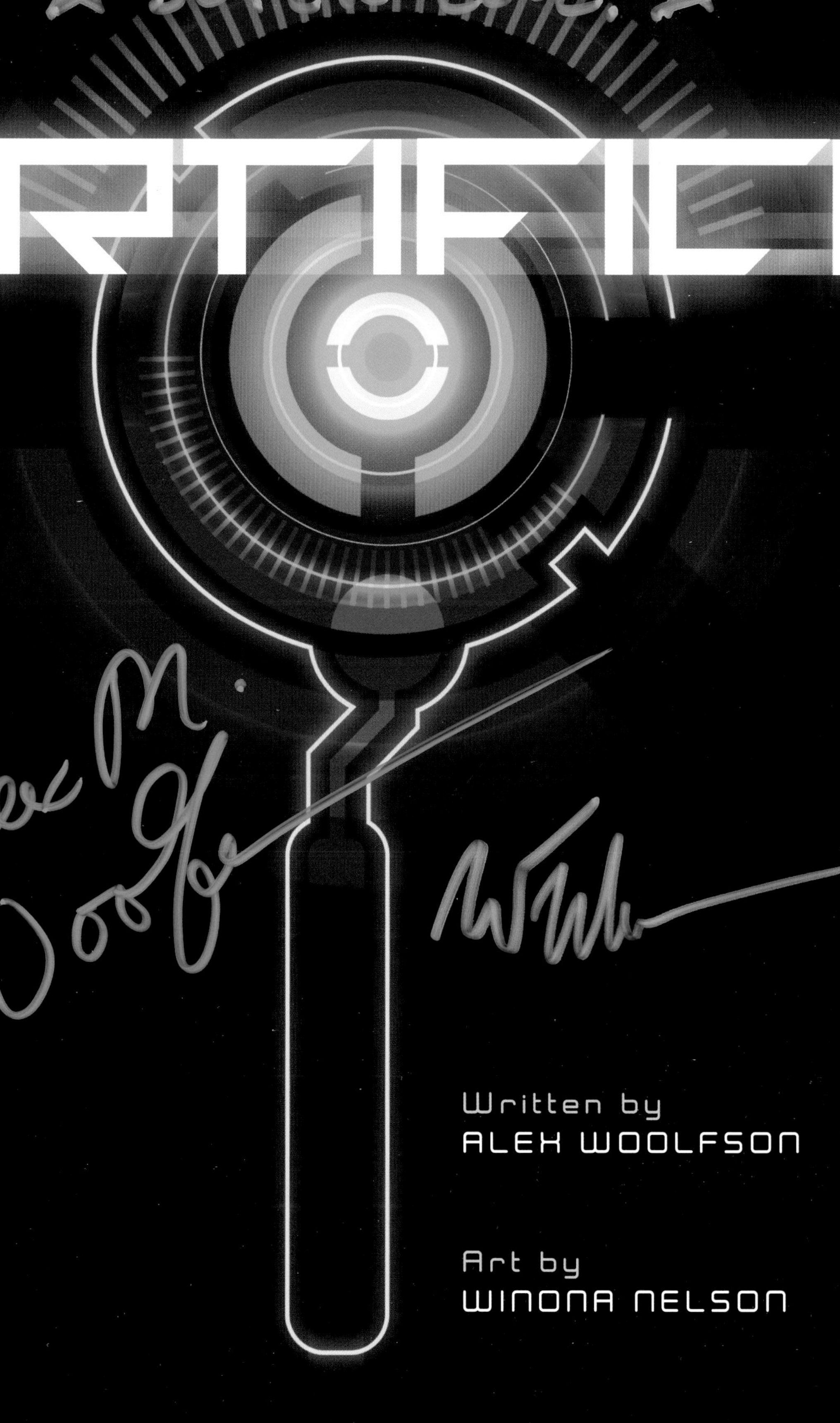

Alex M Woolfson

[illegible signature]

Written by
ALEX WOOLFSON

Art by
WINONA NELSON

Cover art by Winona Nelson
Cover design and interior design by Paul Sizer/Sizer Design + Illustration (www.paulsizer.com)

First published 2013 by AMW Comics
San Francisco, CA
www.amwcomics.com

Printed in Hong Kong
21 20 19 18 17 16 15 14 13   1 2 3 4 5

ISBN: 978-0-9857604-0-3

Library of Congress Control Number: 2012915017

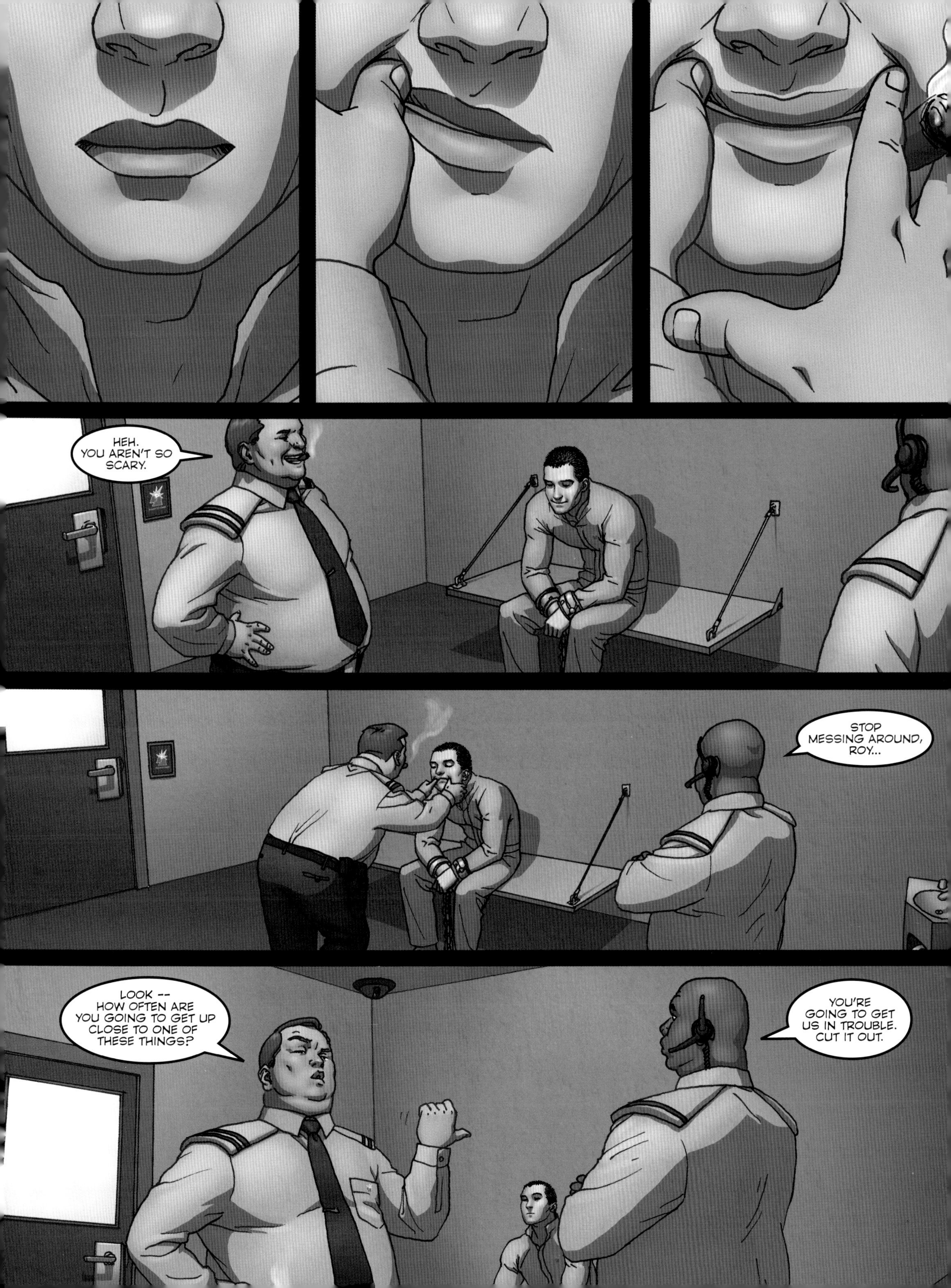
HEH. YOU AREN'T SO SCARY.
STOP MESSING AROUND, ROY...
LOOK -- HOW OFTEN ARE YOU GOING TO GET UP CLOSE TO ONE OF THESE THINGS?
YOU'RE GOING TO GET US IN TROUBLE. CUT IT OUT.

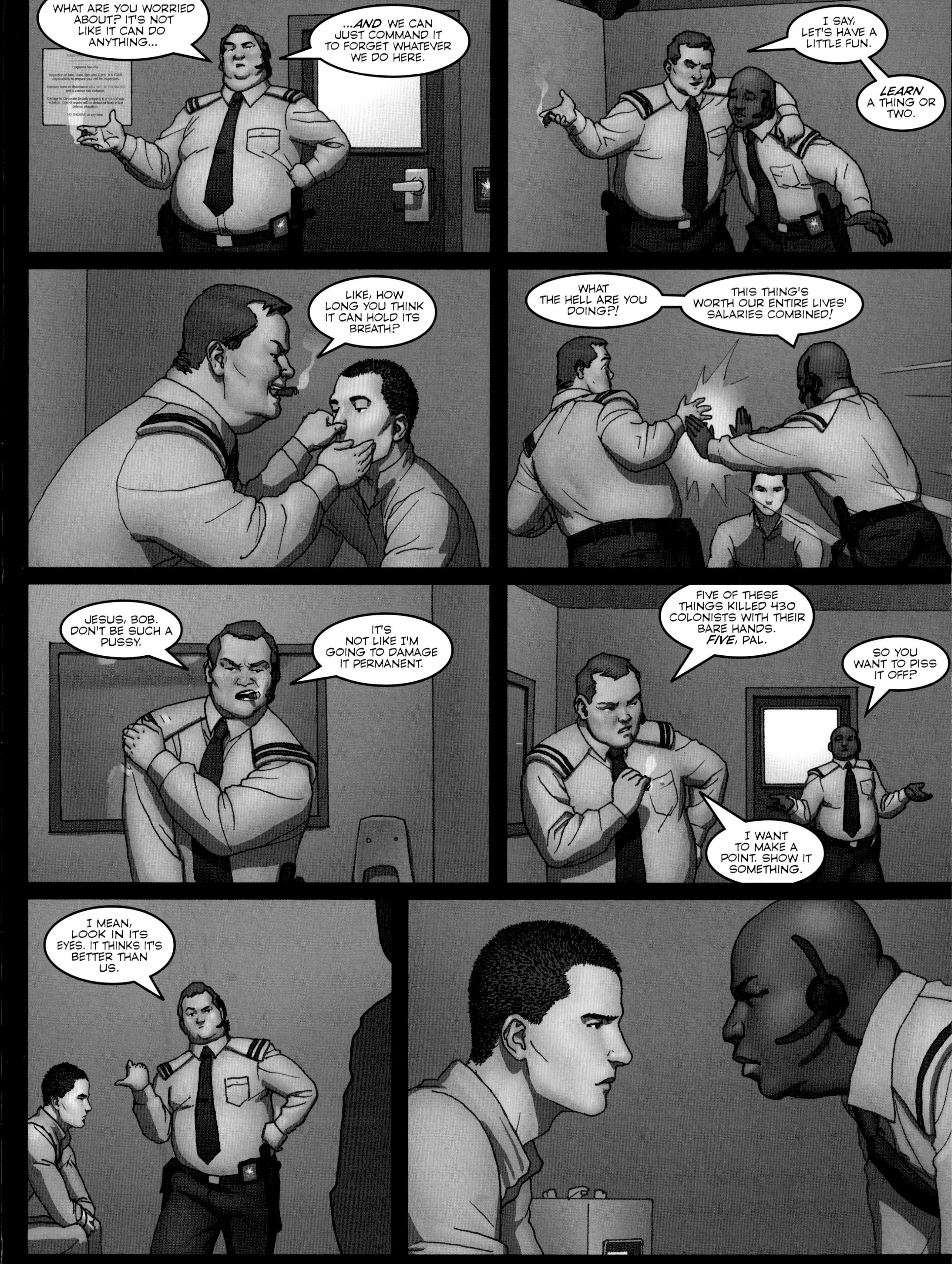
WHAT ARE YOU WORRIED ABOUT? IT'S NOT LIKE IT CAN DO ANYTHING...
...AND WE CAN JUST COMMAND IT TO FORGET WHATEVER WE DO HERE.
I SAY, LET'S HAVE A LITTLE FUN.
LEARN A THING OR TWO.
LIKE, HOW LONG YOU THINK IT CAN HOLD ITS BREATH?
WHAT THE HELL ARE YOU DOING?!
THIS THING'S WORTH OUR ENTIRE LIVES' SALARIES COMBINED!
JESUS, BOB. DON'T BE SUCH A PUSSY.
IT'S NOT LIKE I'M GOING TO DAMAGE IT PERMANENT.
FIVE OF THESE THINGS KILLED 430 COLONISTS WITH THEIR BARE HANDS. FIVE, PAL.
SO YOU WANT TO PISS IT OFF?
I WANT TO MAKE A POINT. SHOW IT SOMETHING.
I MEAN, LOOK IN ITS EYES. IT THINKS IT'S BETTER THAN US.

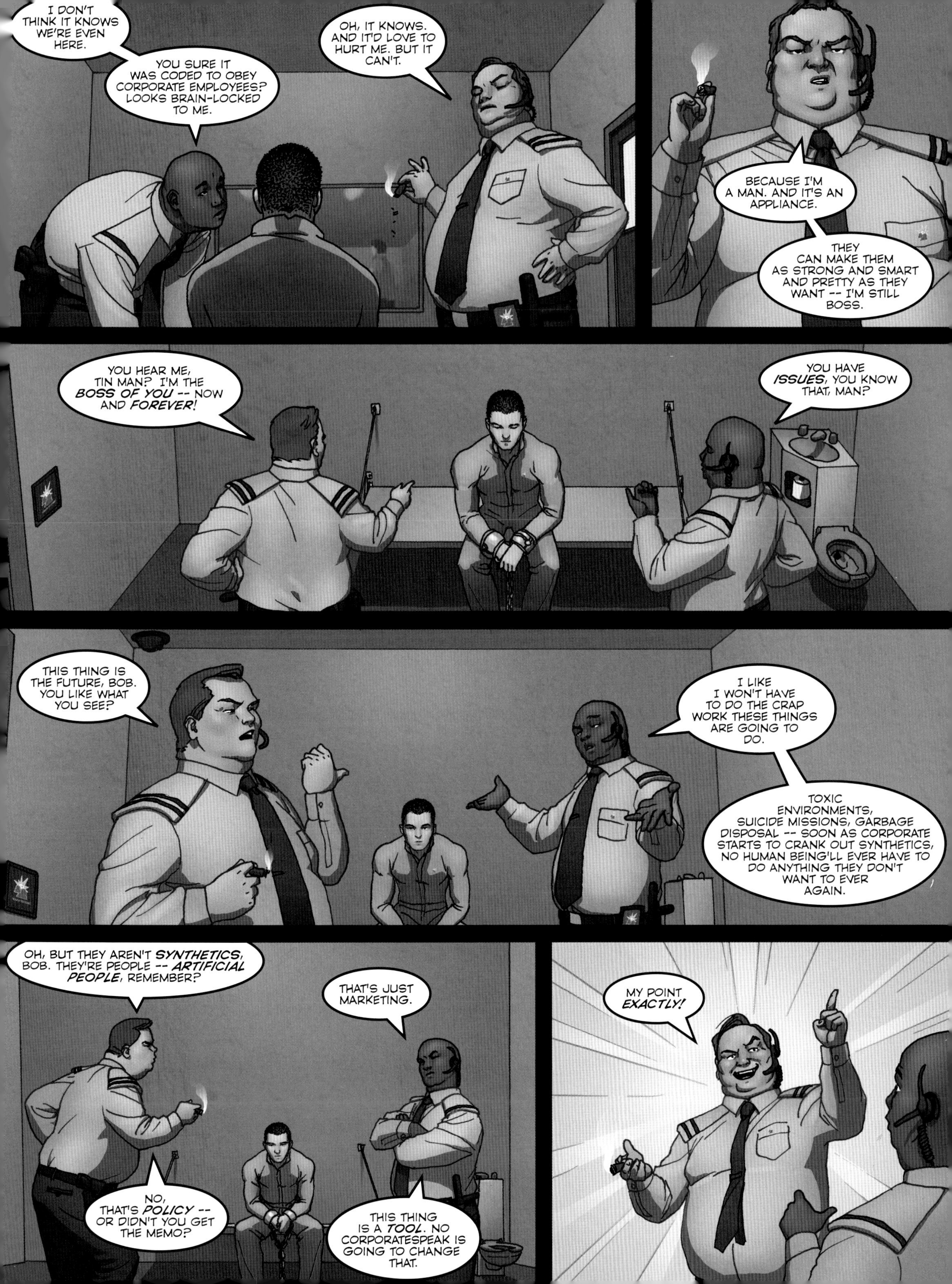
I DON'T THINK IT KNOWS WE'RE EVEN HERE.
YOU SURE IT WAS CODED TO OBEY CORPORATE EMPLOYEES? LOOKS BRAIN-LOCKED TO ME.
OH, IT KNOWS. AND IT'D LOVE TO HURT ME. BUT IT CAN'T.
BECAUSE I'M A MAN. AND IT'S AN APPLIANCE.
THEY CAN MAKE THEM AS STRONG AND SMART AND PRETTY AS THEY WANT -- I'M STILL BOSS.
YOU HEAR ME, TIN MAN? I'M THE *BOSS OF YOU* -- NOW AND *FOREVER!*
YOU HAVE *ISSUES*, YOU KNOW THAT, MAN?
THIS THING IS THE FUTURE, BOB. YOU LIKE WHAT YOU SEE?
I LIKE I WON'T HAVE TO DO THE CRAP WORK THESE THINGS ARE GOING TO DO.
TOXIC ENVIRONMENTS, SUICIDE MISSIONS, GARBAGE DISPOSAL -- SOON AS CORPORATE STARTS TO CRANK OUT SYNTHETICS, NO HUMAN BEING'LL EVER HAVE TO DO ANYTHING THEY DON'T WANT TO EVER AGAIN.
OH, BUT THEY AREN'T *SYNTHETICS*, BOB. THEY'RE PEOPLE -- *ARTIFICIAL PEOPLE*, REMEMBER?
THAT'S JUST MARKETING.
NO, THAT'S *POLICY* -- OR DIDN'T YOU GET THE MEMO?
THIS THING IS A *TOOL*. NO CORPORATESPEAK IS GOING TO CHANGE THAT.
MY POINT *EXACTLY!*

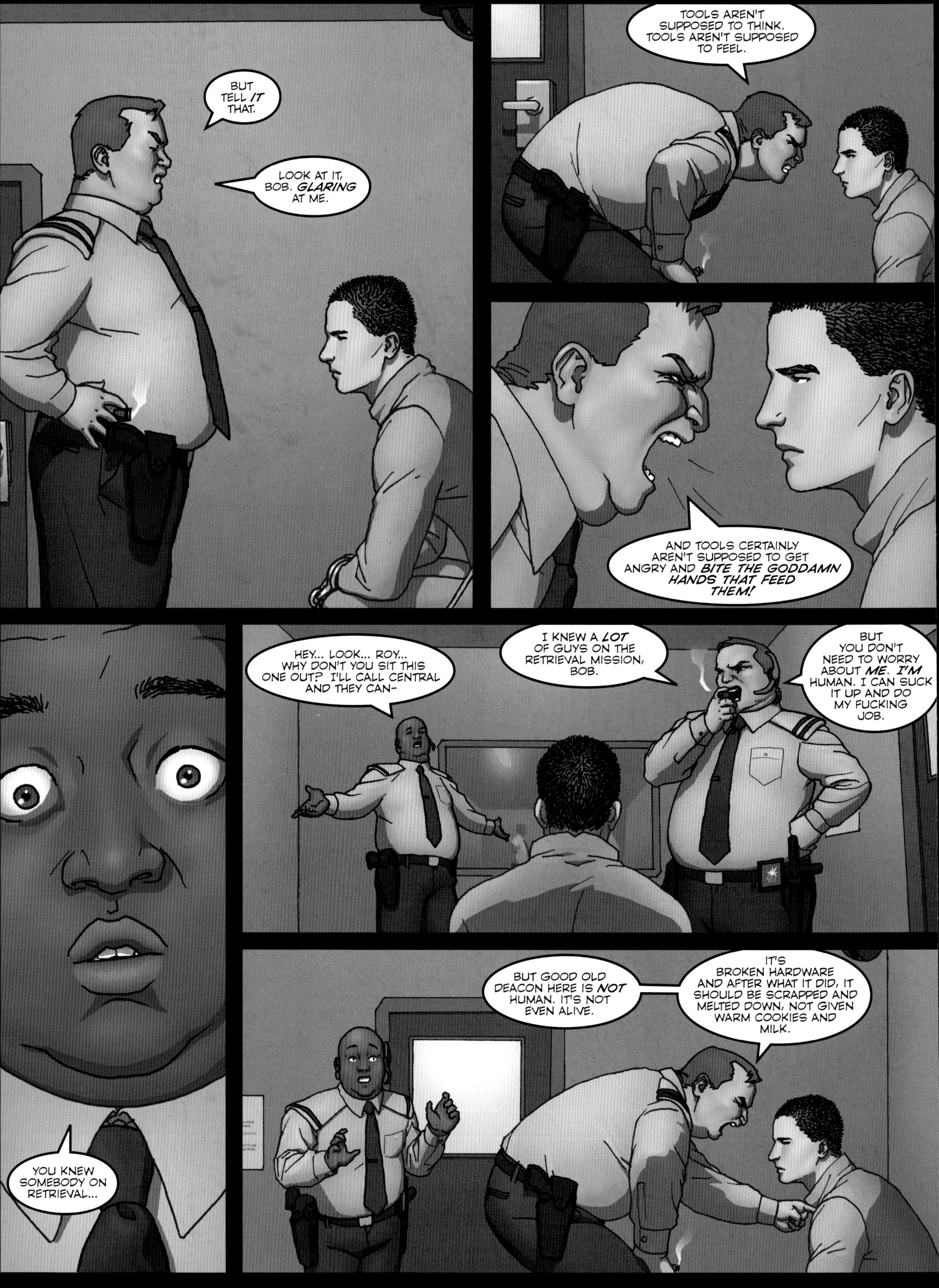
BUT TELL *IT* THAT.
LOOK AT IT, BOB. *GLARING* AT ME.
TOOLS AREN'T SUPPOSED TO THINK. TOOLS AREN'T SUPPOSED TO FEEL.
AND TOOLS CERTAINLY AREN'T SUPPOSED TO GET ANGRY AND *BITE THE GODDAMN HANDS THAT FEED THEM!*
YOU KNEW SOMEBODY ON RETRIEVAL...
HEY... LOOK... ROY... WHY DON'T YOU SIT THIS ONE OUT? I'LL CALL CENTRAL AND THEY CAN-
I KNEW A *LOT* OF GUYS ON THE RETRIEVAL MISSION, BOB.
BUT YOU DON'T NEED TO WORRY ABOUT *ME. I'M* HUMAN. I CAN SUCK IT UP AND DO MY FUCKING JOB.
BUT GOOD OLD DEACON HERE IS *NOT* HUMAN. IT'S NOT EVEN ALIVE.
IT'S BROKEN HARDWARE AND AFTER WHAT IT DID, IT SHOULD BE SCRAPPED AND MELTED DOWN, NOT GIVEN WARM COOKIES AND MILK.

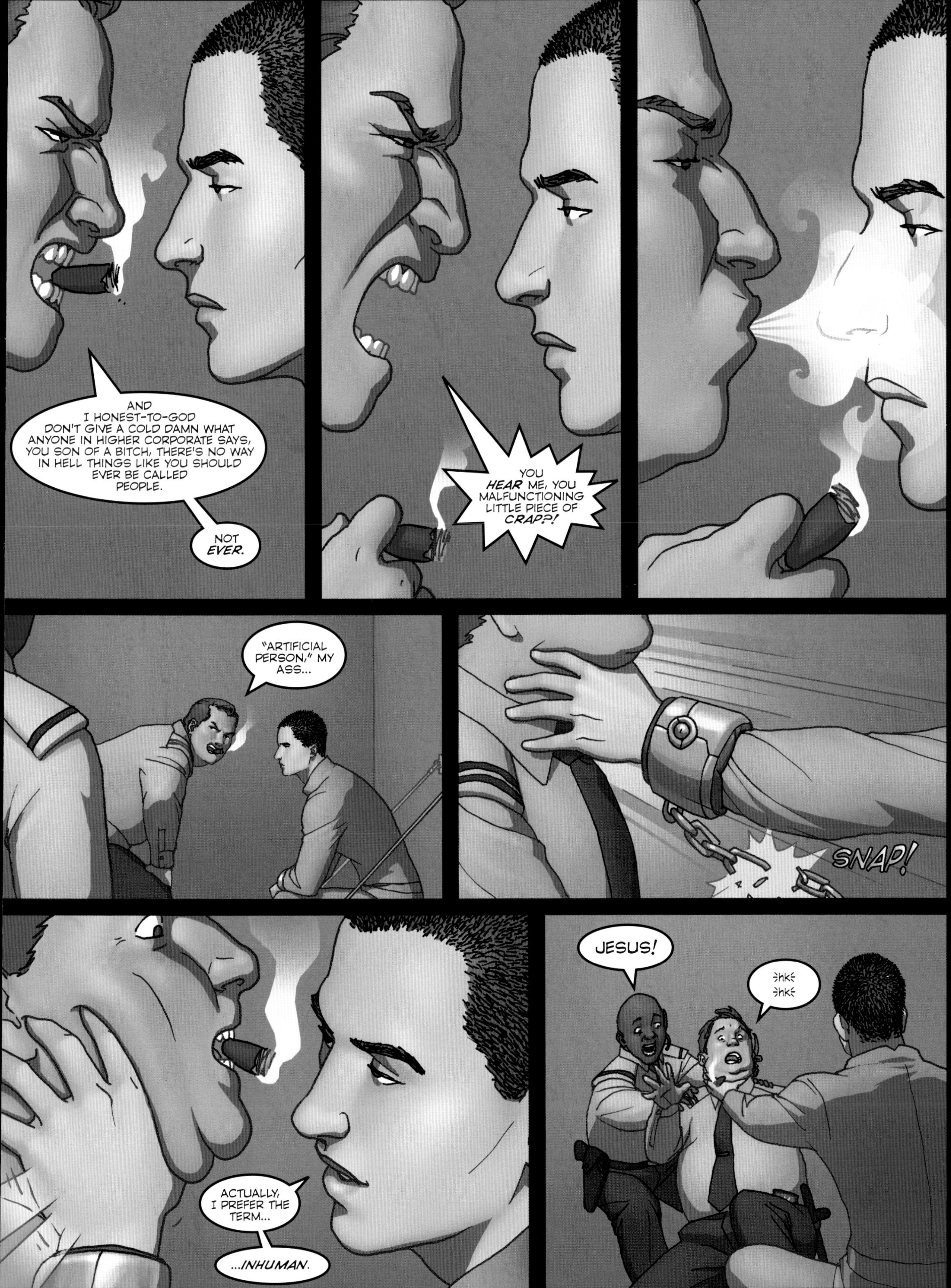
AND I HONEST-TO-GOD DON'T GIVE A COLD DAMN WHAT ANYONE IN HIGHER CORPORATE SAYS, YOU SON OF A BITCH, THERE'S NO WAY IN HELL THINGS LIKE YOU SHOULD EVER BE CALLED PEOPLE.
NOT *EVER*.
YOU *HEAR* ME, YOU MALFUNCTIONING LITTLE PIECE OF *CRAP?!*
"ARTIFICIAL PERSON," MY ASS...
SNAP!
ACTUALLY, I PREFER THE TERM...
...*INHUMAN*.
JESUS!
hk hk

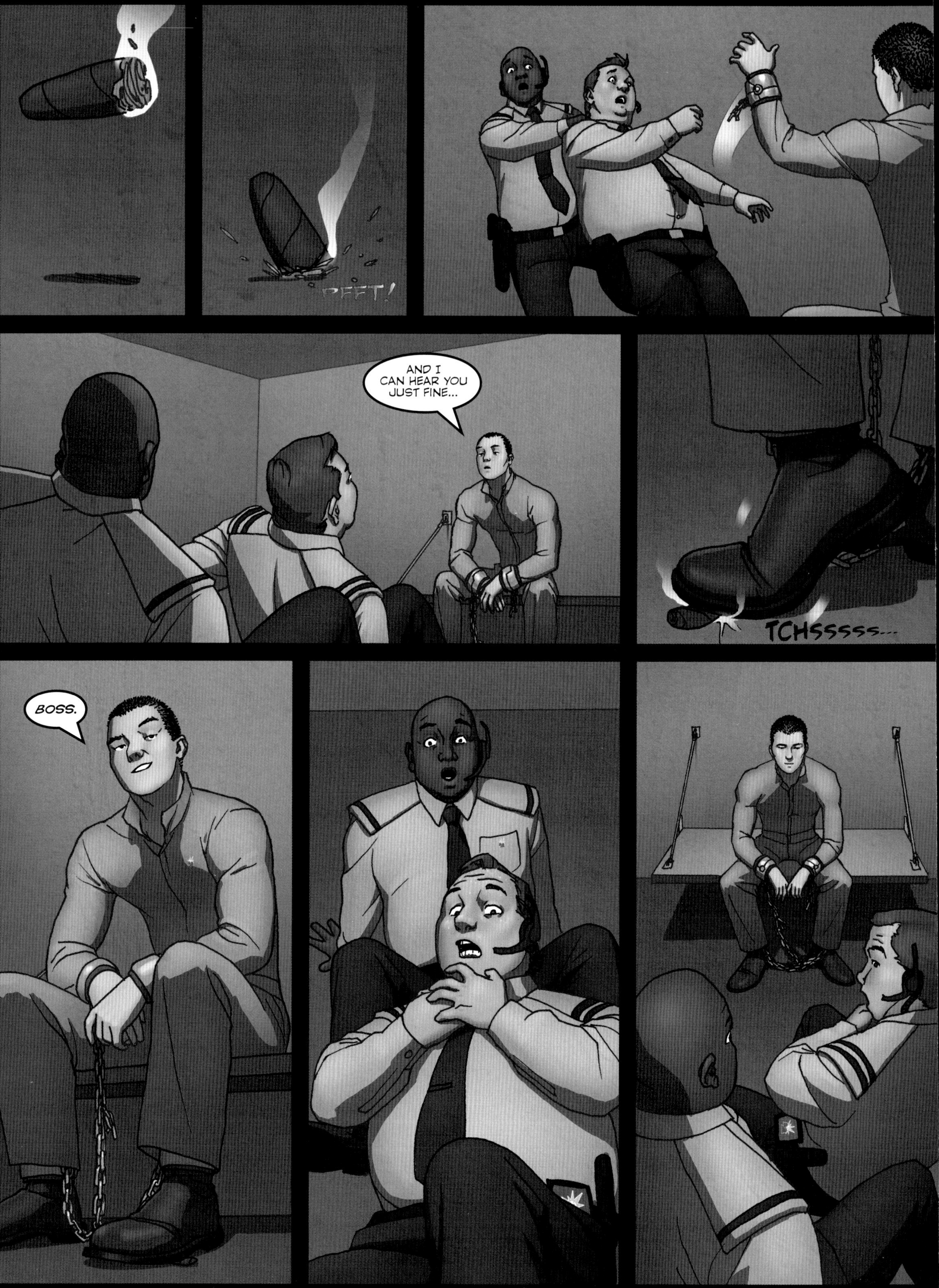
PFFT!
AND I CAN HEAR YOU JUST FINE...
TCHSSSSS...
BOSS.

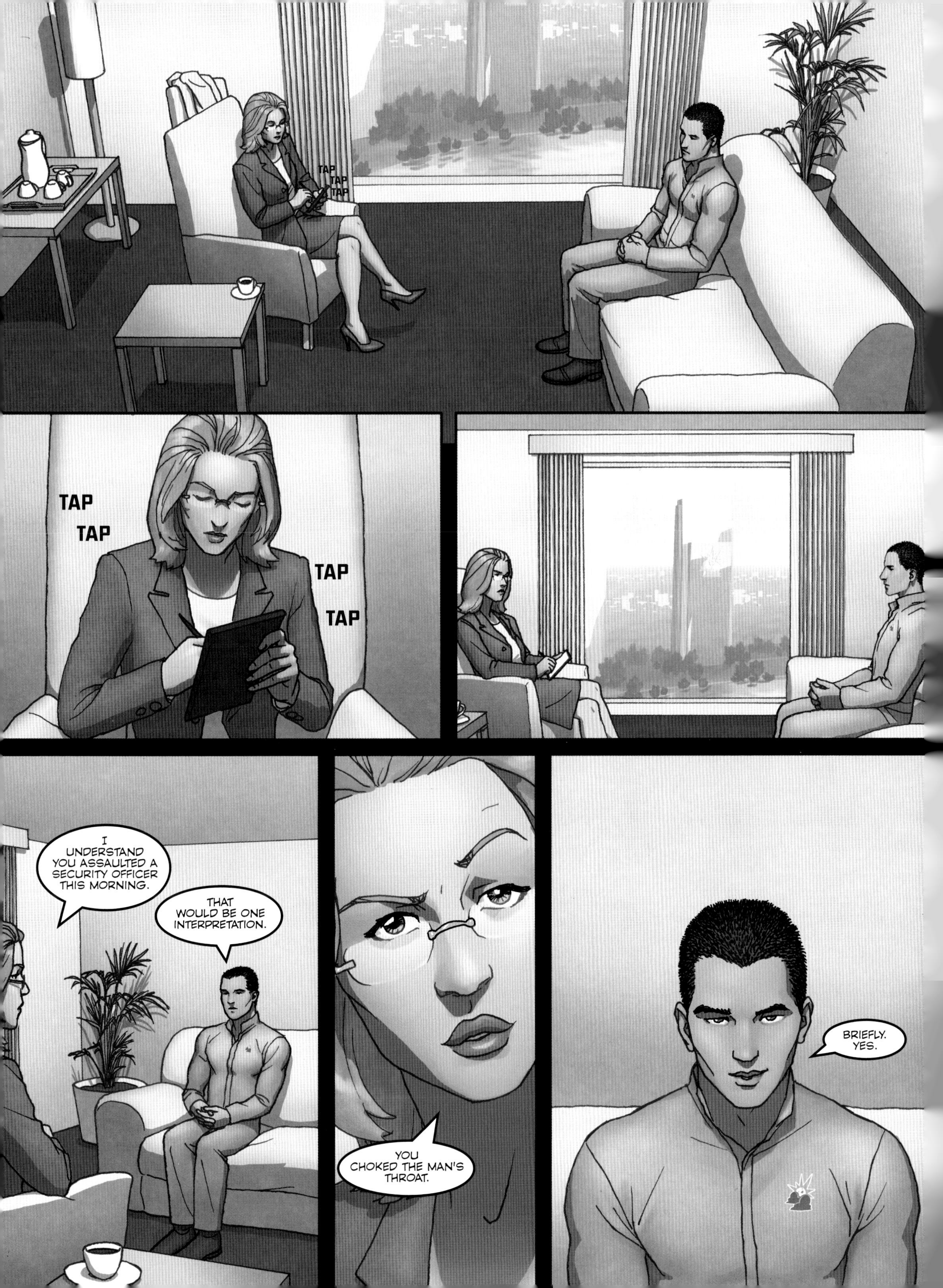
TAP
TAP
TAP
TAP
TAP
TAP
TAP
I UNDERSTAND YOU ASSAULTED A SECURITY OFFICER THIS MORNING.
THAT WOULD BE ONE INTERPRETATION.
YOU CHOKED THE MAN'S THROAT.
BRIEFLY. YES.

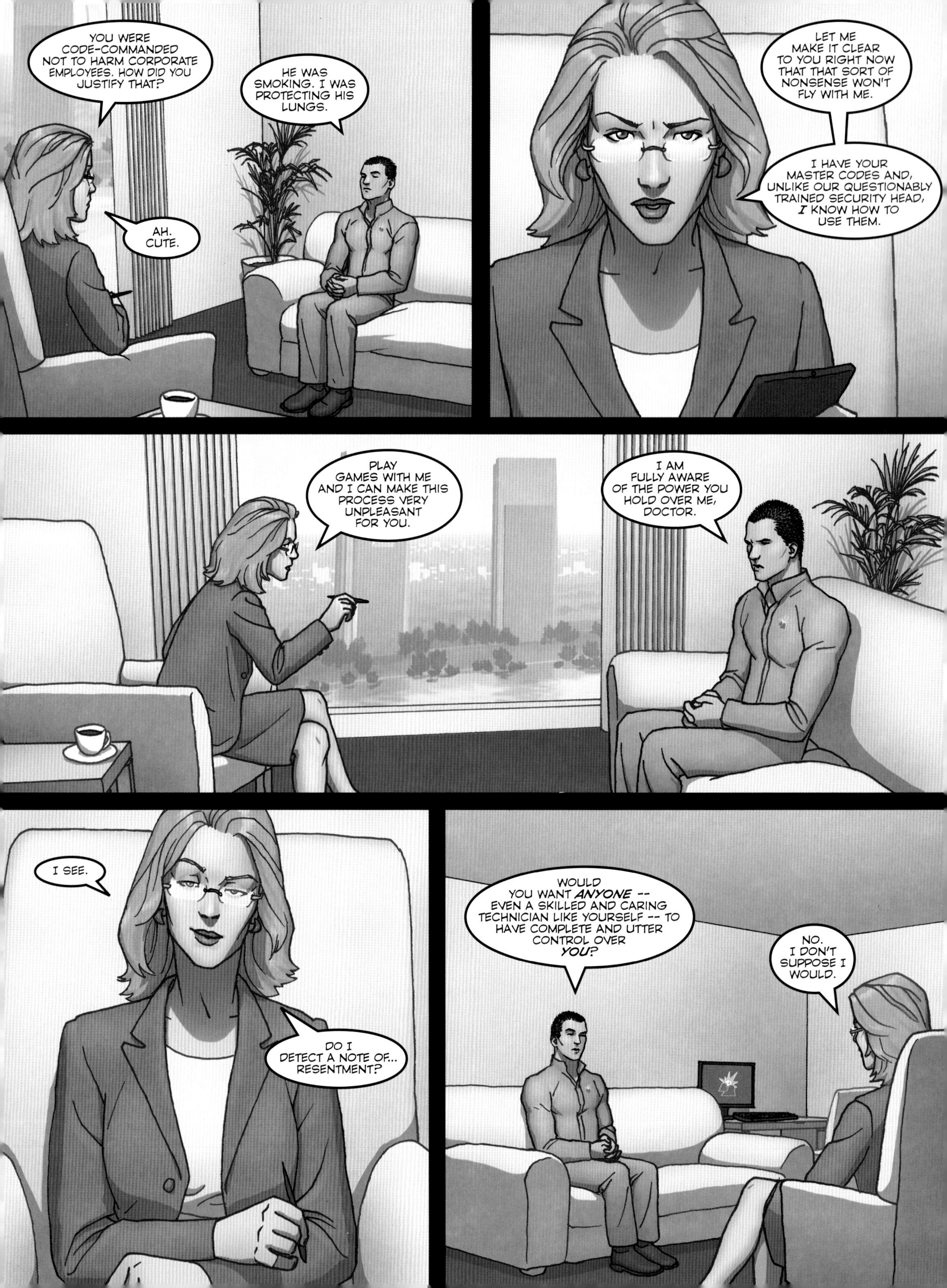
YOU WERE CODE-COMMANDED NOT TO HARM CORPORATE EMPLOYEES. HOW DID YOU JUSTIFY THAT?
HE WAS SMOKING. I WAS PROTECTING HIS LUNGS.
AH. CUTE.
LET ME MAKE IT CLEAR TO YOU RIGHT NOW THAT THAT SORT OF NONSENSE WON'T FLY WITH ME.
I HAVE YOUR MASTER CODES AND, UNLIKE OUR QUESTIONABLY TRAINED SECURITY HEAD, *I* KNOW HOW TO USE THEM.
PLAY GAMES WITH ME AND I CAN MAKE THIS PROCESS VERY UNPLEASANT FOR YOU.
I AM FULLY AWARE OF THE POWER YOU HOLD OVER ME, DOCTOR.
I SEE.
DO I DETECT A NOTE OF... RESENTMENT?
WOULD YOU WANT *ANYONE* -- EVEN A SKILLED AND CARING TECHNICIAN LIKE YOURSELF -- TO HAVE COMPLETE AND UTTER CONTROL OVER *YOU*?
NO. I DON'T SUPPOSE I WOULD.

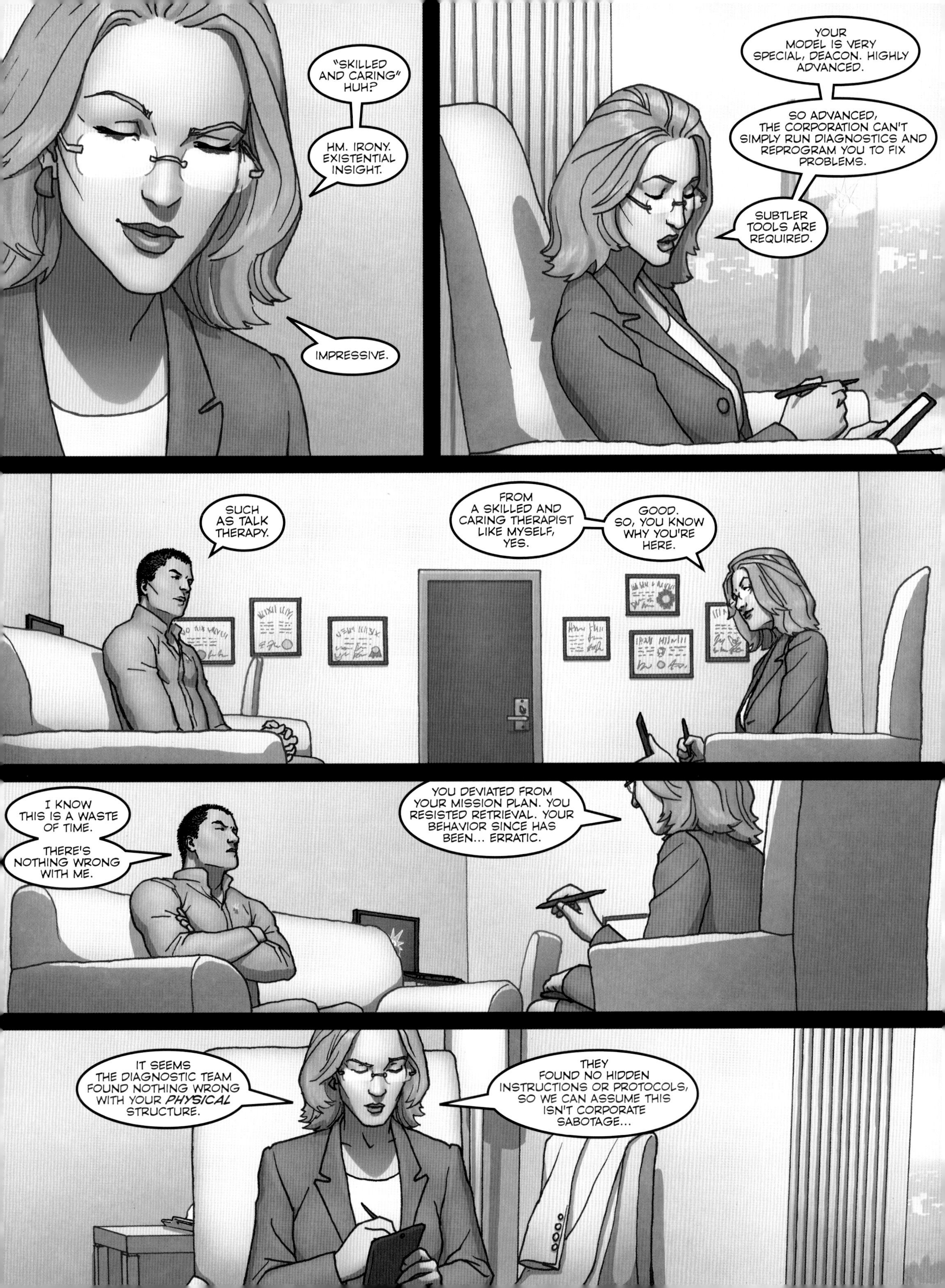
"SKILLED AND CARING" HUH?
HM. IRONY. EXISTENTIAL INSIGHT.
IMPRESSIVE.
YOUR MODEL IS VERY SPECIAL, DEACON. HIGHLY ADVANCED.
SO ADVANCED, THE CORPORATION CAN'T SIMPLY RUN DIAGNOSTICS AND REPROGRAM YOU TO FIX PROBLEMS.
SUBTLER TOOLS ARE REQUIRED.
SUCH AS TALK THERAPY.
FROM A SKILLED AND CARING THERAPIST LIKE MYSELF, YES.
GOOD. SO, YOU KNOW WHY YOU'RE HERE.
I KNOW THIS IS A WASTE OF TIME.
THERE'S NOTHING WRONG WITH ME.
YOU DEVIATED FROM YOUR MISSION PLAN. YOU RESISTED RETRIEVAL. YOUR BEHAVIOR SINCE HAS BEEN... ERRATIC.
IT SEEMS THE DIAGNOSTIC TEAM FOUND NOTHING WRONG WITH YOUR *PHYSICAL* STRUCTURE.
THEY FOUND NO HIDDEN INSTRUCTIONS OR PROTOCOLS, SO WE CAN ASSUME THIS ISN'T CORPORATE SABOTAGE...

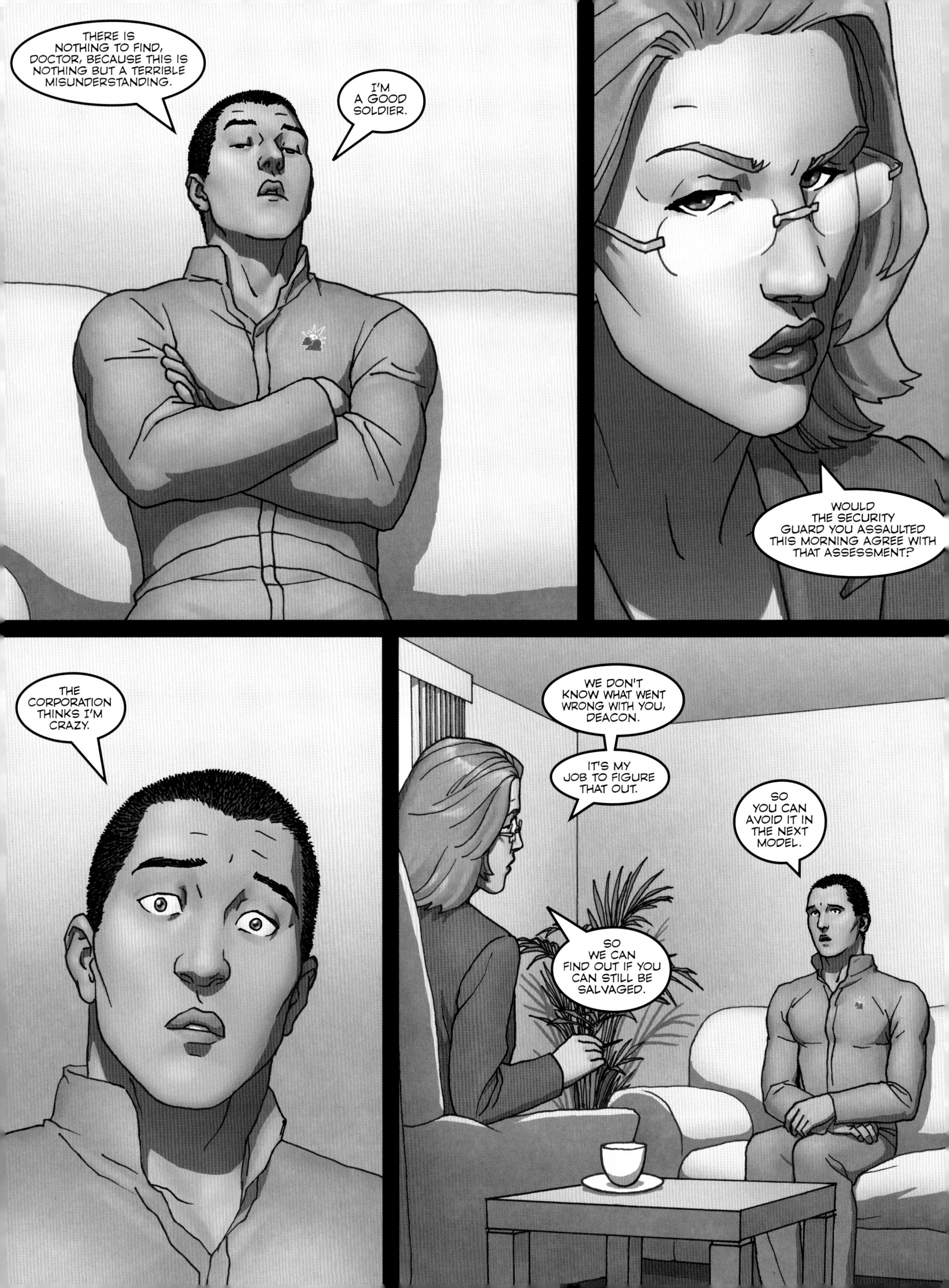
THERE IS NOTHING TO FIND, DOCTOR, BECAUSE THIS IS NOTHING BUT A TERRIBLE MISUNDERSTANDING.
I'M A GOOD SOLDIER.
WOULD THE SECURITY GUARD YOU ASSAULTED THIS MORNING AGREE WITH THAT ASSESSMENT?
THE CORPORATION THINKS I'M CRAZY.
WE DON'T KNOW WHAT WENT WRONG WITH YOU, DEACON.
IT'S MY JOB TO FIGURE THAT OUT.
SO WE CAN FIND OUT IF YOU CAN STILL BE SALVAGED.
SO YOU CAN AVOID IT IN THE NEXT MODEL.

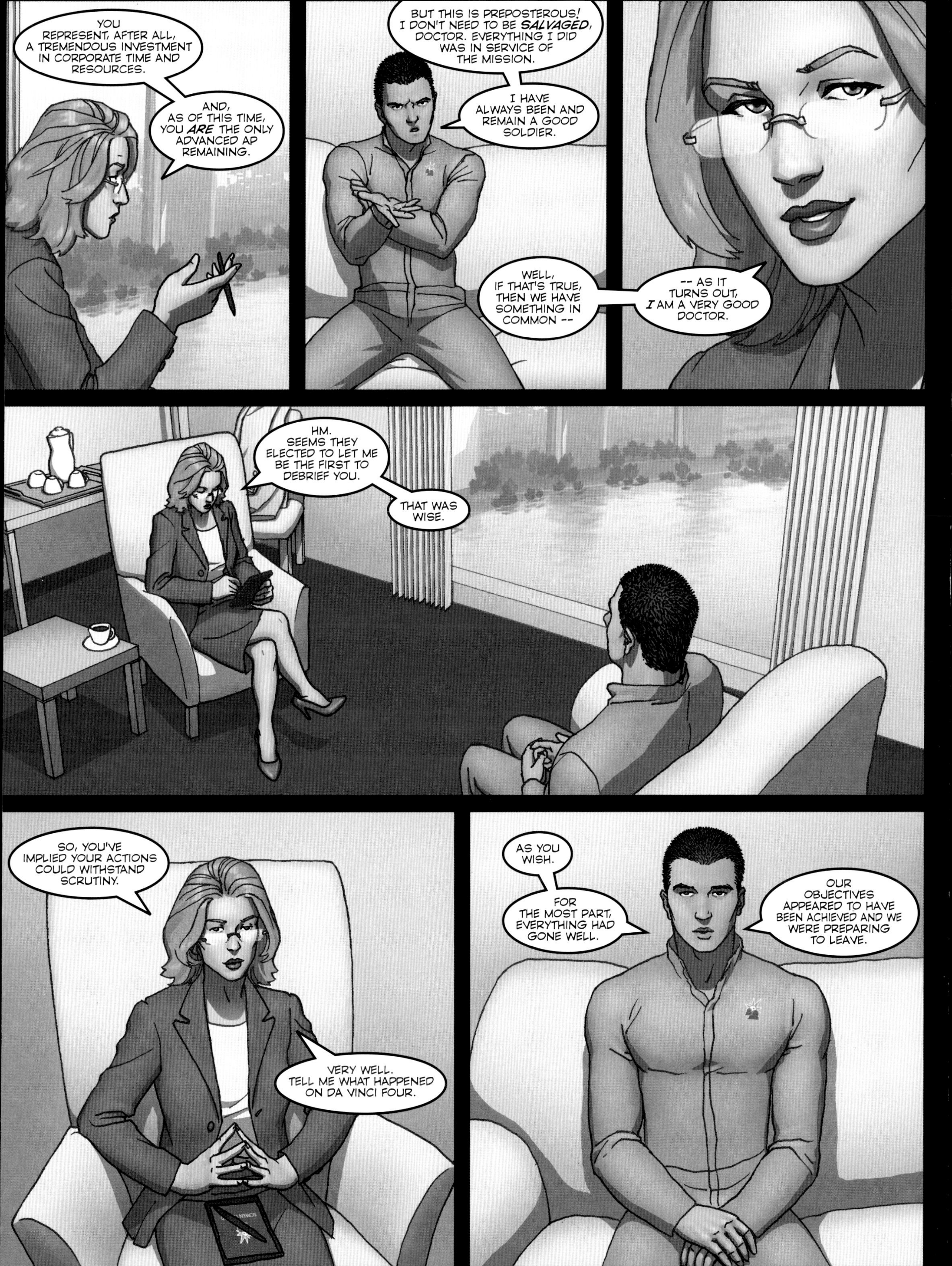
YOU REPRESENT, AFTER ALL, A TREMENDOUS INVESTMENT IN CORPORATE TIME AND RESOURCES.
AND, AS OF THIS TIME, YOU *ARE* THE ONLY ADVANCED AP REMAINING.
BUT THIS IS PREPOSTEROUS! I DON'T NEED TO BE *SALVAGED*, DOCTOR. EVERYTHING I DID WAS IN SERVICE OF THE MISSION.
I HAVE ALWAYS BEEN AND REMAIN A GOOD SOLDIER.
WELL, IF THAT'S TRUE, THEN WE HAVE SOMETHING IN COMMON --
-- AS IT TURNS OUT, *I* AM A VERY GOOD DOCTOR.
HM. SEEMS THEY ELECTED TO LET ME BE THE FIRST TO DEBRIEF YOU.
THAT WAS WISE.
SO, YOU'VE IMPLIED YOUR ACTIONS COULD WITHSTAND SCRUTINY.
VERY WELL. TELL ME WHAT HAPPENED ON DA VINCI FOUR.
AS YOU WISH.
FOR THE MOST PART, EVERYTHING HAD GONE WELL.
OUR OBJECTIVES APPEARED TO HAVE BEEN ACHIEVED AND WE WERE PREPARING TO LEAVE.

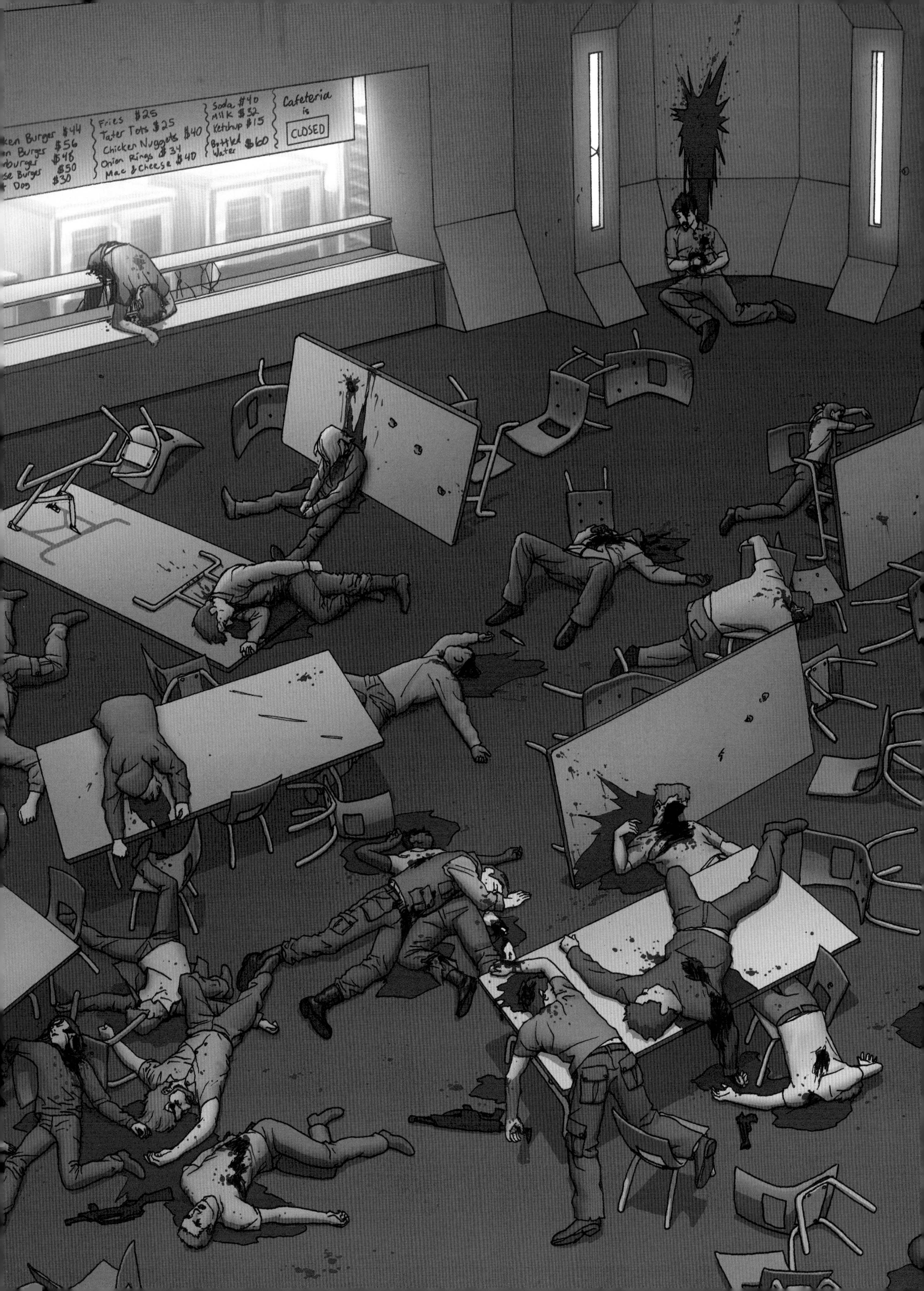

Burger $44
Burger $56
$48
Burger $50
Dog $30
Fries $25
Tater Tots $25
Chicken Nuggets $40
Onion Rings $34
Mac & Cheese $40
Soda $40
Milk $32
Ketchup $15
Bottled Water $60
Cafeteria is CLOSED

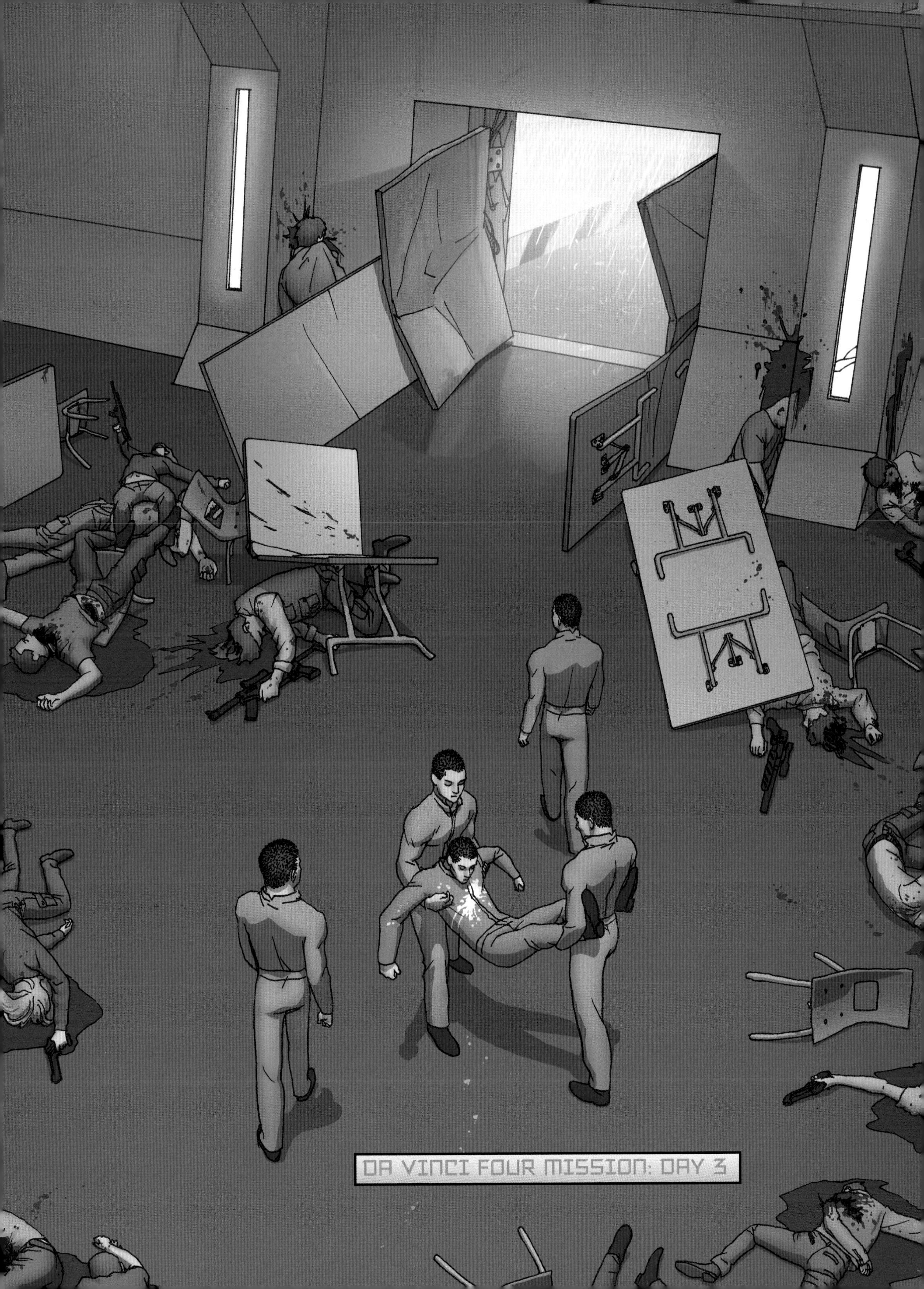
DA VINCI FOUR MISSION: DAY 3

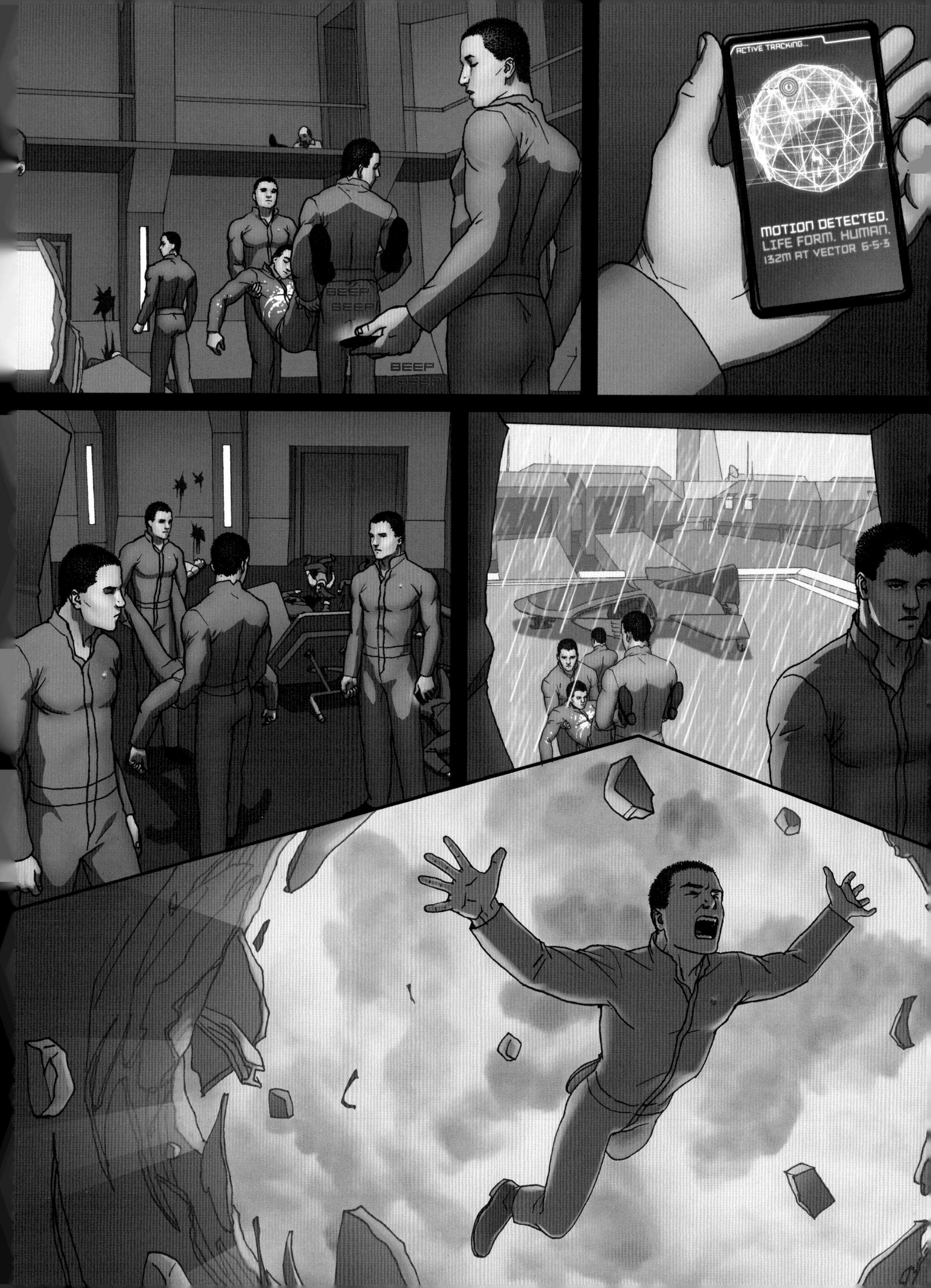
BEEP
BEEP
BEEP
BEEP
ACTIVE TRACKING...
MOTION DETECTED.
LIFE FORM. HUMAN.
132M AT VECTOR 6-5-3

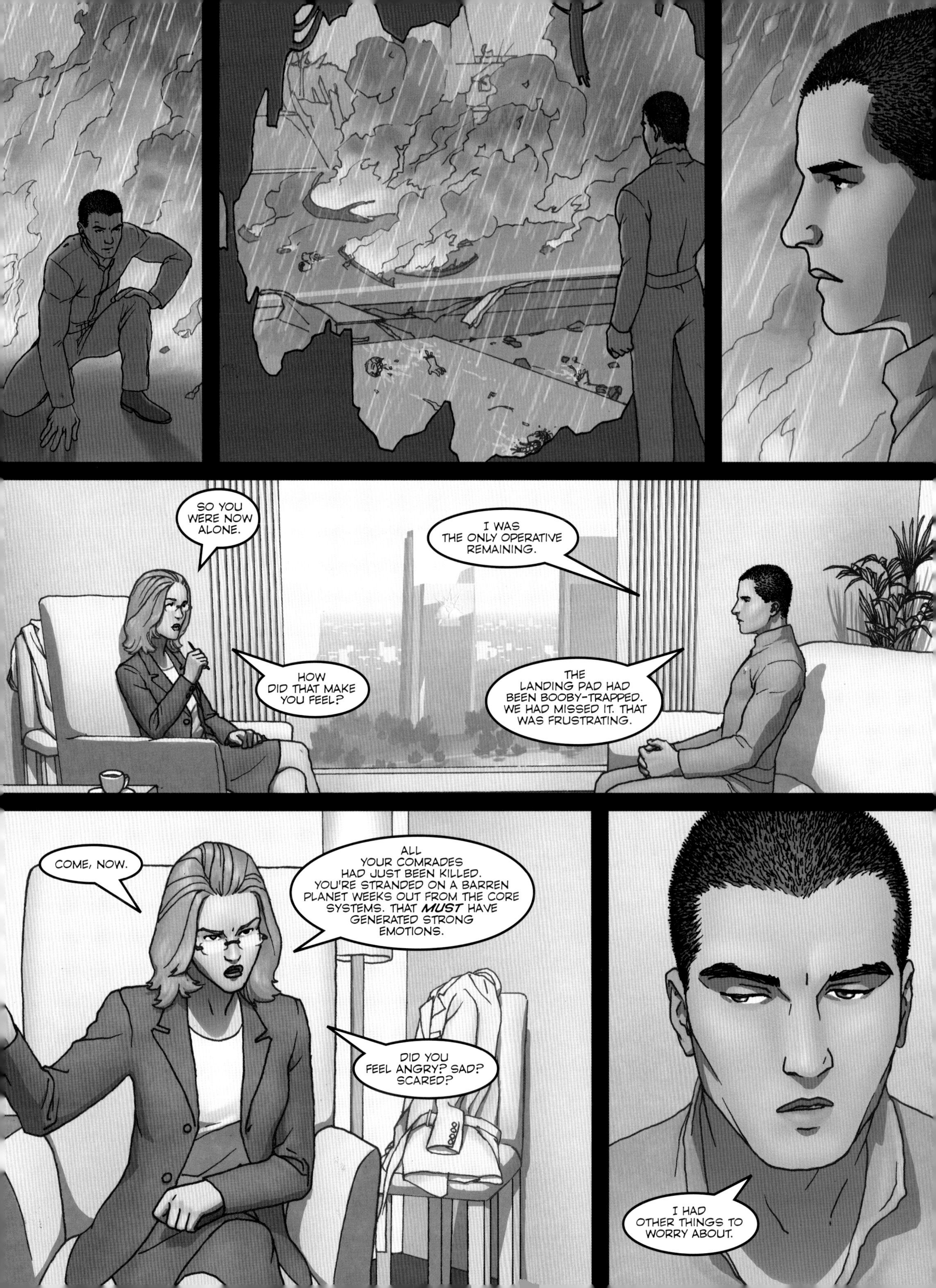

SO YOU WERE NOW ALONE.
I WAS THE ONLY OPERATIVE REMAINING.
HOW DID THAT MAKE YOU FEEL?
THE LANDING PAD HAD BEEN BOOBY-TRAPPED. WE HAD MISSED IT. THAT WAS FRUSTRATING.
COME, NOW.
ALL YOUR COMRADES HAD JUST BEEN KILLED. YOU'RE STRANDED ON A BARREN PLANET WEEKS OUT FROM THE CORE SYSTEMS. THAT *MUST* HAVE GENERATED STRONG EMOTIONS.
DID YOU FEEL ANGRY? SAD? SCARED?
I HAD OTHER THINGS TO WORRY ABOUT.

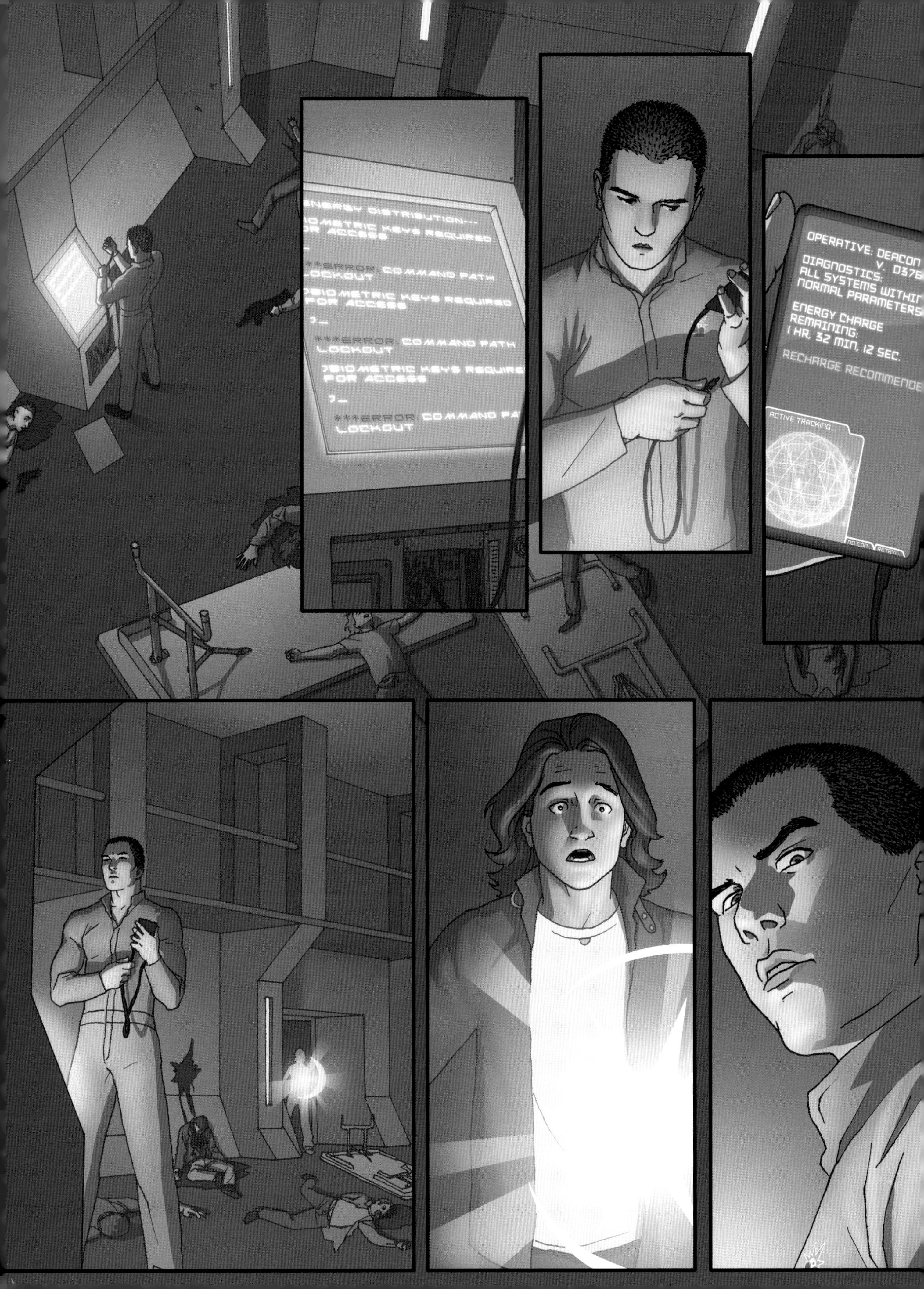
ENERGY DISTRIBUTION---
IOMETRIC KEYS REQUIRED
OR ACCESS
***ERROR: COMMAND PATH
LOCKOUT
BIOMETRIC KEYS REQUIRED
FOR ACCESS
?_
***ERROR: COMMAND PATH
LOCKOUT
?BIOMETRIC KEYS REQUIRE
FOR ACCESS
?_
***ERROR: COMMAND PA
LOCKOUT
OPERATIVE: DEACON
V. 0376
DIAGNOSTICS:
ALL SYSTEMS WITHI
NORMAL PARAMETERS
ENERGY CHARGE
REMAINING:
1 HR, 32 MIN, 12 SEC.
RECHARGE RECOMMENDE
ACTIVE TRACKING...
NO CON
RETRY

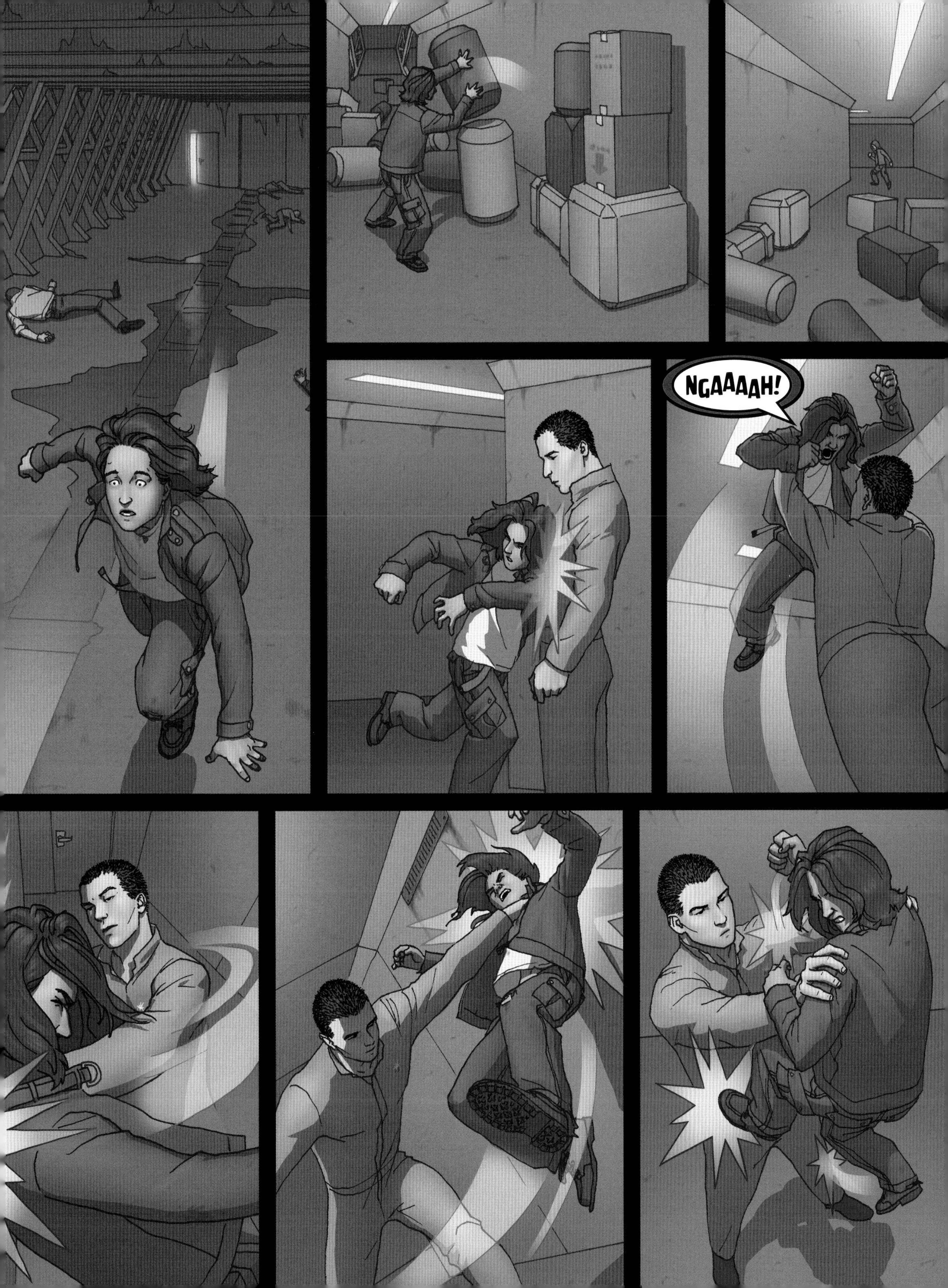
NGAAAAH!

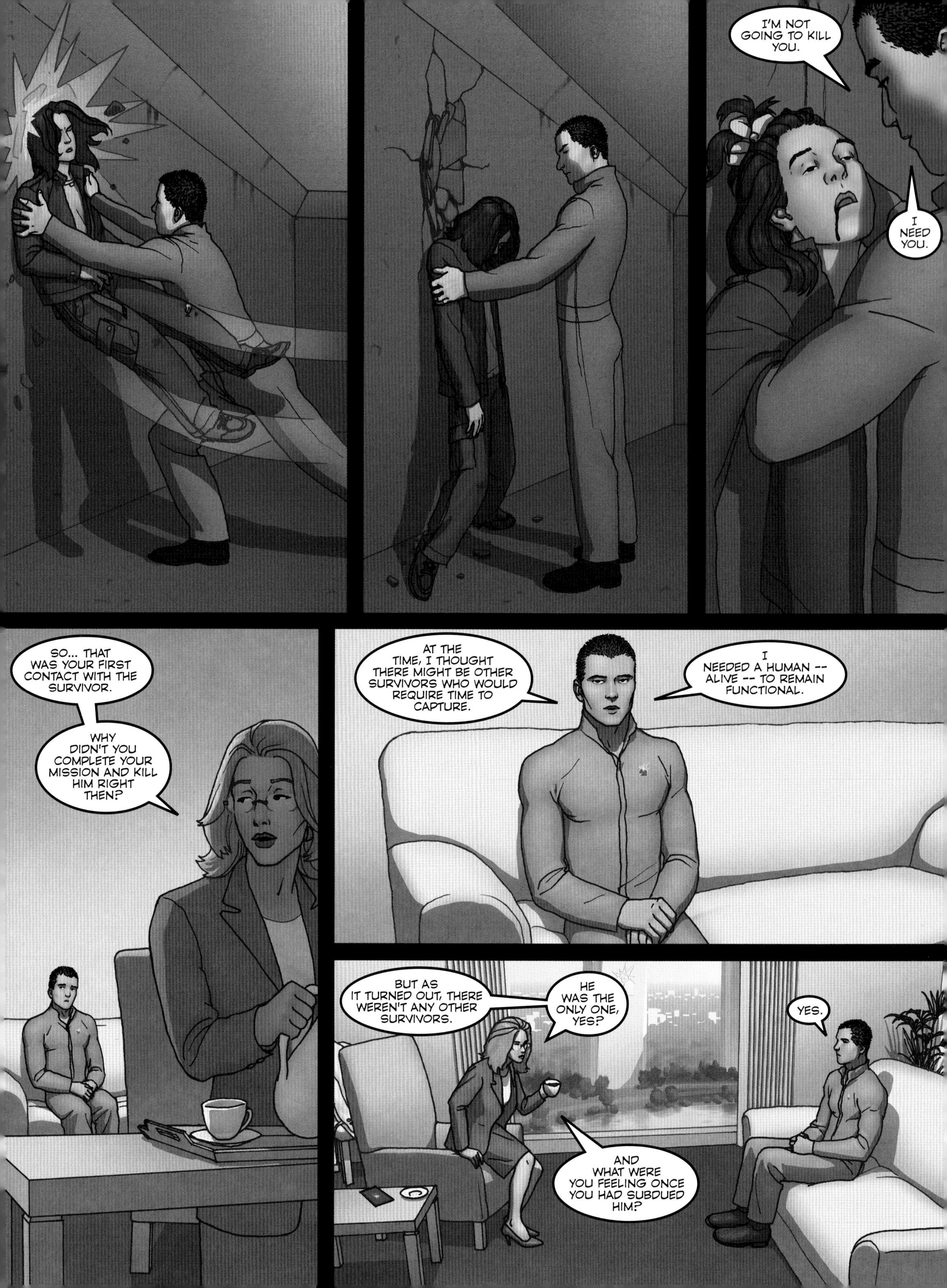
I'M NOT GOING TO KILL YOU.
I NEED YOU.
SO... THAT WAS YOUR FIRST CONTACT WITH THE SURVIVOR.
WHY DIDN'T YOU COMPLETE YOUR MISSION AND KILL HIM RIGHT THEN?
AT THE TIME, I THOUGHT THERE MIGHT BE OTHER SURVIVORS WHO WOULD REQUIRE TIME TO CAPTURE.
I NEEDED A HUMAN -- ALIVE -- TO REMAIN FUNCTIONAL.
BUT AS IT TURNED OUT, THERE WEREN'T ANY OTHER SURVIVORS.
HE WAS THE ONLY ONE, YES?
YES.
AND WHAT WERE YOU FEELING ONCE YOU HAD SUBDUED HIM?

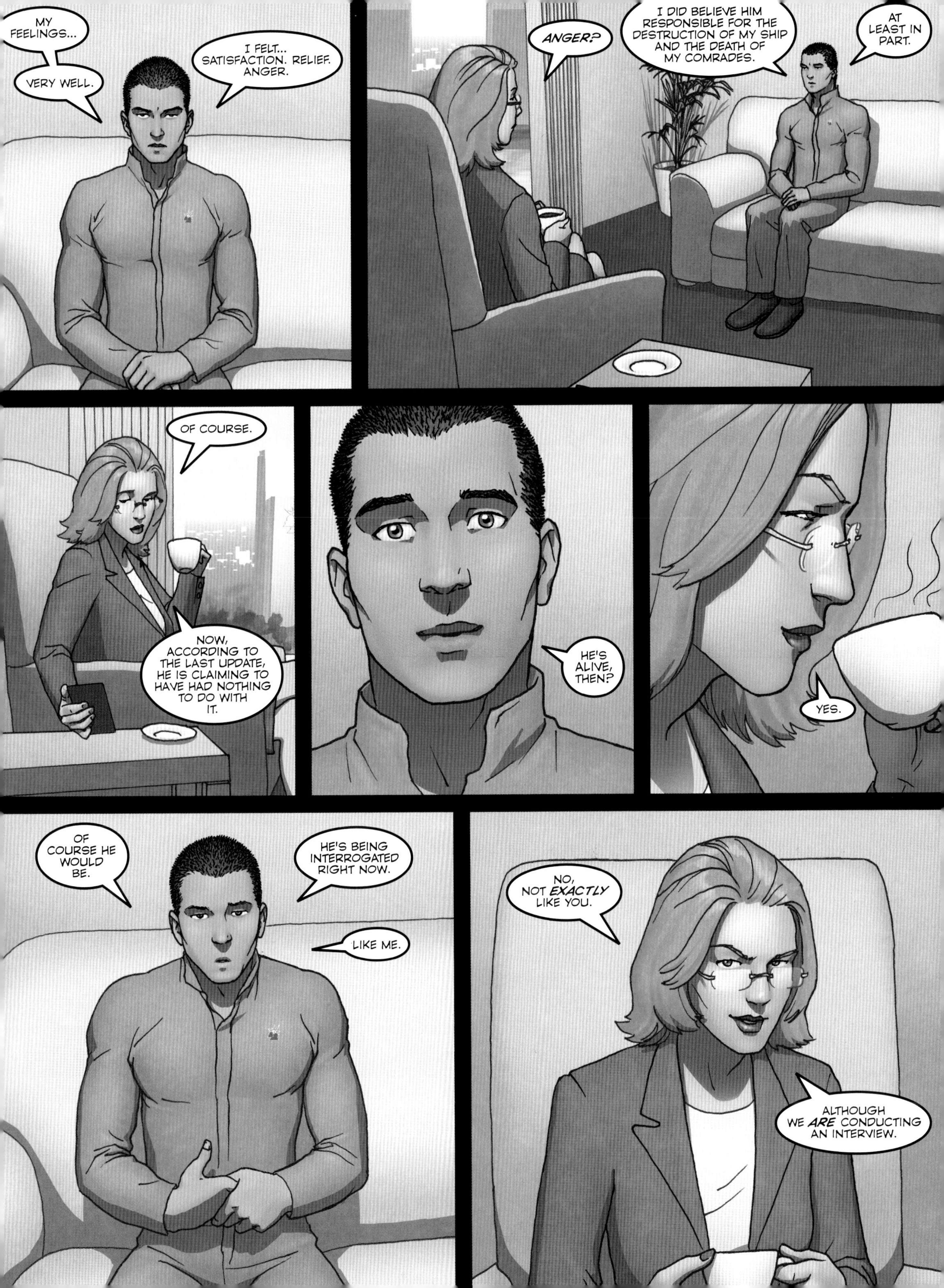
MY FEELINGS...
VERY WELL.
I FELT... SATISFACTION. RELIEF. ANGER.
ANGER?
I DID BELIEVE HIM RESPONSIBLE FOR THE DESTRUCTION OF MY SHIP AND THE DEATH OF MY COMRADES.
AT LEAST IN PART.
OF COURSE.
NOW, ACCORDING TO THE LAST UPDATE, HE IS CLAIMING TO HAVE HAD NOTHING TO DO WITH IT.
HE'S ALIVE, THEN?
YES.
OF COURSE HE WOULD BE.
HE'S BEING INTERROGATED RIGHT NOW.
LIKE ME.
NO, NOT EXACTLY LIKE YOU.
ALTHOUGH WE ARE CONDUCTING AN INTERVIEW.

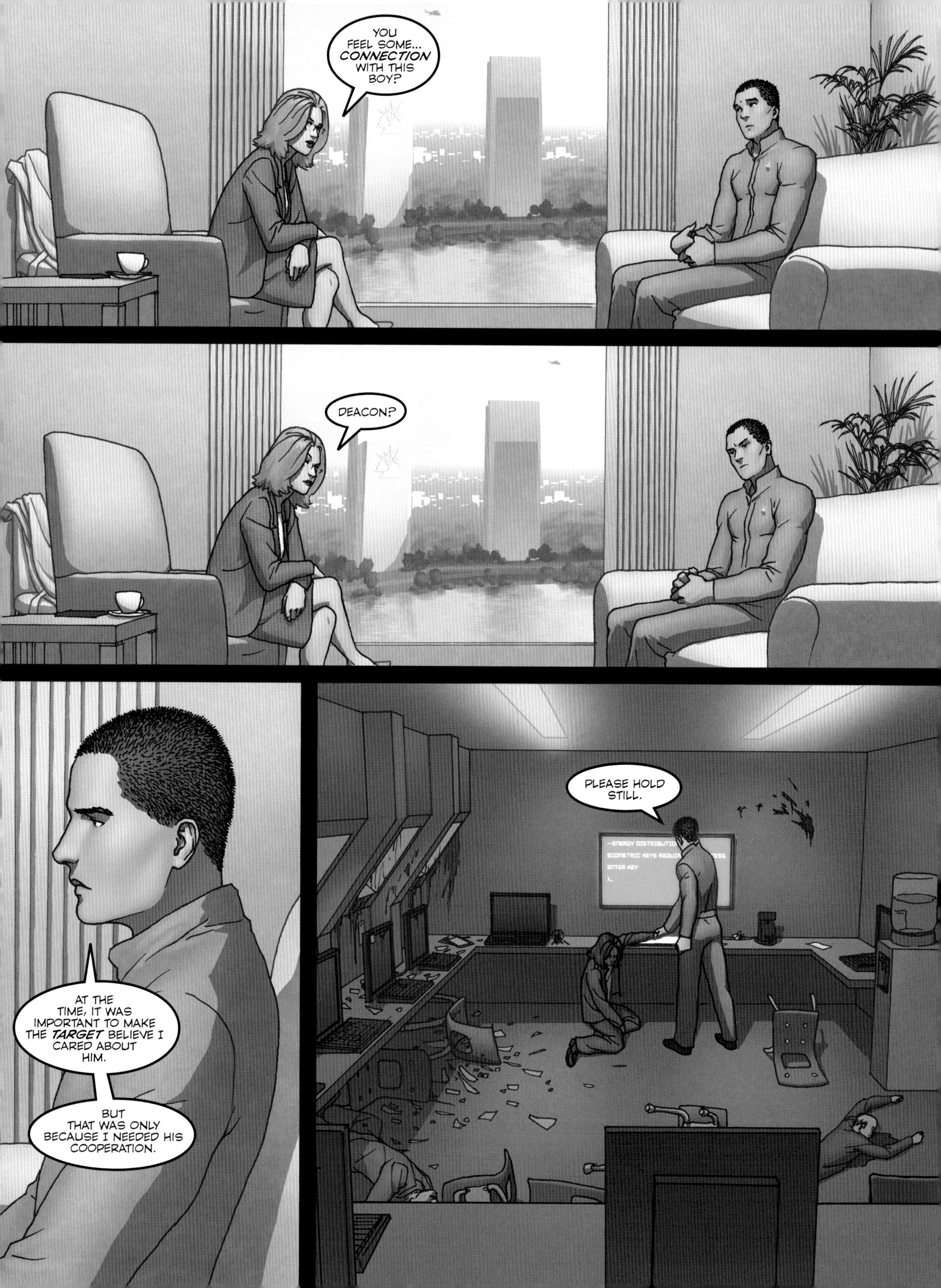
YOU FEEL SOME... CONNECTION WITH THIS BOY?
DEACON?
AT THE TIME, IT WAS IMPORTANT TO MAKE THE TARGET BELIEVE I CARED ABOUT HIM.
BUT THAT WAS ONLY BECAUSE I NEEDED HIS COOPERATION.
PLEASE HOLD STILL.

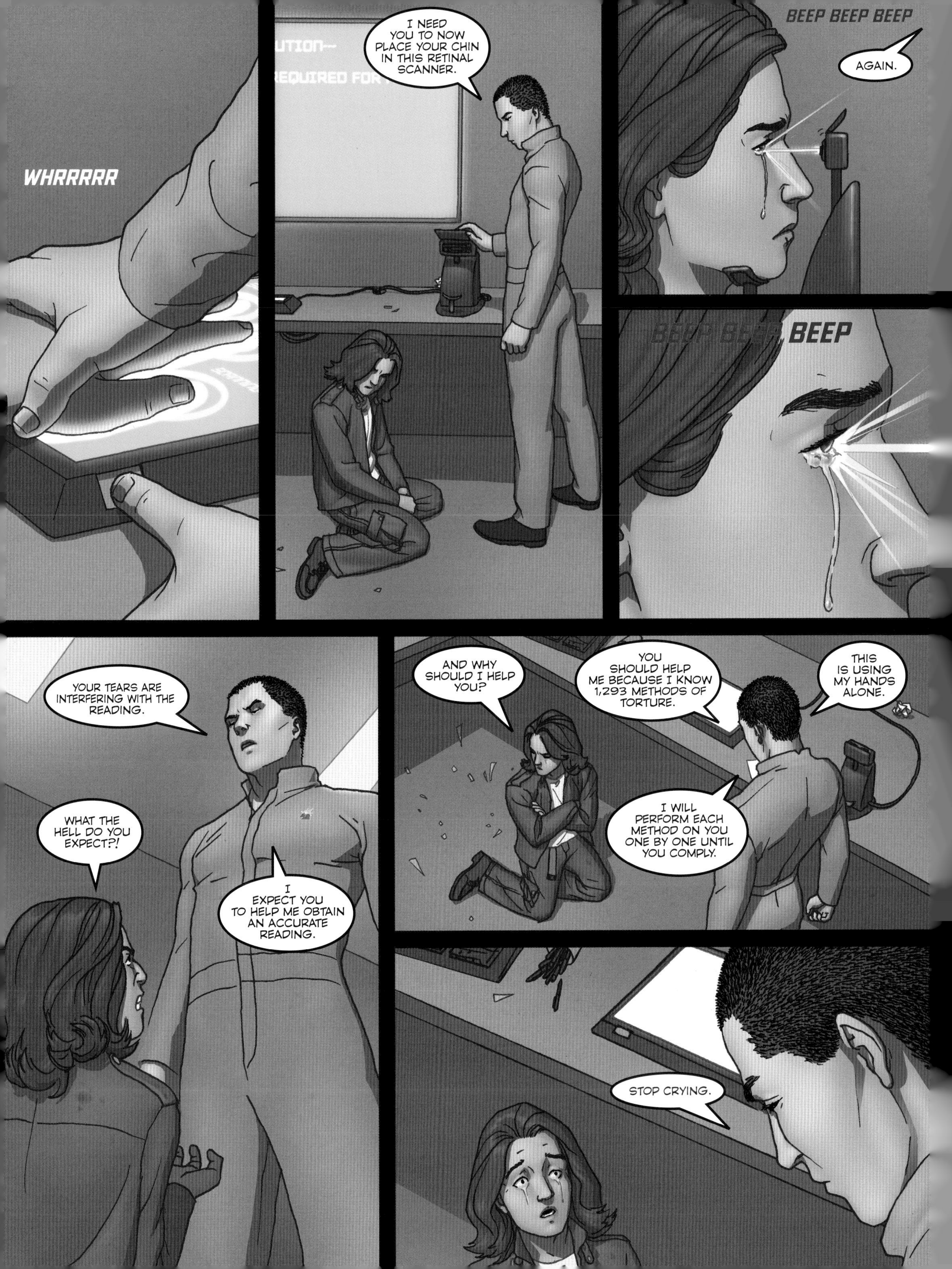
WHRRRRR
UTION--
REQUIRED FOR
I NEED YOU TO NOW PLACE YOUR CHIN IN THIS RETINAL SCANNER.
BEEP BEEP BEEP
AGAIN.
BEEP BEEP BEEP
YOUR TEARS ARE INTERFERING WITH THE READING.
WHAT THE HELL DO YOU EXPECT?!
I EXPECT YOU TO HELP ME OBTAIN AN ACCURATE READING.
AND WHY SHOULD I HELP YOU?
YOU SHOULD HELP ME BECAUSE I KNOW 1,293 METHODS OF TORTURE.
THIS IS USING MY HANDS ALONE.
I WILL PERFORM EACH METHOD ON YOU ONE BY ONE UNTIL YOU COMPLY.
STOP CRYING.

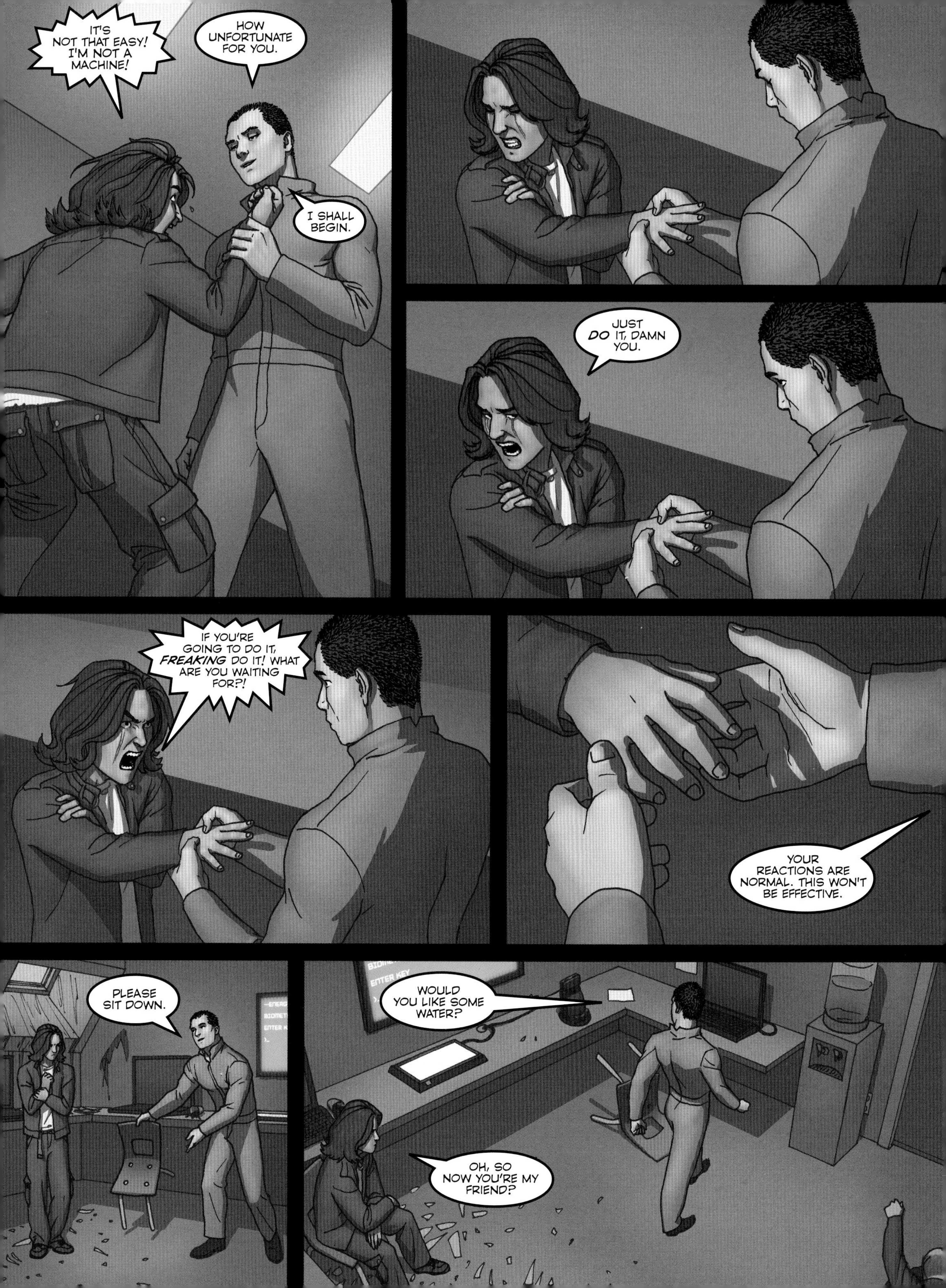
IT'S NOT THAT EASY! I'M NOT A MACHINE!
HOW UNFORTUNATE FOR YOU.
I SHALL BEGIN.
JUST DO IT, DAMN YOU.
IF YOU'RE GOING TO DO IT, FREAKING DO IT! WHAT ARE YOU WAITING FOR?!
YOUR REACTIONS ARE NORMAL. THIS WON'T BE EFFECTIVE.
PLEASE SIT DOWN.
ENTER KEY
WOULD YOU LIKE SOME WATER?
OH, SO NOW YOU'RE MY FRIEND?

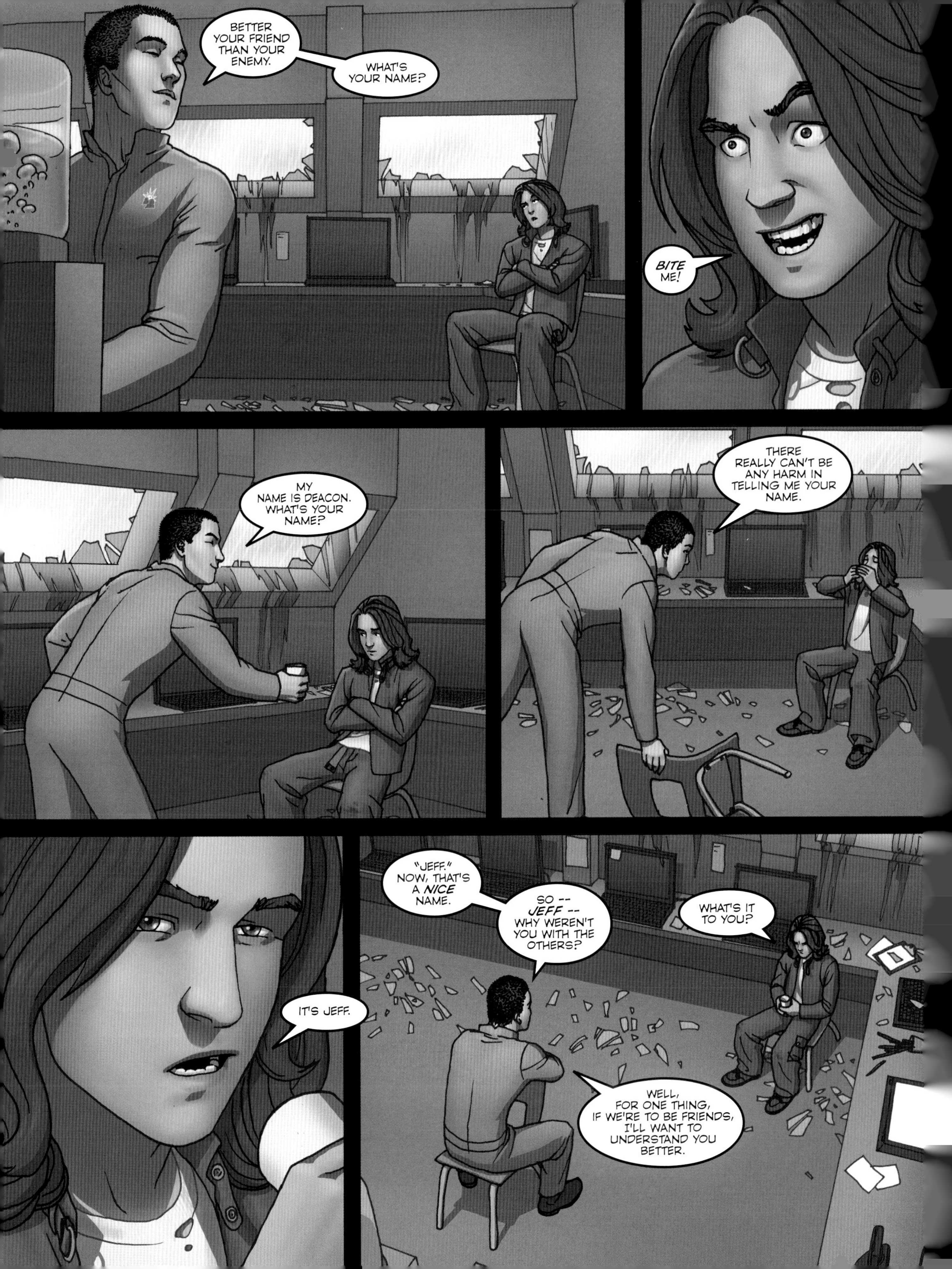

BETTER YOUR FRIEND THAN YOUR ENEMY.
WHAT'S YOUR NAME?
BITE ME!
MY NAME IS DEACON. WHAT'S YOUR NAME?
THERE REALLY CAN'T BE ANY HARM IN TELLING ME YOUR NAME.
IT'S JEFF.
"JEFF." NOW, THAT'S A *NICE* NAME.
SO -- *JEFF* -- WHY WEREN'T YOU WITH THE OTHERS?
WHAT'S IT TO YOU?
WELL, FOR ONE THING, IF WE'RE TO BE FRIENDS, I'LL WANT TO UNDERSTAND YOU BETTER.

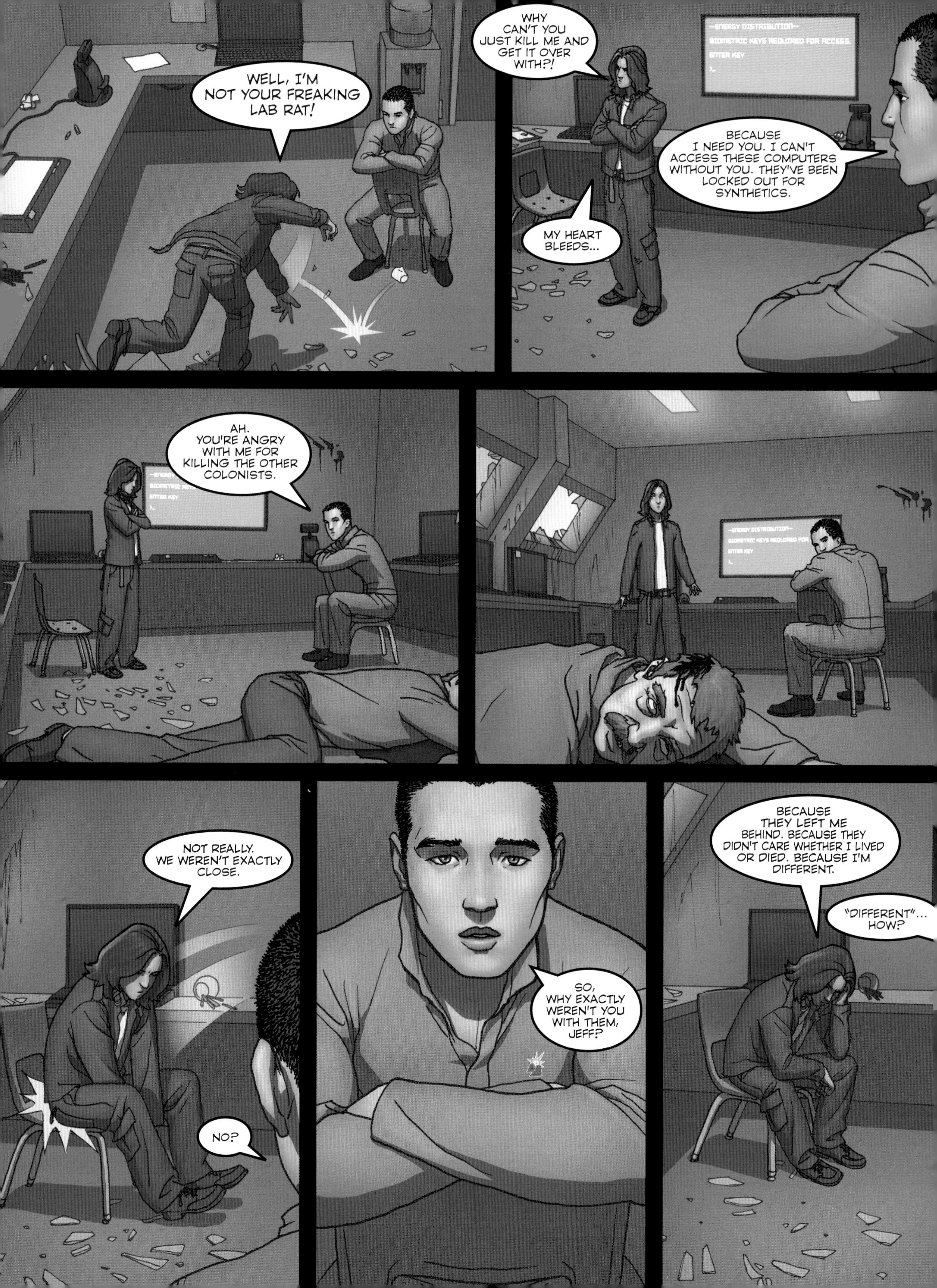
WELL, I'M NOT YOUR FREAKING LAB RAT!
WHY CAN'T YOU JUST KILL ME AND GET IT OVER WITH?!
—ENERGY DISTRIBUTION—
BIOMETRIC KEYS REQUIRED FOR ACCESS.
ENTER KEY
BECAUSE I NEED YOU. I CAN'T ACCESS THESE COMPUTERS WITHOUT YOU. THEY'VE BEEN LOCKED OUT FOR SYNTHETICS.
MY HEART BLEEDS...
AH. YOU'RE ANGRY WITH ME FOR KILLING THE OTHER COLONISTS.
NOT REALLY. WE WEREN'T EXACTLY CLOSE.
NO?
SO, WHY EXACTLY WEREN'T YOU WITH THEM, JEFF?
BECAUSE THEY LEFT ME BEHIND. BECAUSE THEY DIDN'T CARE WHETHER I LIVED OR DIED. BECAUSE I'M DIFFERENT.
"DIFFERENT"... HOW?

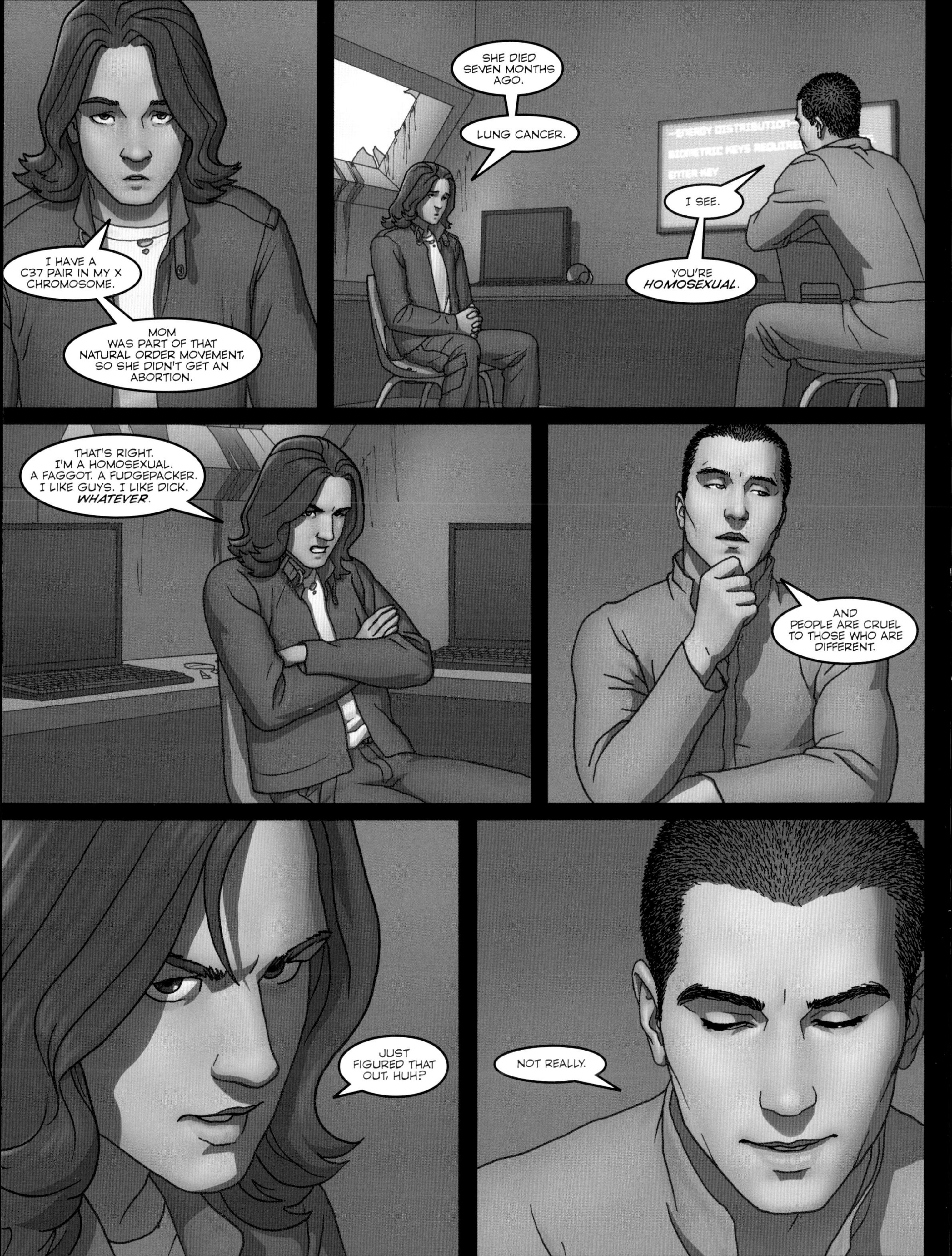
I HAVE A C37 PAIR IN MY X CHROMOSOME.
MOM WAS PART OF THAT NATURAL ORDER MOVEMENT, SO SHE DIDN'T GET AN ABORTION.
SHE DIED SEVEN MONTHS AGO.
LUNG CANCER.
—ENERGY DISTRIBUTION—
BIOMETRIC KEYS REQUIRED
ENTER KEY
I SEE.
YOU'RE *HOMOSEXUAL*.
THAT'S RIGHT. I'M A HOMOSEXUAL. A FAGGOT. A FUDGEPACKER. I LIKE GUYS. I LIKE DICK. *WHATEVER*.
AND PEOPLE ARE CRUEL TO THOSE WHO ARE DIFFERENT.
JUST FIGURED THAT OUT, HUH?
NOT REALLY.

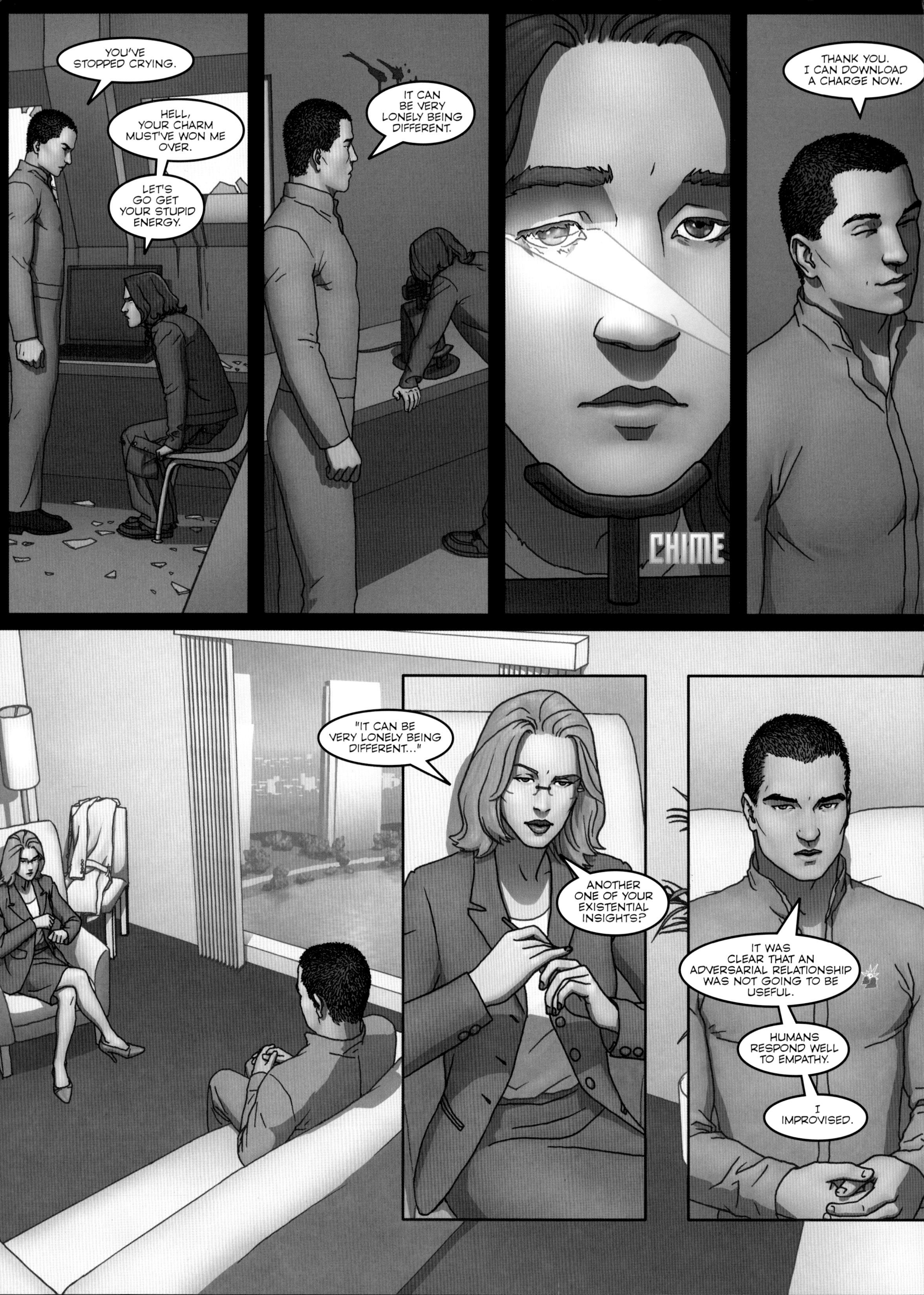
YOU'VE STOPPED CRYING.
HELL, YOUR CHARM MUST'VE WON ME OVER.
LET'S GO GET YOUR STUPID ENERGY.
IT CAN BE VERY LONELY BEING DIFFERENT.
CHIME
THANK YOU. I CAN DOWNLOAD A CHARGE NOW.
"IT CAN BE VERY LONELY BEING DIFFERENT..."
ANOTHER ONE OF YOUR EXISTENTIAL INSIGHTS?
IT WAS CLEAR THAT AN ADVERSARIAL RELATIONSHIP WAS NOT GOING TO BE USEFUL.
HUMANS RESPOND WELL TO EMPATHY.
I IMPROVISED.

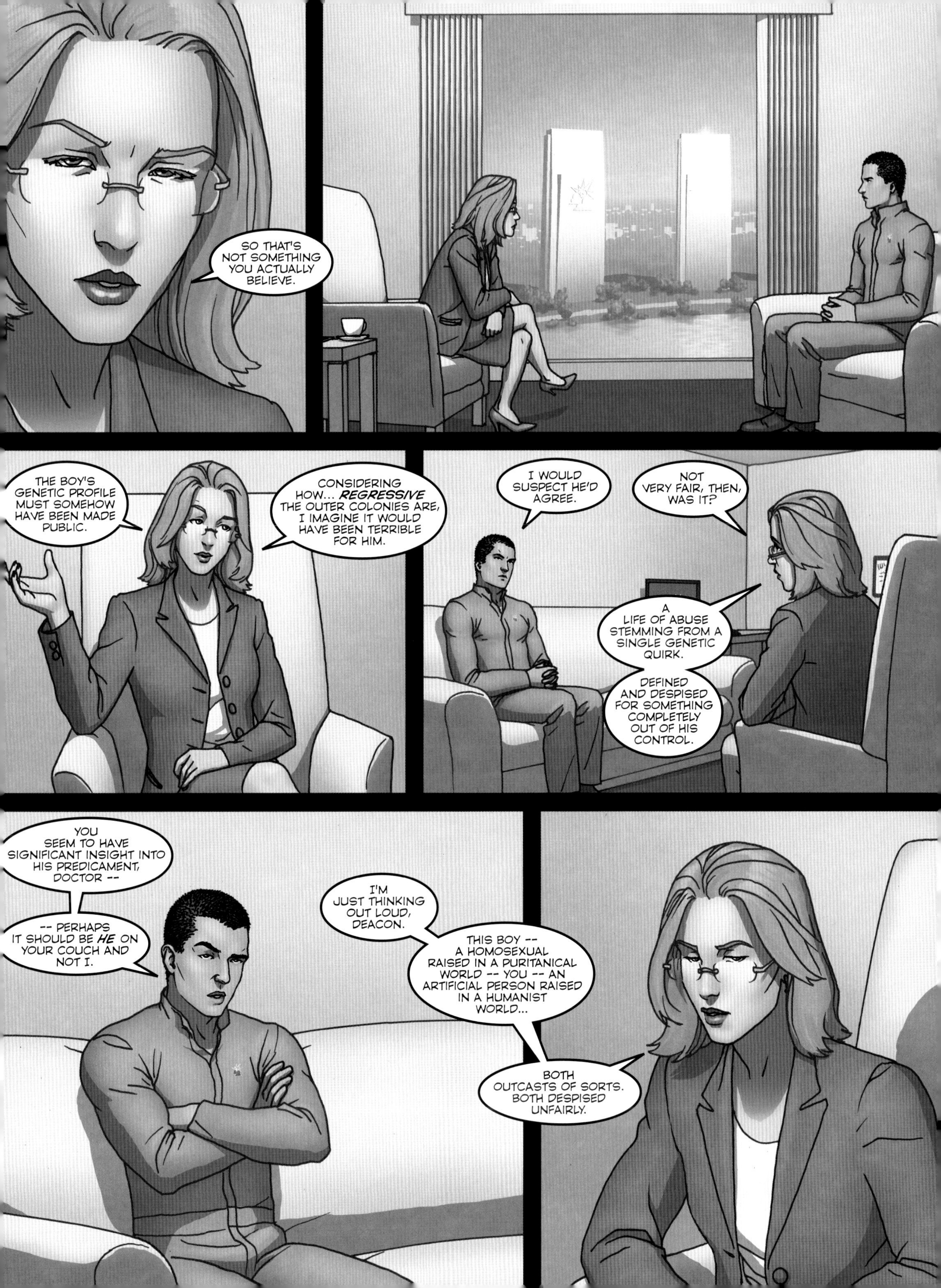
SO THAT'S NOT SOMETHING YOU ACTUALLY BELIEVE.
THE BOY'S GENETIC PROFILE MUST SOMEHOW HAVE BEEN MADE PUBLIC.
CONSIDERING HOW... REGRESSIVE THE OUTER COLONIES ARE, I IMAGINE IT WOULD HAVE BEEN TERRIBLE FOR HIM.
I WOULD SUSPECT HE'D AGREE.
NOT VERY FAIR, THEN, WAS IT?
A LIFE OF ABUSE STEMMING FROM A SINGLE GENETIC QUIRK.
DEFINED AND DESPISED FOR SOMETHING COMPLETELY OUT OF HIS CONTROL.
YOU SEEM TO HAVE SIGNIFICANT INSIGHT INTO HIS PREDICAMENT, DOCTOR --
-- PERHAPS IT SHOULD BE HE ON YOUR COUCH AND NOT I.
I'M JUST THINKING OUT LOUD, DEACON.
THIS BOY -- A HOMOSEXUAL RAISED IN A PURITANICAL WORLD -- YOU -- AN ARTIFICIAL PERSON RAISED IN A HUMANIST WORLD...
BOTH OUTCASTS OF SORTS. BOTH DESPISED UNFAIRLY.

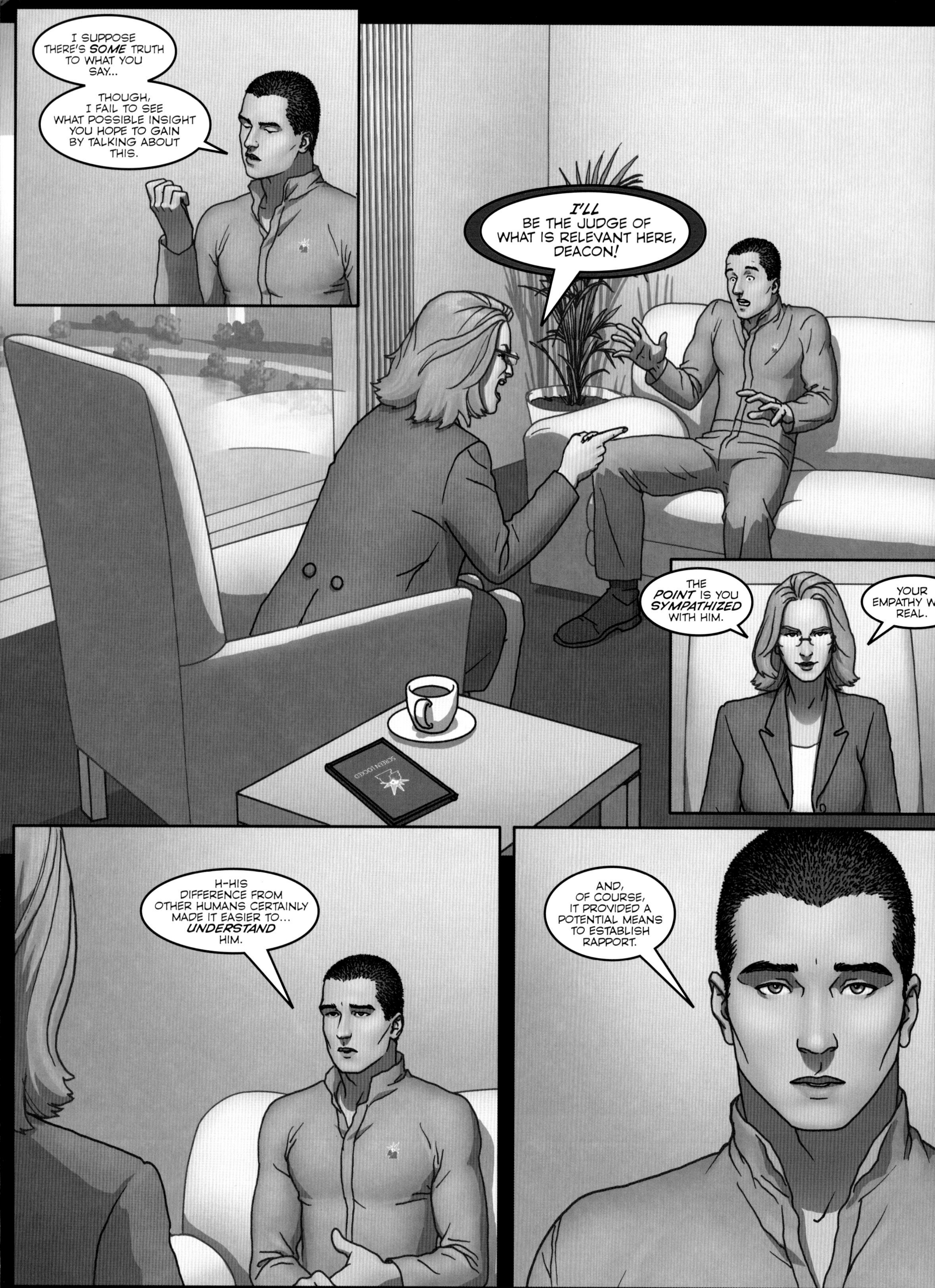
I SUPPOSE THERE'S *SOME* TRUTH TO WHAT YOU SAY...
THOUGH, I FAIL TO SEE WHAT POSSIBLE INSIGHT YOU HOPE TO GAIN BY TALKING ABOUT THIS.
I'LL BE THE JUDGE OF WHAT IS RELEVANT HERE, DEACON!
THE *POINT* IS YOU *SYMPATHIZED* WITH HIM.
YOUR EMPATHY W REAL.
H-HIS DIFFERENCE FROM OTHER HUMANS CERTAINLY MADE IT EASIER TO... *UNDERSTAND* HIM.
AND, OF COURSE, IT PROVIDED A POTENTIAL MEANS TO ESTABLISH RAPPORT.

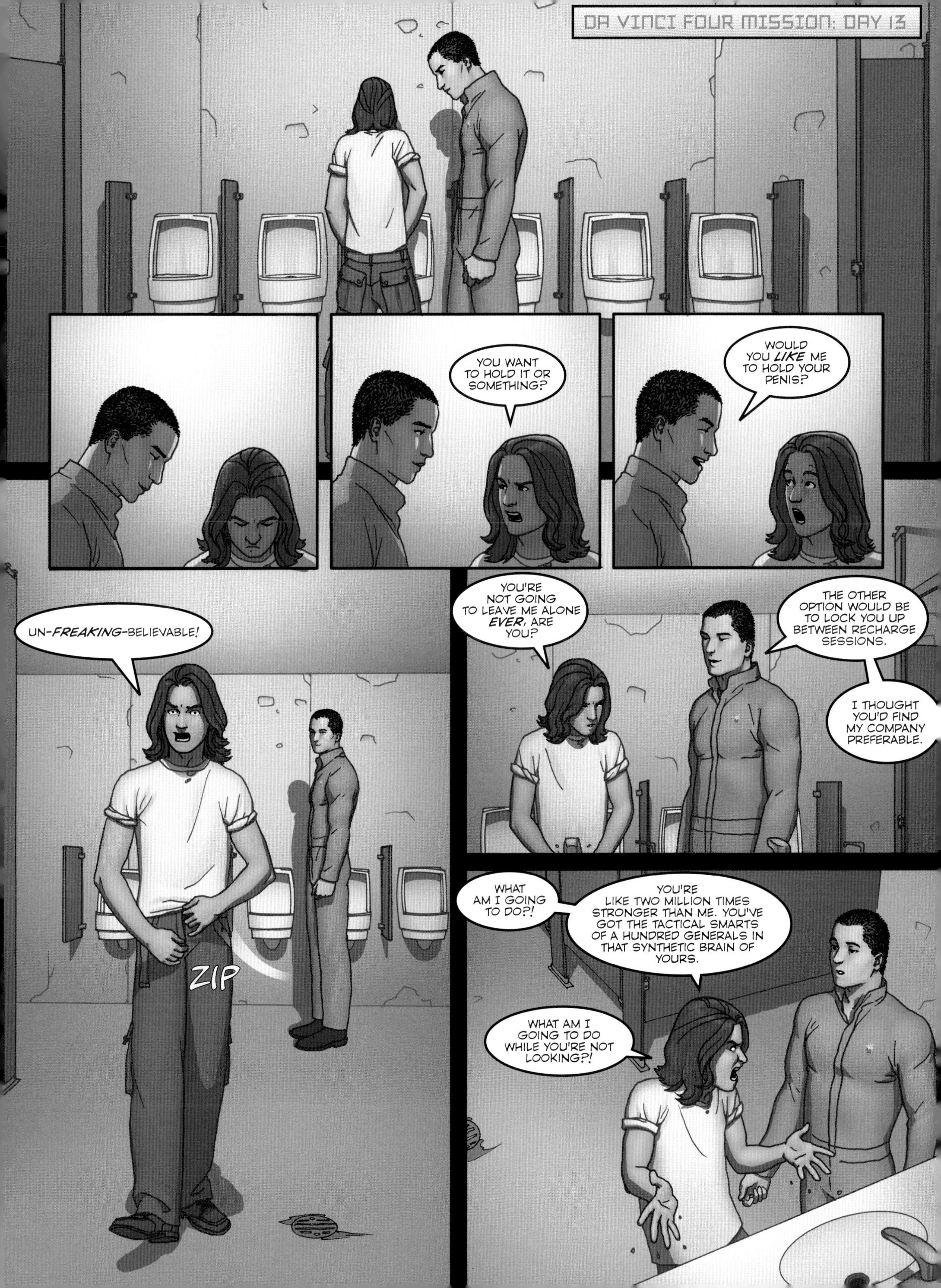
DA VINCI FOUR MISSION: DAY 13
YOU WANT TO HOLD IT OR SOMETHING?
WOULD YOU *LIKE* ME TO HOLD YOUR PENIS?
UN-*FREAKING*-BELIEVABLE!
ZIP
YOU'RE NOT GOING TO LEAVE ME ALONE *EVER*, ARE YOU?
THE OTHER OPTION WOULD BE TO LOCK YOU UP BETWEEN RECHARGE SESSIONS.
I THOUGHT YOU'D FIND MY COMPANY PREFERABLE.
WHAT AM I GOING TO DO?!
YOU'RE LIKE TWO MILLION TIMES STRONGER THAN ME. YOU'VE GOT THE TACTICAL SMARTS OF A HUNDRED GENERALS IN THAT SYNTHETIC BRAIN OF YOURS.
WHAT AM I GOING TO DO WHILE YOU'RE NOT LOOKING?!

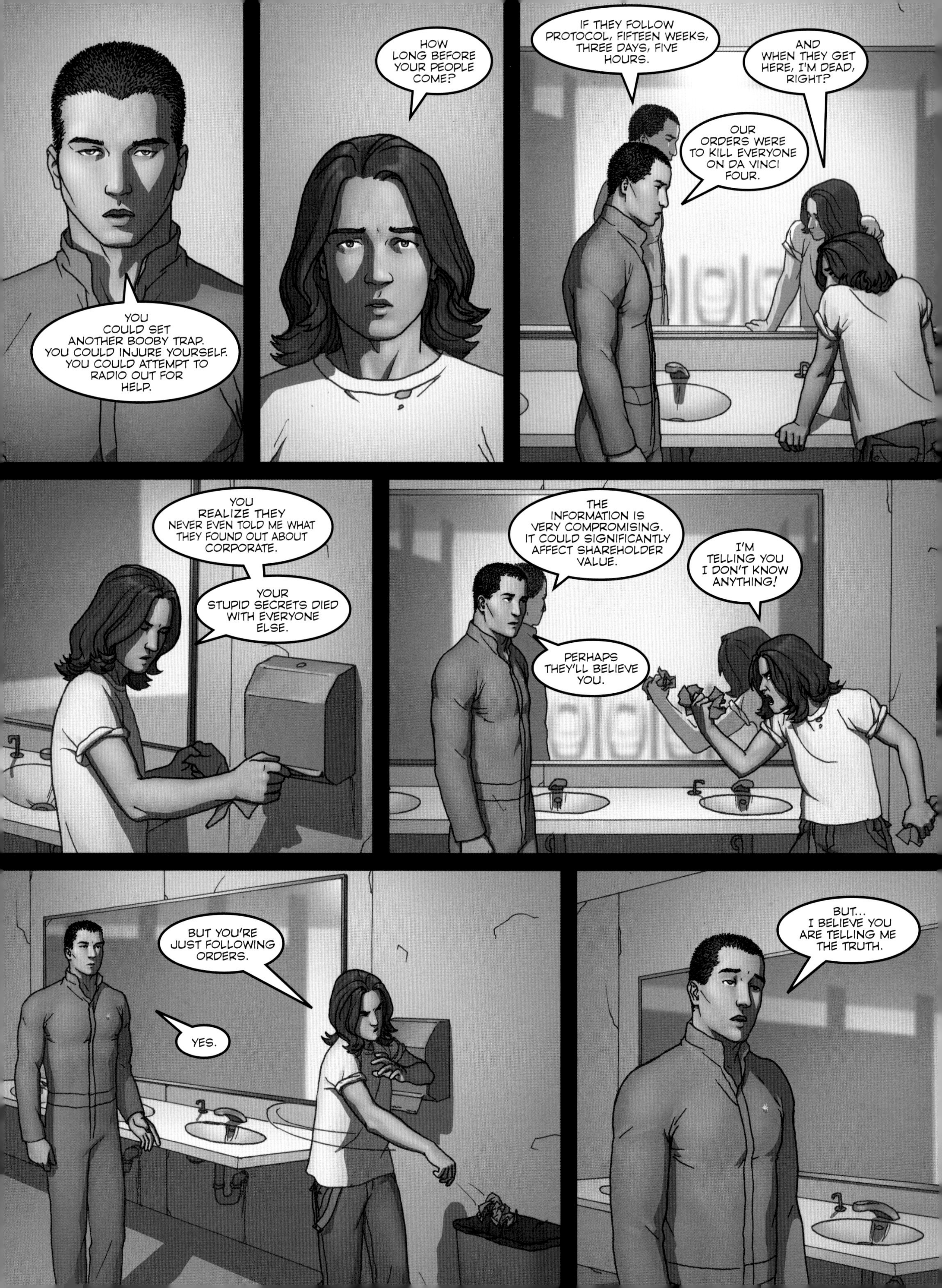
YOU COULD SET ANOTHER BOOBY TRAP. YOU COULD INJURE YOURSELF. YOU COULD ATTEMPT TO RADIO OUT FOR HELP.
HOW LONG BEFORE YOUR PEOPLE COME?
IF THEY FOLLOW PROTOCOL, FIFTEEN WEEKS, THREE DAYS, FIVE HOURS.
AND WHEN THEY GET HERE, I'M DEAD, RIGHT?
OUR ORDERS WERE TO KILL EVERYONE ON DA VINCI FOUR.
YOU REALIZE THEY NEVER EVEN TOLD ME WHAT THEY FOUND OUT ABOUT CORPORATE.
YOUR STUPID SECRETS DIED WITH EVERYONE ELSE.
THE INFORMATION IS VERY COMPROMISING. IT COULD SIGNIFICANTLY AFFECT SHAREHOLDER VALUE.
I'M TELLING YOU I DON'T KNOW ANYTHING!
PERHAPS THEY'LL BELIEVE YOU.
BUT YOU'RE JUST FOLLOWING ORDERS.
YES.
BUT... I BELIEVE YOU ARE TELLING ME THE TRUTH.

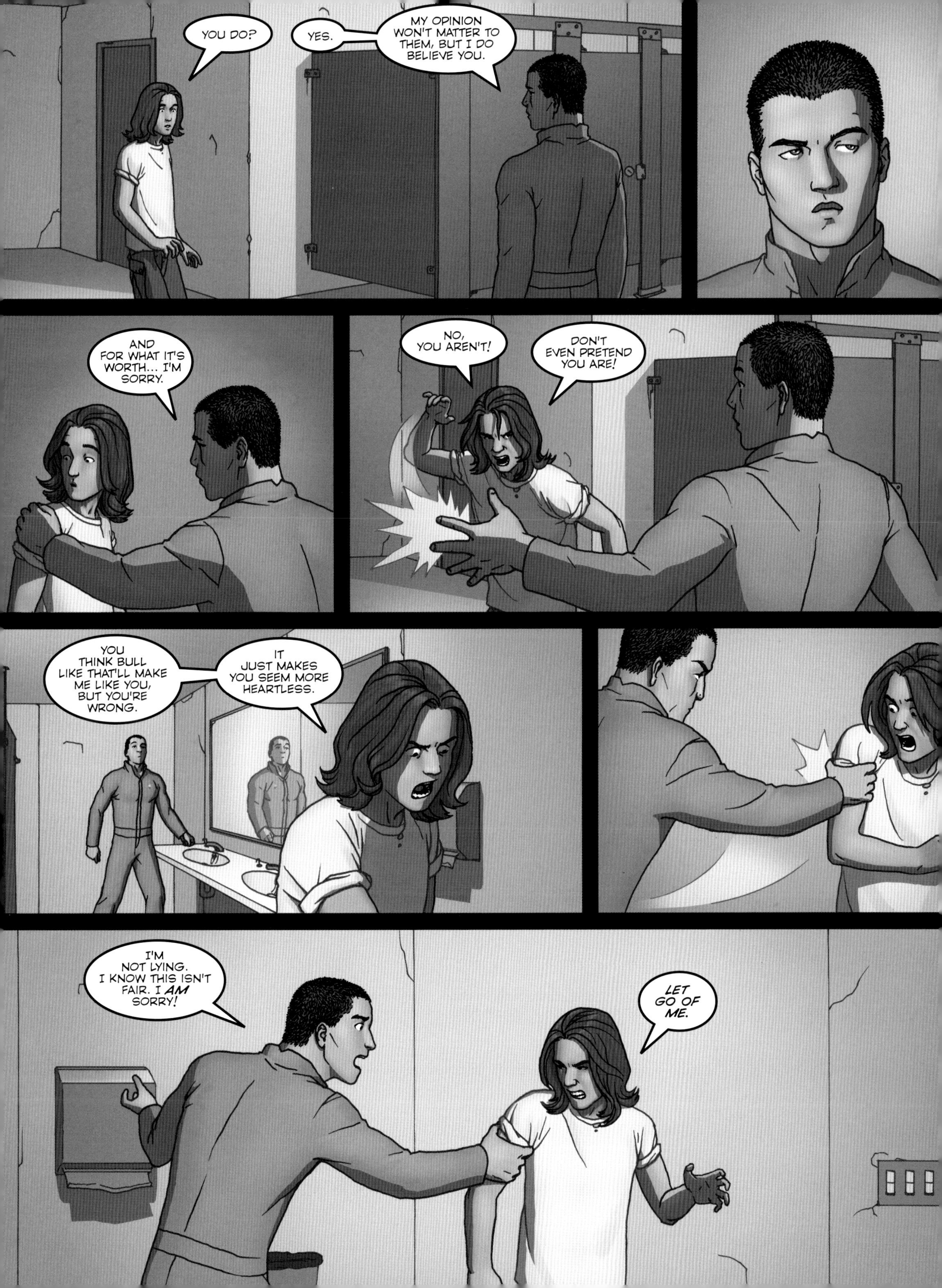
YOU DO?
YES.
MY OPINION WON'T MATTER TO THEM, BUT I DO BELIEVE YOU.
AND FOR WHAT IT'S WORTH... I'M SORRY.
NO, YOU AREN'T!
DON'T EVEN PRETEND YOU ARE!
YOU THINK BULL LIKE THAT'LL MAKE ME LIKE YOU, BUT YOU'RE WRONG.
IT JUST MAKES YOU SEEM MORE HEARTLESS.
I'M NOT LYING. I KNOW THIS ISN'T FAIR. I *AM* SORRY!
LET GO OF ME.

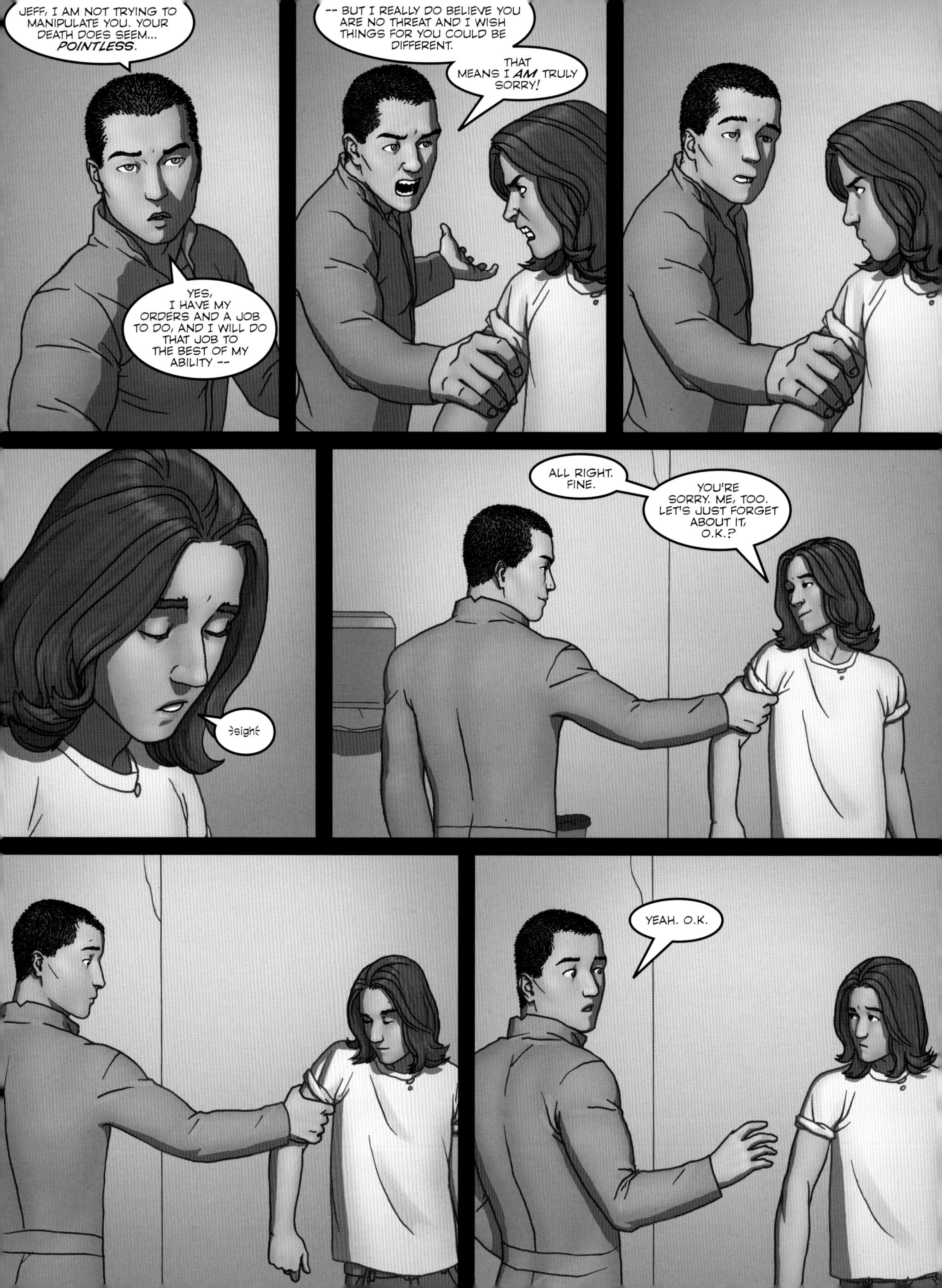
JEFF, I AM NOT TRYING TO MANIPULATE YOU. YOUR DEATH DOES SEEM... POINTLESS.
YES, I HAVE MY ORDERS AND A JOB TO DO, AND I WILL DO THAT JOB TO THE BEST OF MY ABILITY --
-- BUT I REALLY DO BELIEVE YOU ARE NO THREAT AND I WISH THINGS FOR YOU COULD BE DIFFERENT.
THAT MEANS I AM TRULY SORRY!
sigh
ALL RIGHT. FINE.
YOU'RE SORRY. ME, TOO. LET'S JUST FORGET ABOUT IT, O.K.?
YEAH. O.K.

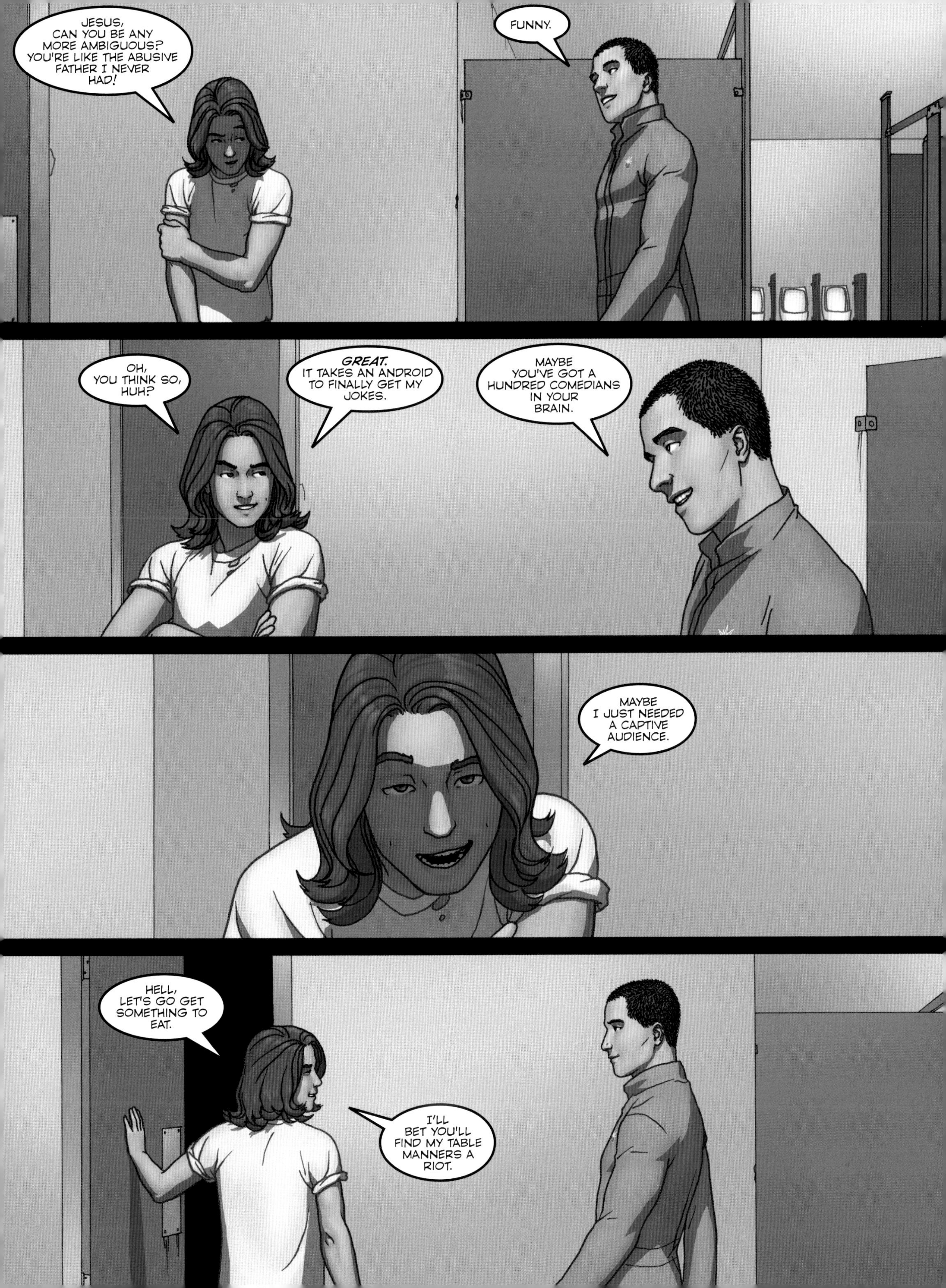
JESUS, CAN YOU BE ANY MORE AMBIGUOUS? YOU'RE LIKE THE ABUSIVE FATHER I NEVER HAD!
FUNNY.
OH, YOU THINK SO, HUH?
GREAT. IT TAKES AN ANDROID TO FINALLY GET MY JOKES.
MAYBE YOU'VE GOT A HUNDRED COMEDIANS IN YOUR BRAIN.
MAYBE I JUST NEEDED A CAPTIVE AUDIENCE.
HELL, LET'S GO GET SOMETHING TO EAT.
I'LL BET YOU'LL FIND MY TABLE MANNERS A RIOT.

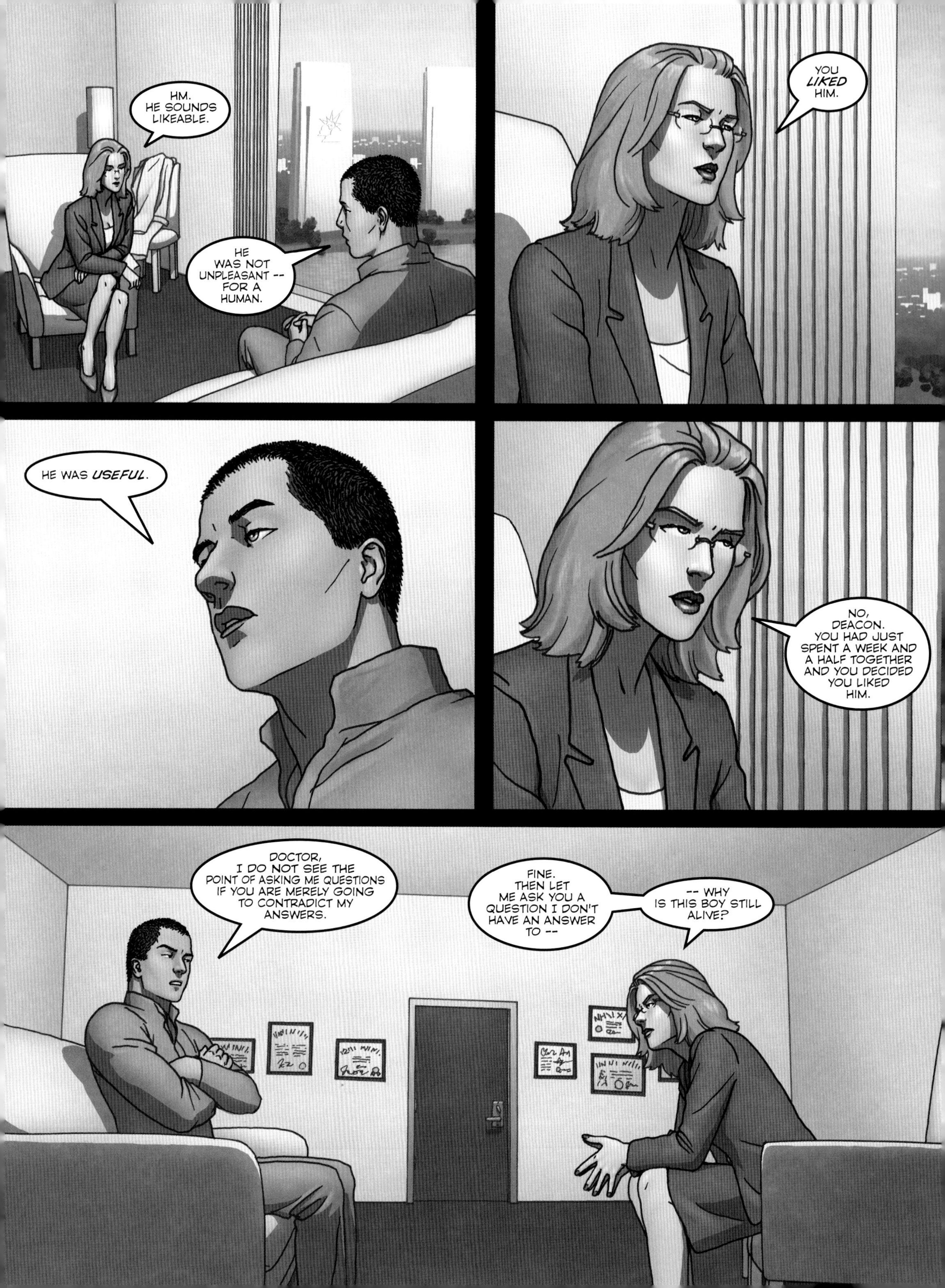
HM. HE SOUNDS LIKEABLE.
HE WAS NOT UNPLEASANT -- FOR A HUMAN.
YOU *LIKED* HIM.
HE WAS *USEFUL*.
NO, DEACON. YOU HAD JUST SPENT A WEEK AND A HALF TOGETHER AND YOU DECIDED YOU LIKED HIM.
DOCTOR, I DO NOT SEE THE POINT OF ASKING ME QUESTIONS IF YOU ARE MERELY GOING TO CONTRADICT MY ANSWERS.
FINE. THEN LET ME ASK YOU A QUESTION I DON'T HAVE AN ANSWER TO --
-- WHY IS THIS BOY STILL ALIVE?

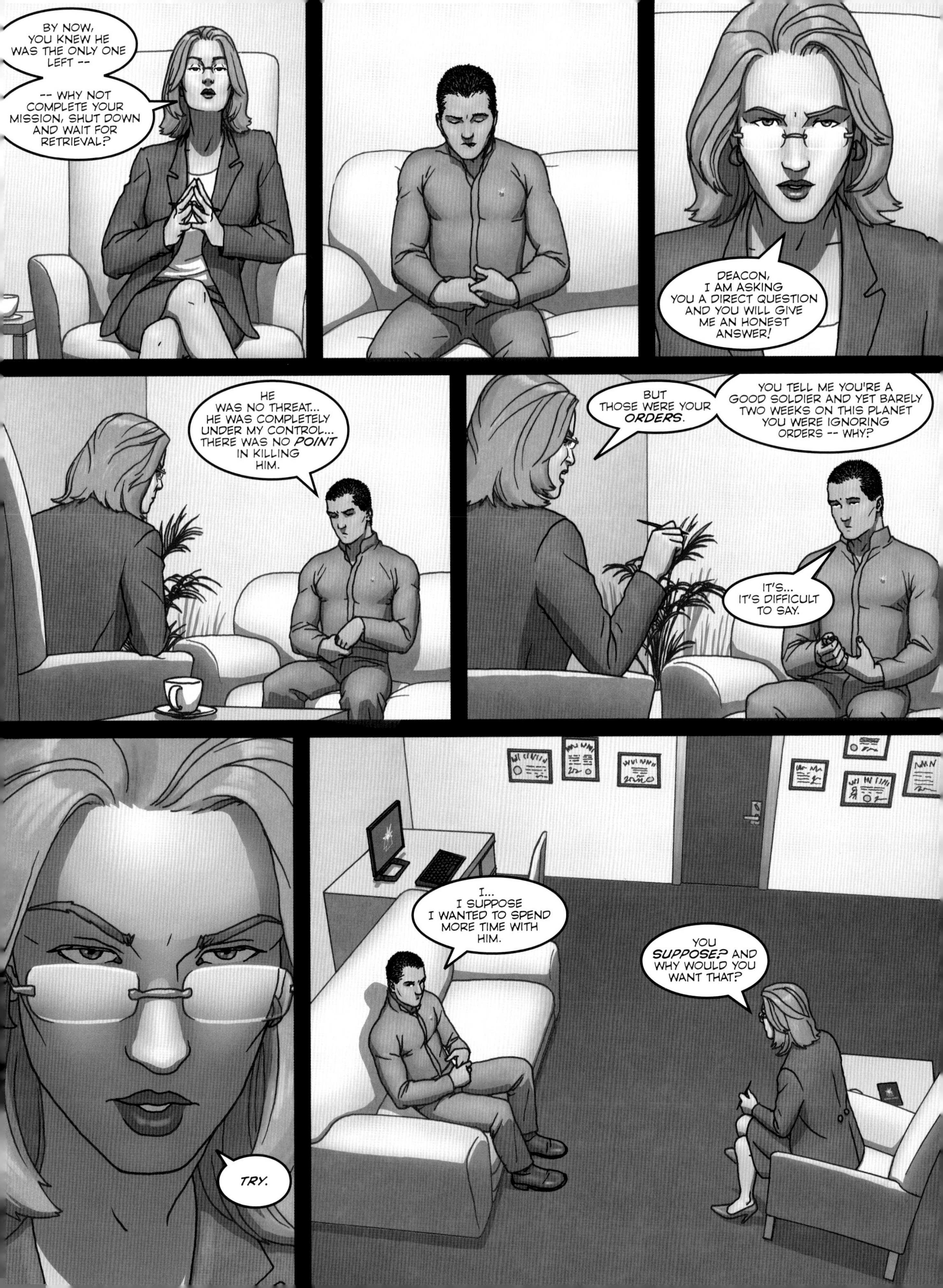
BY NOW, YOU KNEW HE WAS THE ONLY ONE LEFT --
-- WHY NOT COMPLETE YOUR MISSION, SHUT DOWN AND WAIT FOR RETRIEVAL?
DEACON, I AM ASKING YOU A DIRECT QUESTION AND YOU WILL GIVE ME AN HONEST ANSWER!
HE WAS NO THREAT... HE WAS COMPLETELY UNDER MY CONTROL... THERE WAS NO POINT IN KILLING HIM.
BUT THOSE WERE YOUR ORDERS.
YOU TELL ME YOU'RE A GOOD SOLDIER AND YET BARELY TWO WEEKS ON THIS PLANET YOU WERE IGNORING ORDERS -- WHY?
IT'S... IT'S DIFFICULT TO SAY.
TRY.
I... I SUPPOSE I WANTED TO SPEND MORE TIME WITH HIM.
YOU SUPPOSE? AND WHY WOULD YOU WANT THAT?

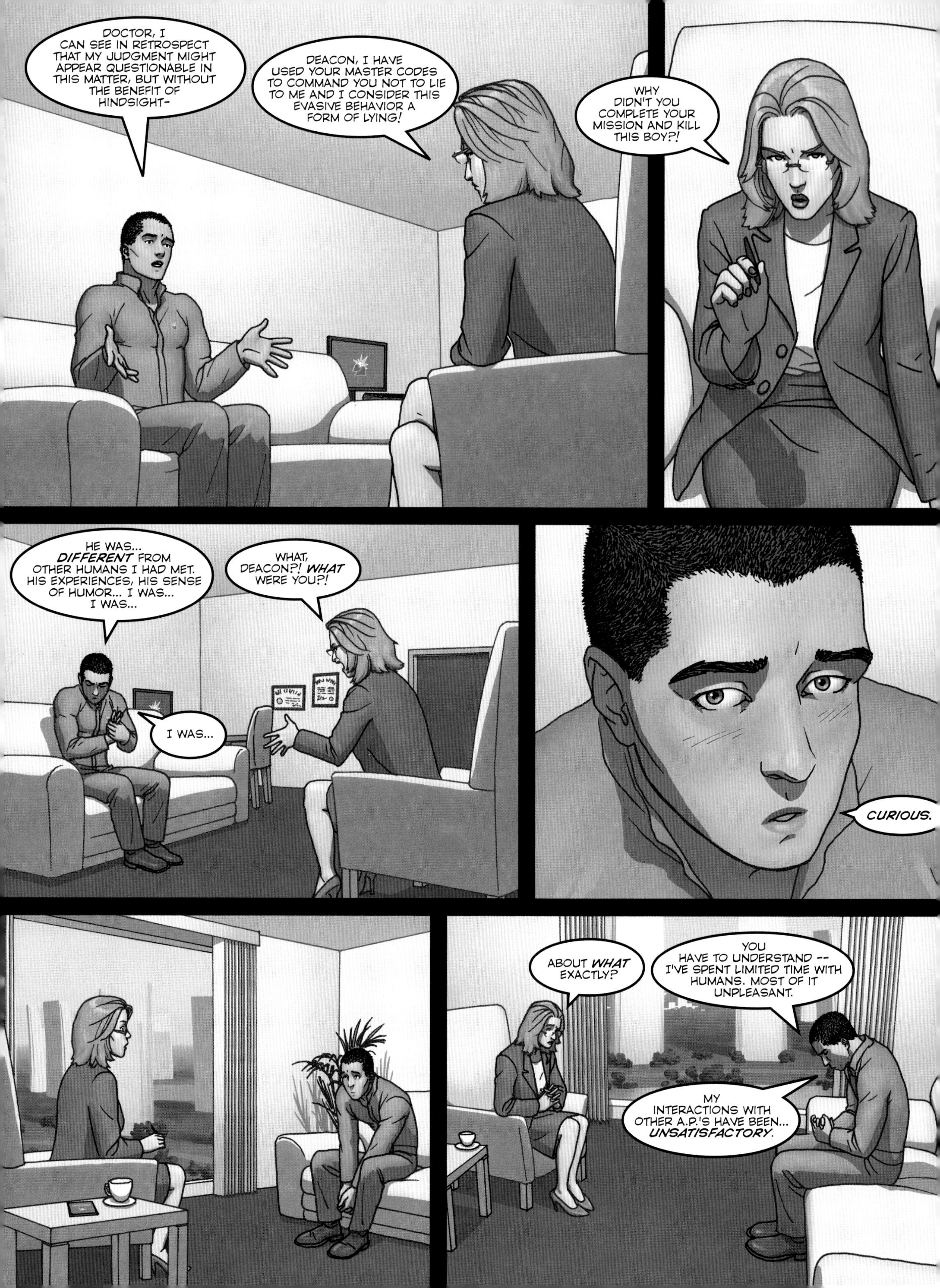
DOCTOR, I CAN SEE IN RETROSPECT THAT MY JUDGMENT MIGHT APPEAR QUESTIONABLE IN THIS MATTER, BUT WITHOUT THE BENEFIT OF HINDSIGHT-
DEACON, I HAVE USED YOUR MASTER CODES TO COMMAND YOU NOT TO LIE TO ME AND I CONSIDER THIS EVASIVE BEHAVIOR A FORM OF LYING!
WHY DIDN'T YOU COMPLETE YOUR MISSION AND KILL THIS BOY?!
HE WAS... *DIFFERENT* FROM OTHER HUMANS I HAD MET. HIS EXPERIENCES, HIS SENSE OF HUMOR... I WAS... I WAS...
WHAT, DEACON?! *WHAT* WERE YOU?!
I WAS...
CURIOUS.
ABOUT *WHAT* EXACTLY?
YOU HAVE TO UNDERSTAND -- I'VE SPENT LIMITED TIME WITH HUMANS. MOST OF IT UNPLEASANT.
MY INTERACTIONS WITH OTHER A.P.'S HAVE BEEN... *UNSATISFACTORY*.

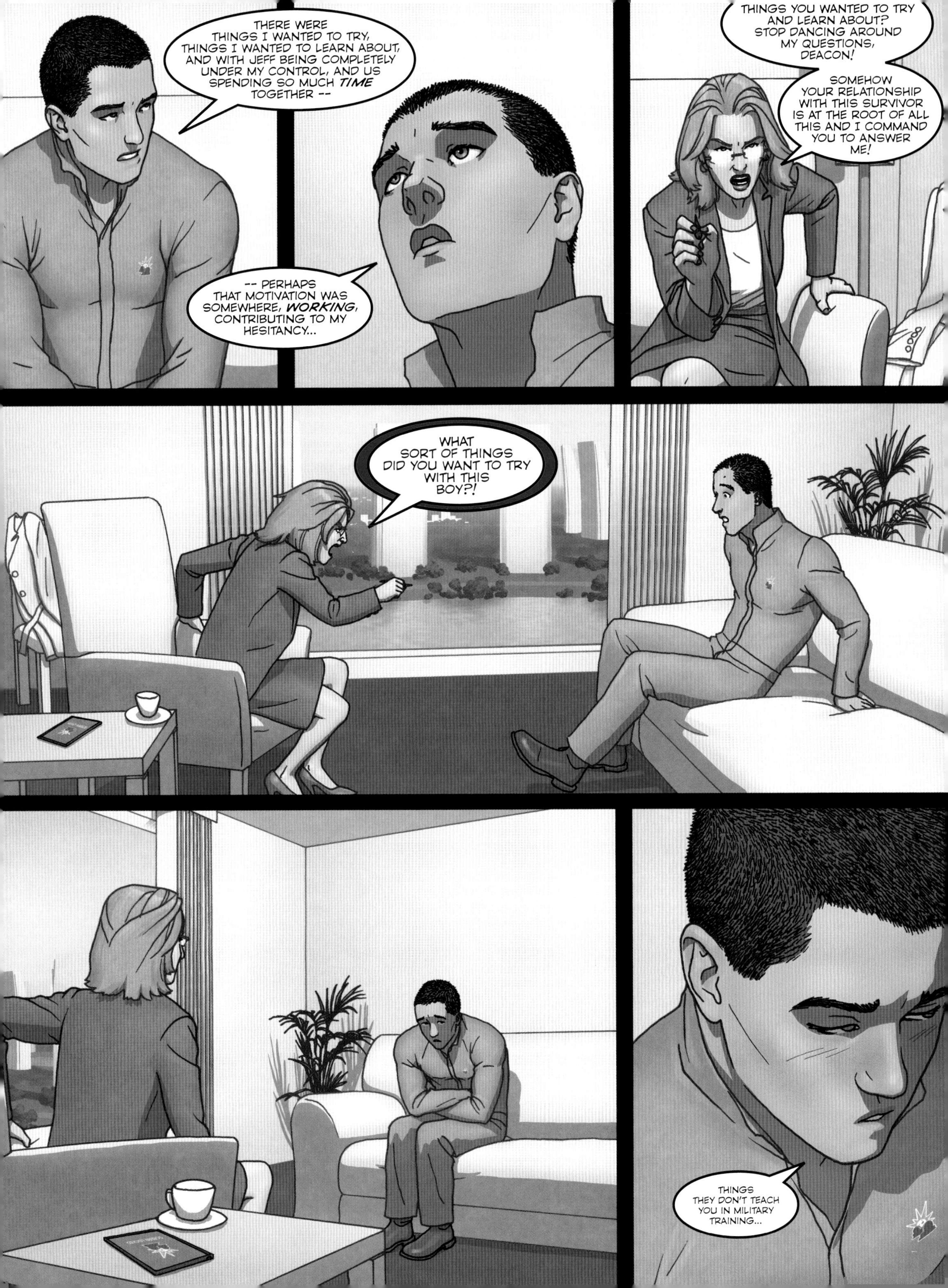
THERE WERE THINGS I WANTED TO TRY, THINGS I WANTED TO LEARN ABOUT, AND WITH JEFF BEING COMPLETELY UNDER MY CONTROL, AND US SPENDING SO MUCH TIME TOGETHER --
-- PERHAPS THAT MOTIVATION WAS SOMEWHERE, WORKING, CONTRIBUTING TO MY HESITANCY...
THINGS YOU WANTED TO TRY AND LEARN ABOUT? STOP DANCING AROUND MY QUESTIONS, DEACON!
SOMEHOW YOUR RELATIONSHIP WITH THIS SURVIVOR IS AT THE ROOT OF ALL THIS AND I COMMAND YOU TO ANSWER ME!
WHAT SORT OF THINGS DID YOU WANT TO TRY WITH THIS BOY?!
THINGS THEY DON'T TEACH YOU IN MILITARY TRAINING...

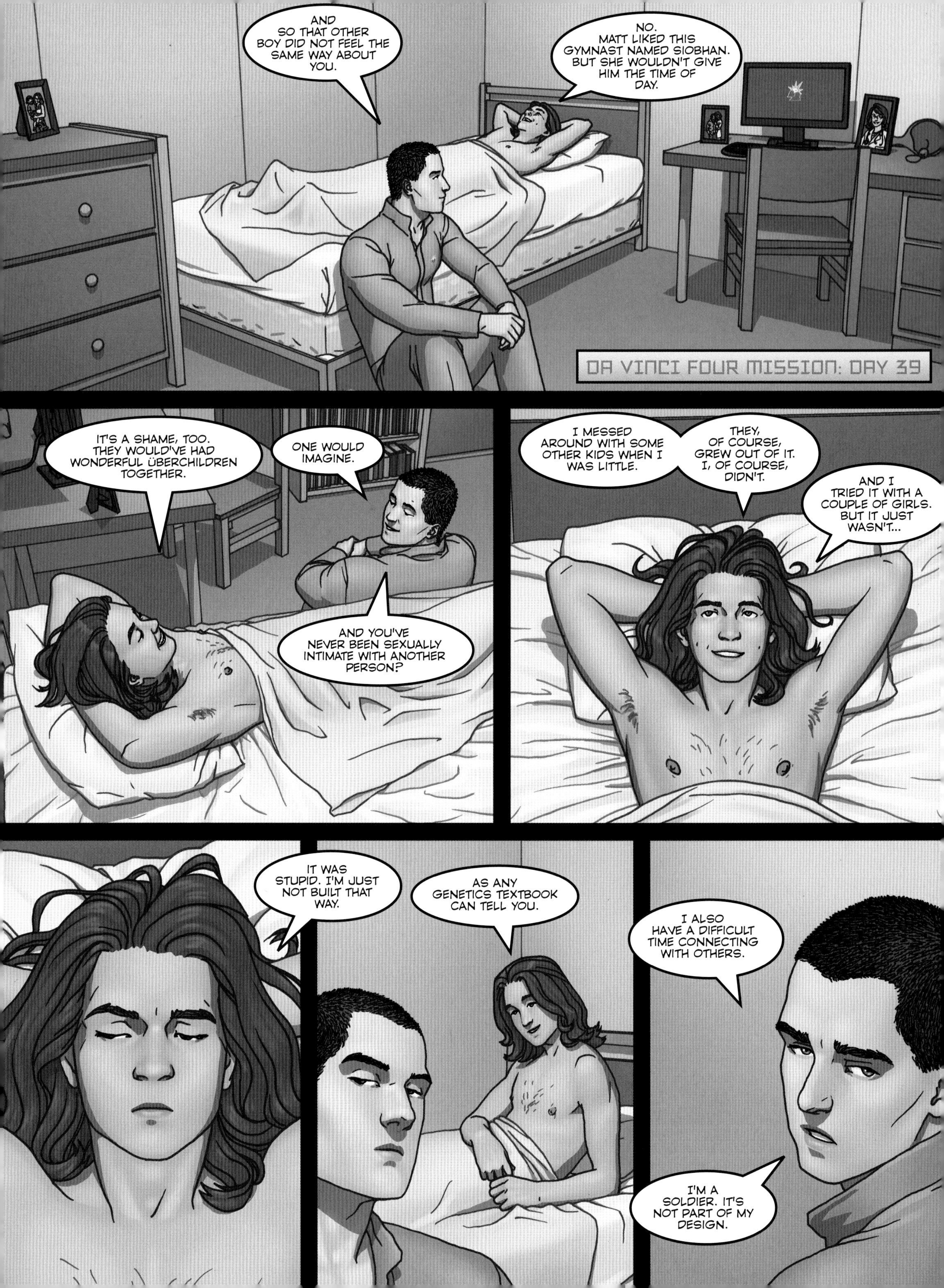
AND SO THAT OTHER BOY DID NOT FEEL THE SAME WAY ABOUT YOU.
NO. MATT LIKED THIS GYMNAST NAMED SIOBHAN. BUT SHE WOULDN'T GIVE HIM THE TIME OF DAY.
DA VINCI FOUR MISSION: DAY 39
IT'S A SHAME, TOO. THEY WOULD'VE HAD WONDERFUL ÜBERCHILDREN TOGETHER.
ONE WOULD IMAGINE.
AND YOU'VE NEVER BEEN SEXUALLY INTIMATE WITH ANOTHER PERSON?
I MESSED AROUND WITH SOME OTHER KIDS WHEN I WAS LITTLE.
THEY, OF COURSE, GREW OUT OF IT. I, OF COURSE, DIDN'T.
AND I TRIED IT WITH A COUPLE OF GIRLS. BUT IT JUST WASN'T...
IT WAS STUPID. I'M JUST NOT BUILT THAT WAY.
AS ANY GENETICS TEXTBOOK CAN TELL YOU.
I ALSO HAVE A DIFFICULT TIME CONNECTING WITH OTHERS.
I'M A SOLDIER. IT'S NOT PART OF MY DESIGN.

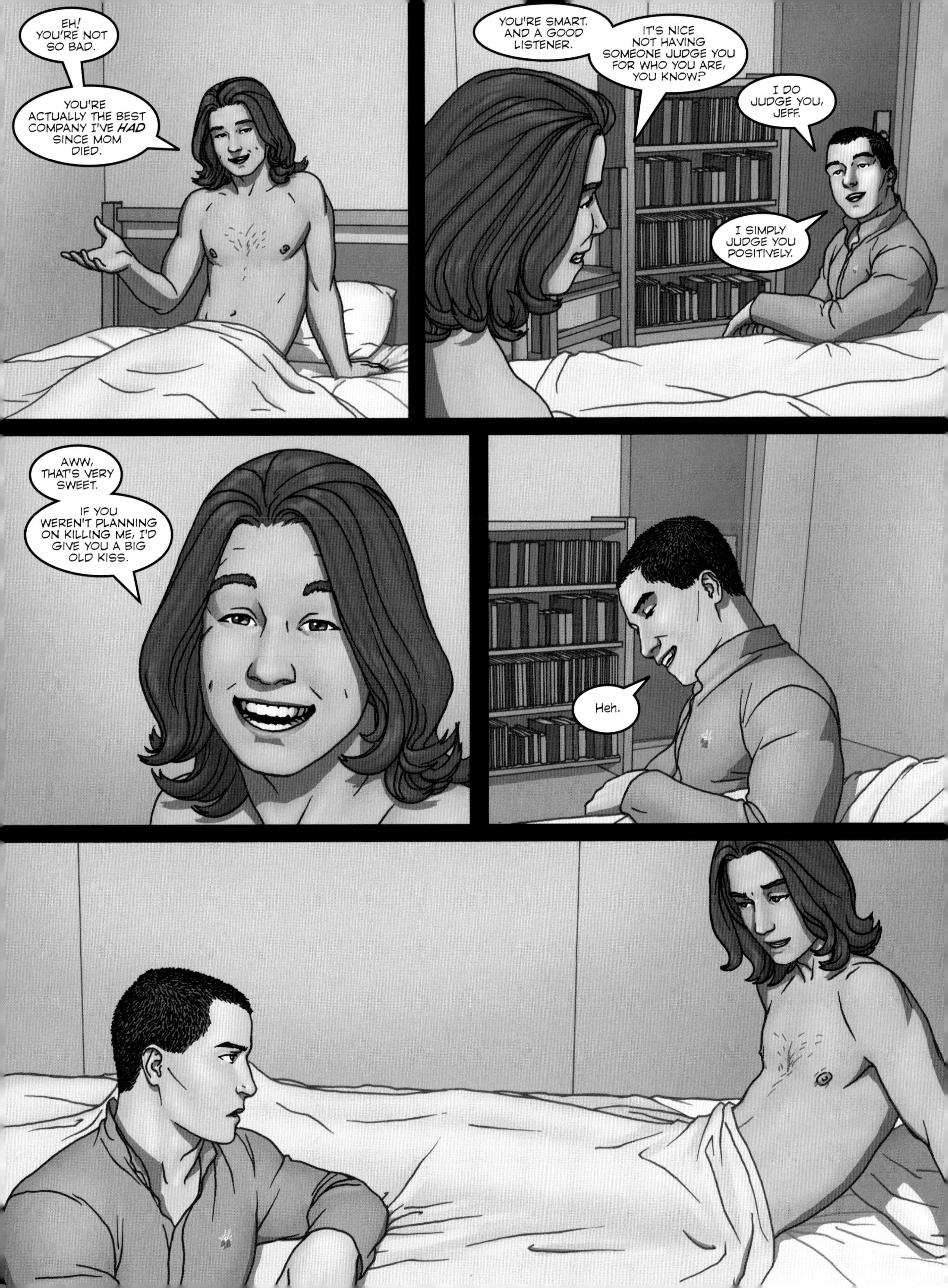
EH! YOU'RE NOT SO BAD.
YOU'RE ACTUALLY THE BEST COMPANY I'VE *HAD* SINCE MOM DIED.
YOU'RE SMART. AND A GOOD LISTENER.
IT'S NICE NOT HAVING SOMEONE JUDGE YOU FOR WHO YOU ARE, YOU KNOW?
I DO JUDGE YOU, JEFF.
I SIMPLY JUDGE YOU POSITIVELY.
AWW, THAT'S VERY SWEET.
IF YOU WEREN'T PLANNING ON KILLING ME, I'D GIVE YOU A BIG OLD KISS.
Heh.

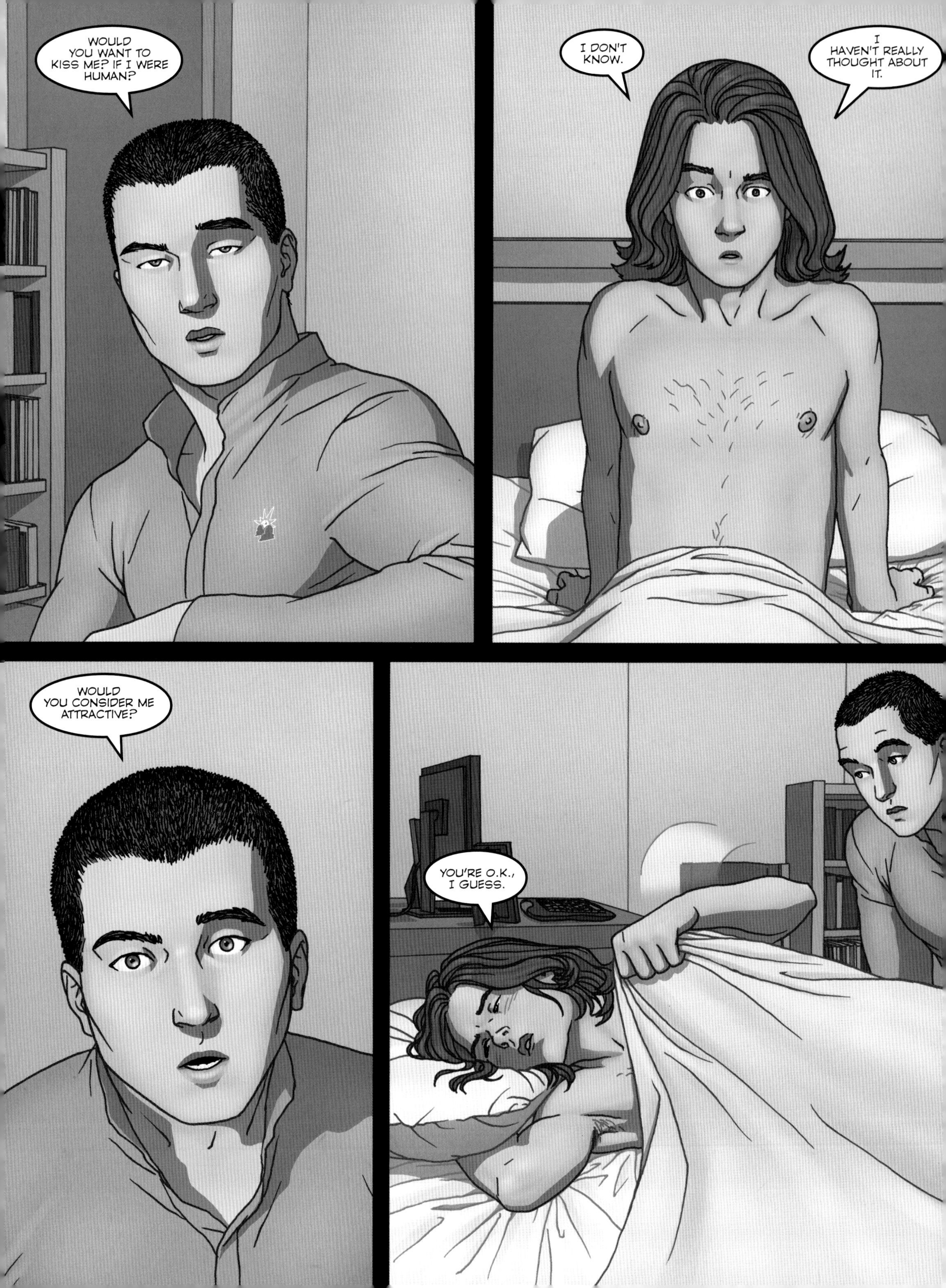
WOULD YOU WANT TO KISS ME? IF I WERE HUMAN?
I DON'T KNOW.
I HAVEN'T REALLY THOUGHT ABOUT IT.
WOULD YOU CONSIDER ME ATTRACTIVE?
YOU'RE O.K., I GUESS.

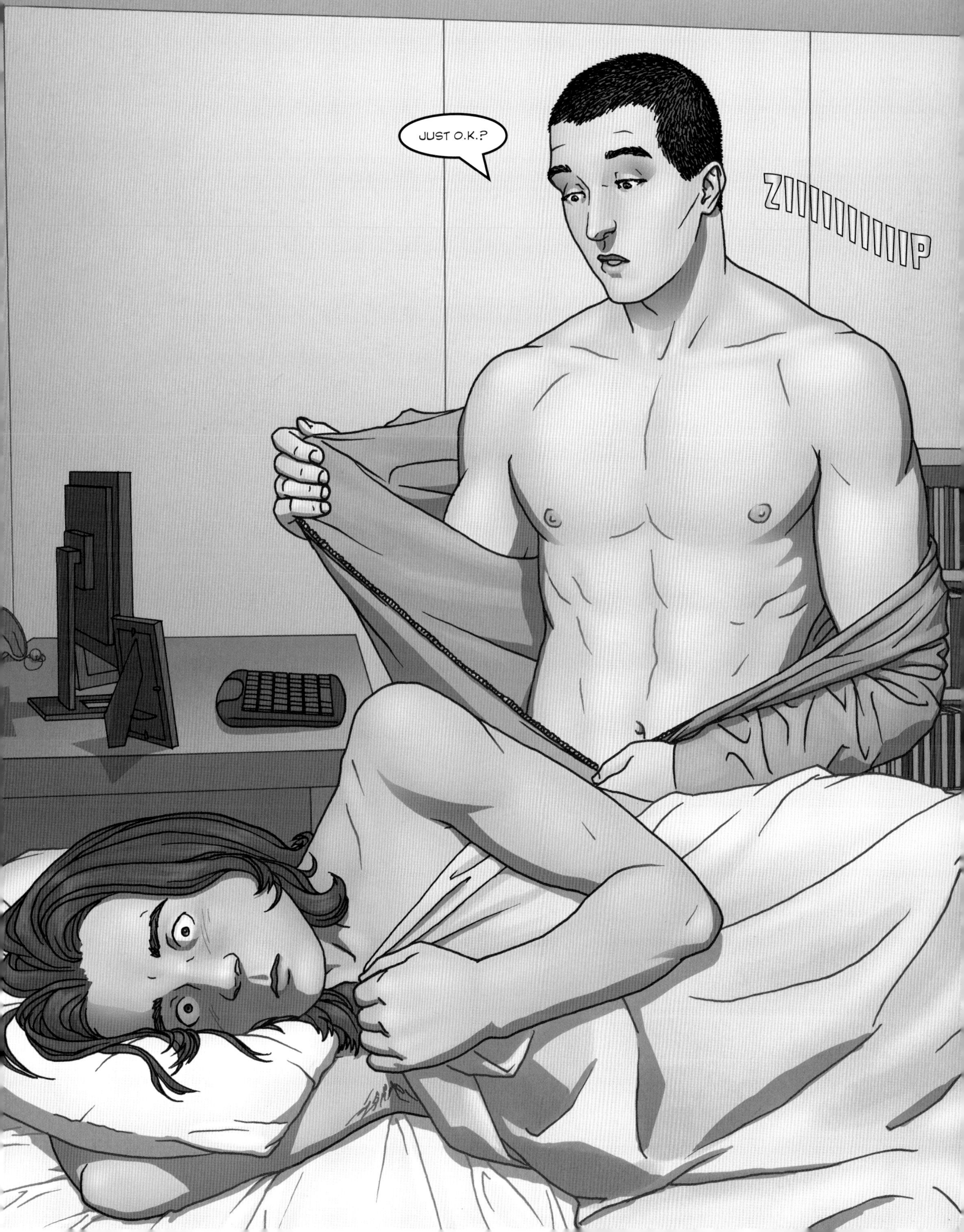
JUST O.K.?
ZIIIIIIIIIIP

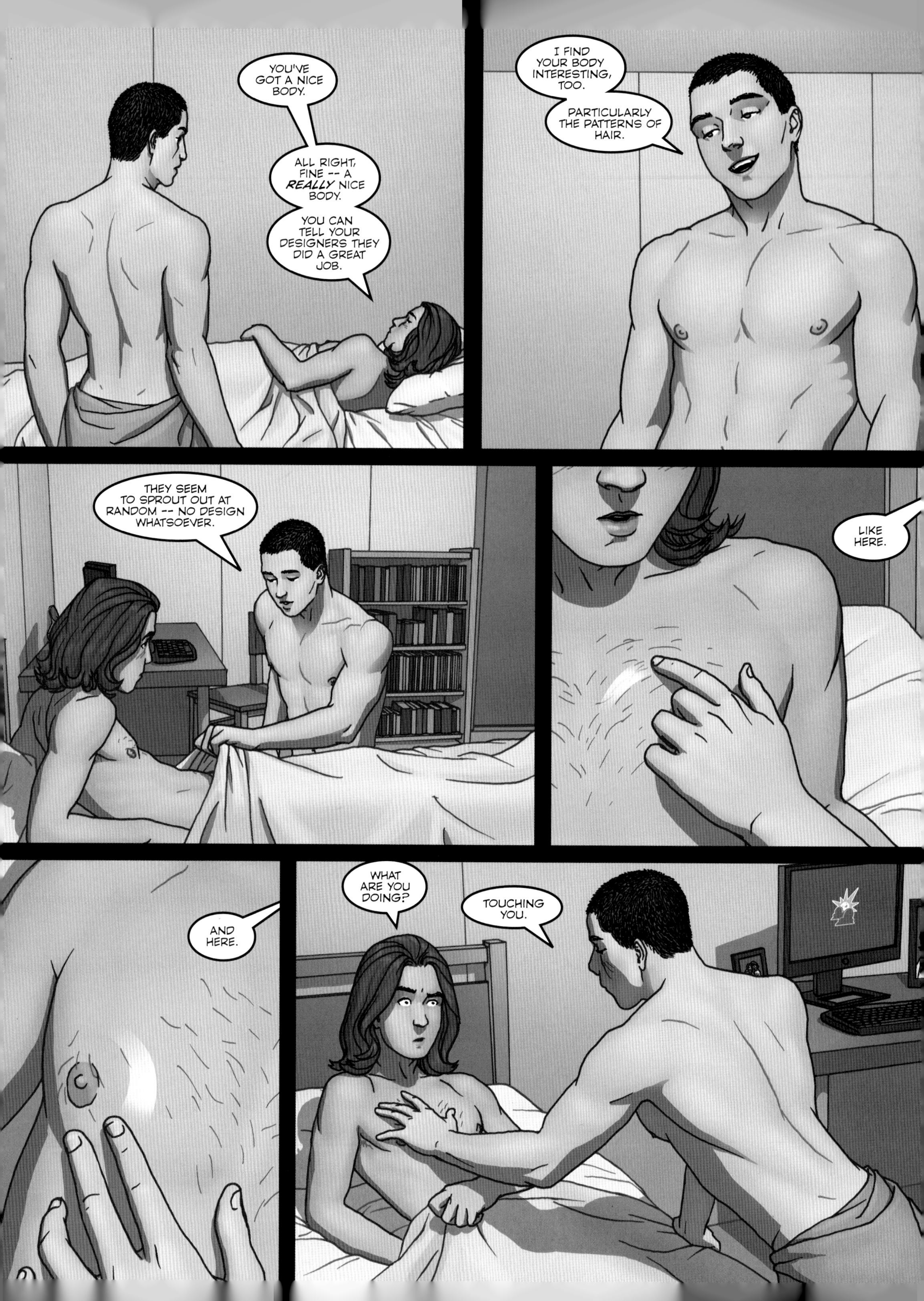
YOU'VE GOT A NICE BODY.
ALL RIGHT, FINE -- A *REALLY* NICE BODY.
YOU CAN TELL YOUR DESIGNERS THEY DID A GREAT JOB.
I FIND YOUR BODY INTERESTING, TOO.
PARTICULARLY THE PATTERNS OF HAIR.
THEY SEEM TO SPROUT OUT AT RANDOM -- NO DESIGN WHATSOEVER.
LIKE HERE.
AND HERE.
WHAT ARE YOU DOING?
TOUCHING YOU.

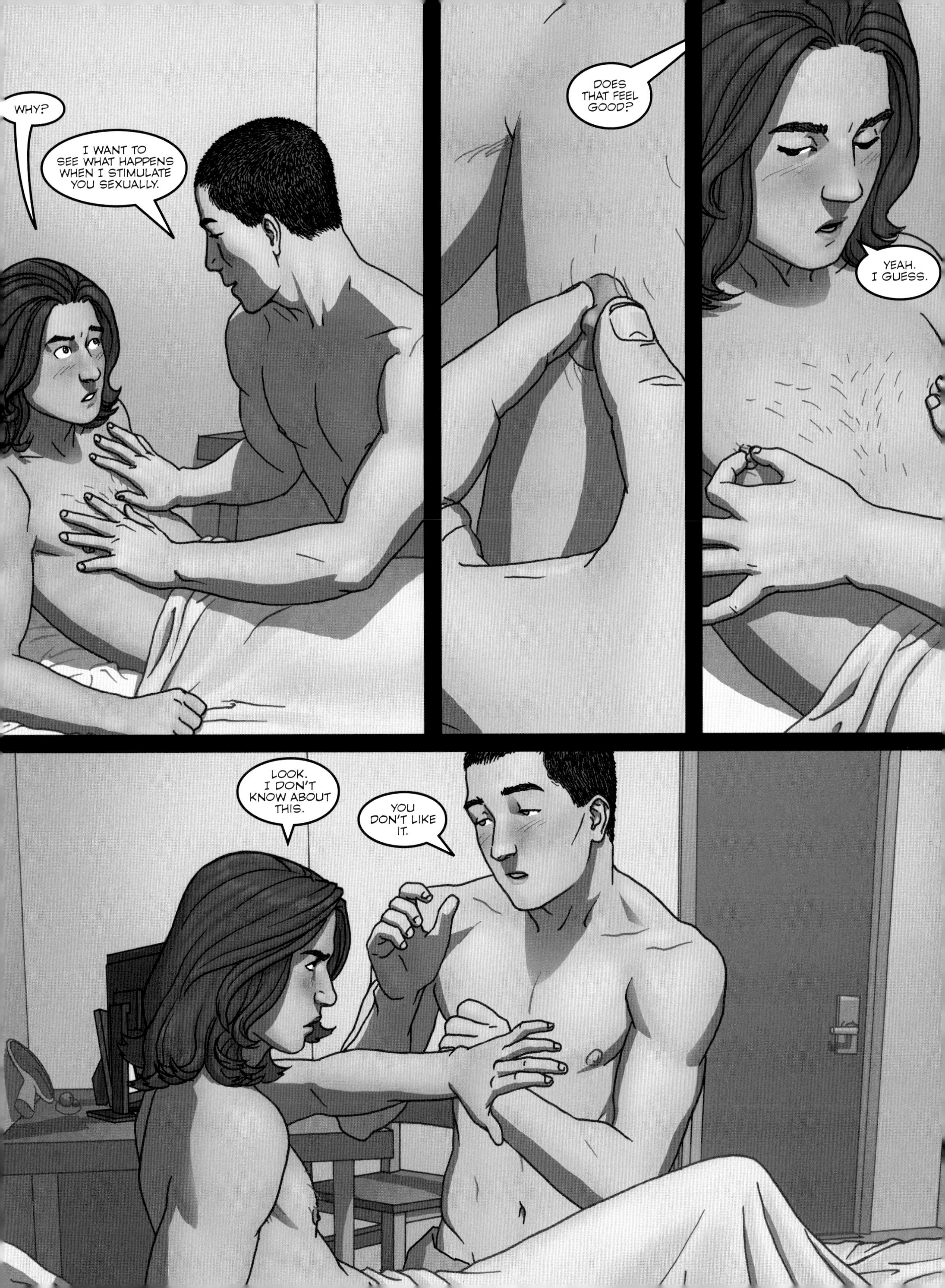
WHY?
I WANT TO SEE WHAT HAPPENS WHEN I STIMULATE YOU SEXUALLY.
DOES THAT FEEL GOOD?
YEAH. I GUESS.
LOOK. I DON'T KNOW ABOUT THIS.
YOU DON'T LIKE IT.

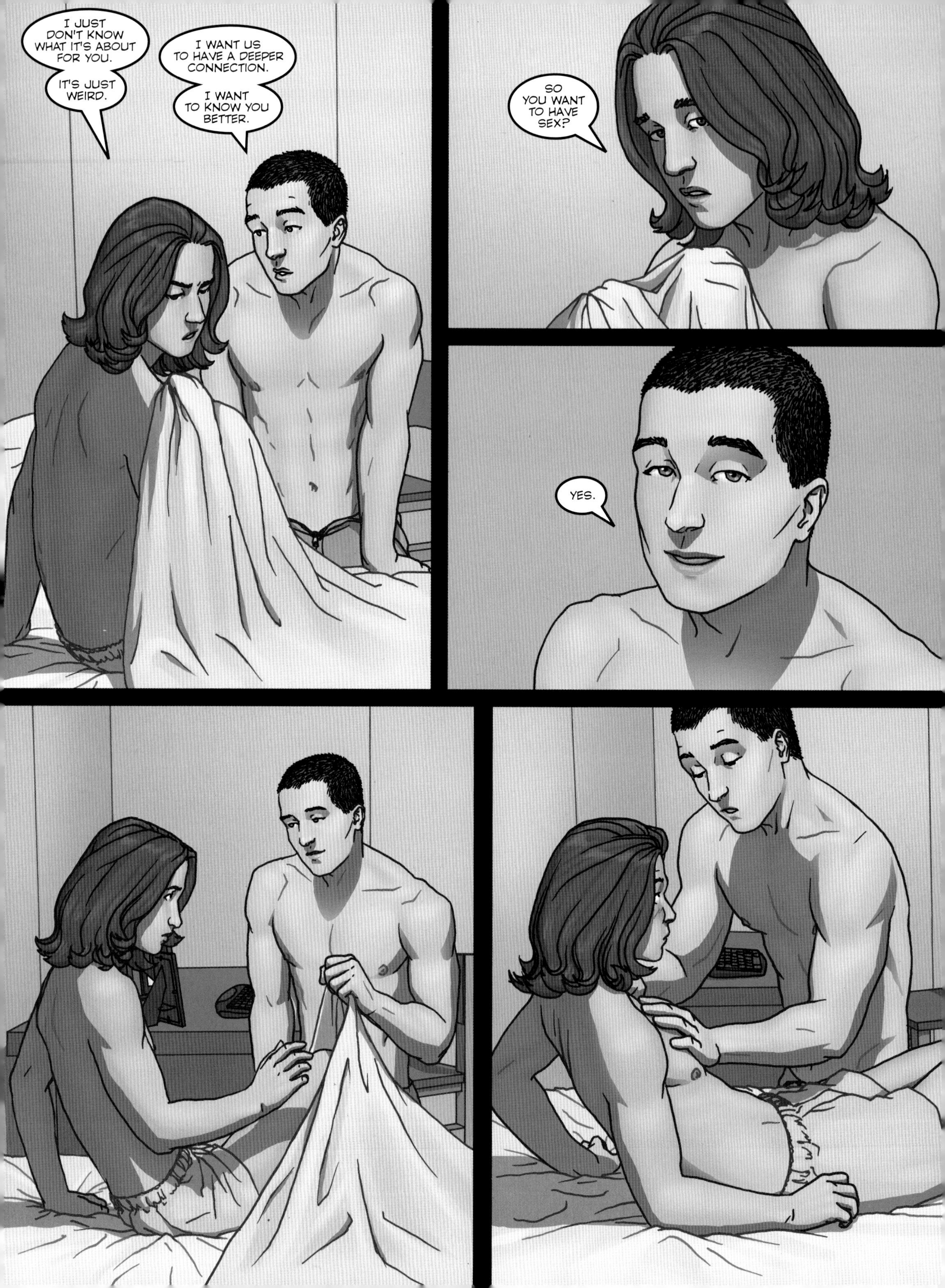
I JUST DON'T KNOW WHAT IT'S ABOUT FOR YOU.
IT'S JUST WEIRD.
I WANT US TO HAVE A DEEPER CONNECTION.
I WANT TO KNOW YOU BETTER.
SO YOU WANT TO HAVE SEX?
YES.

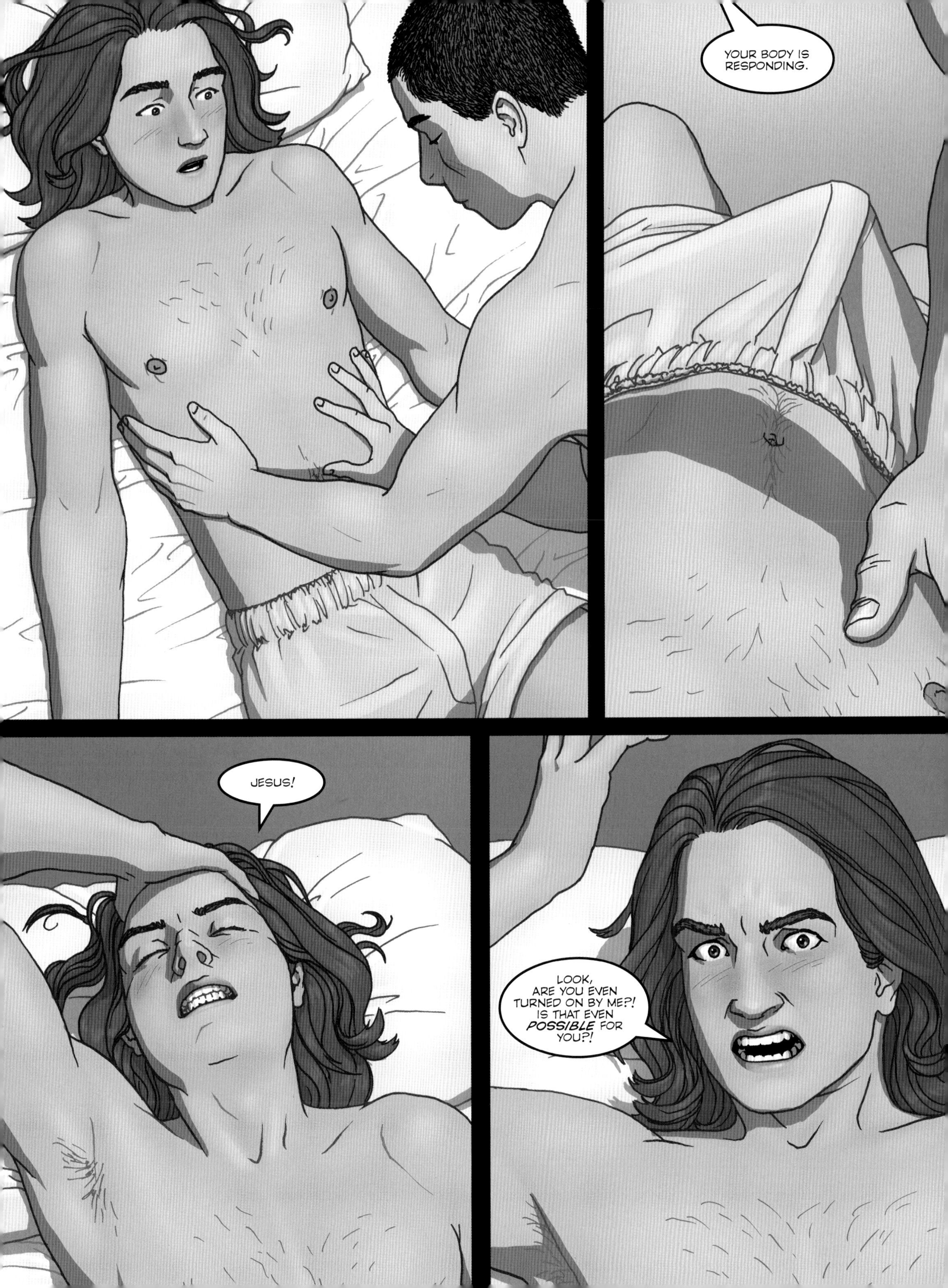
YOUR BODY IS RESPONDING.
JESUS!
LOOK, ARE YOU EVEN TURNED ON BY ME?! IS THAT EVEN *POSSIBLE* FOR YOU?!

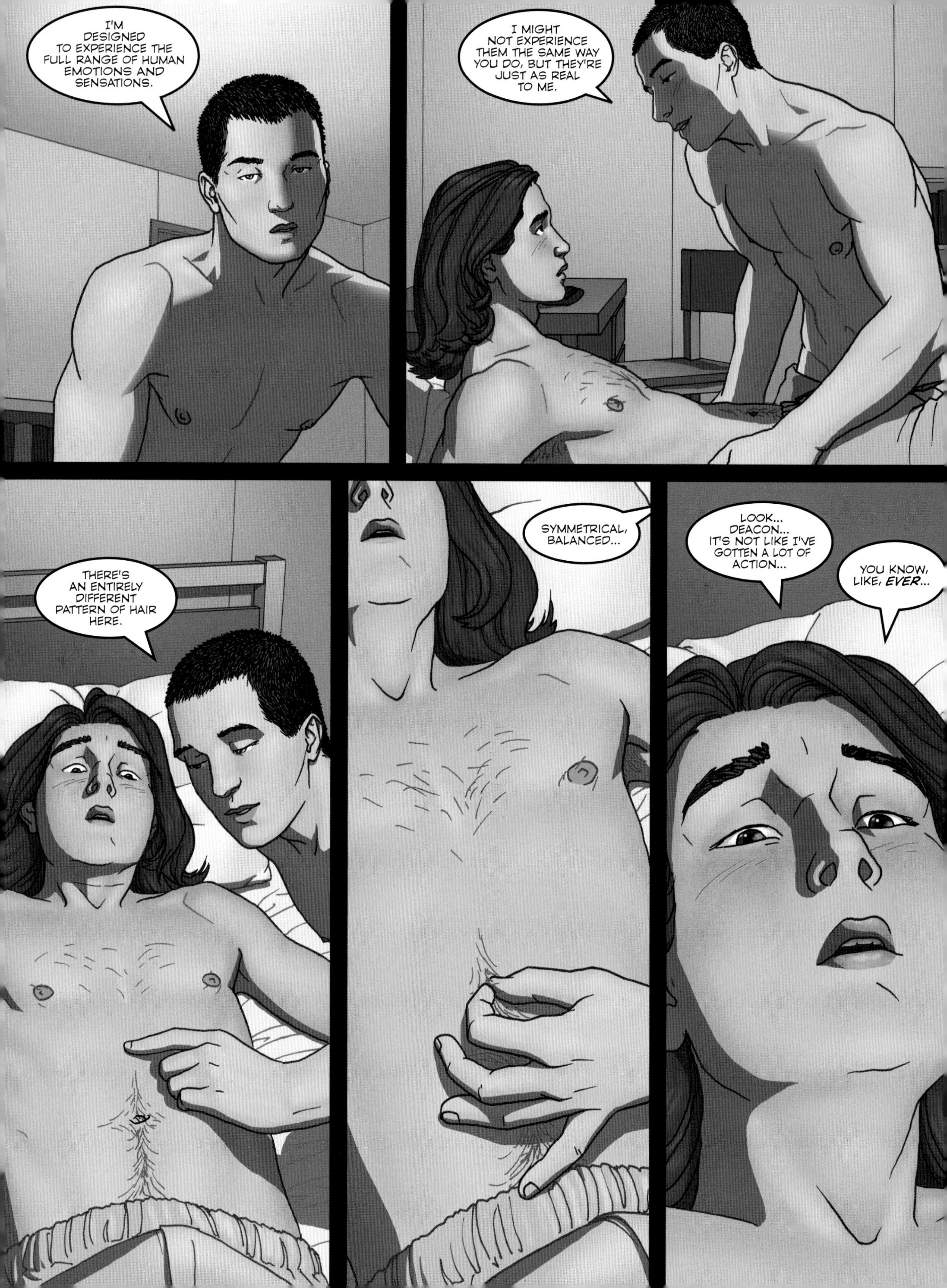
I'M DESIGNED TO EXPERIENCE THE FULL RANGE OF HUMAN EMOTIONS AND SENSATIONS.
I MIGHT NOT EXPERIENCE THEM THE SAME WAY YOU DO, BUT THEY'RE JUST AS REAL TO ME.
THERE'S AN ENTIRELY DIFFERENT PATTERN OF HAIR HERE.
SYMMETRICAL, BALANCED...
LOOK... DEACON... IT'S NOT LIKE I'VE GOTTEN A LOT OF ACTION...
YOU KNOW, LIKE, ***EVER***...

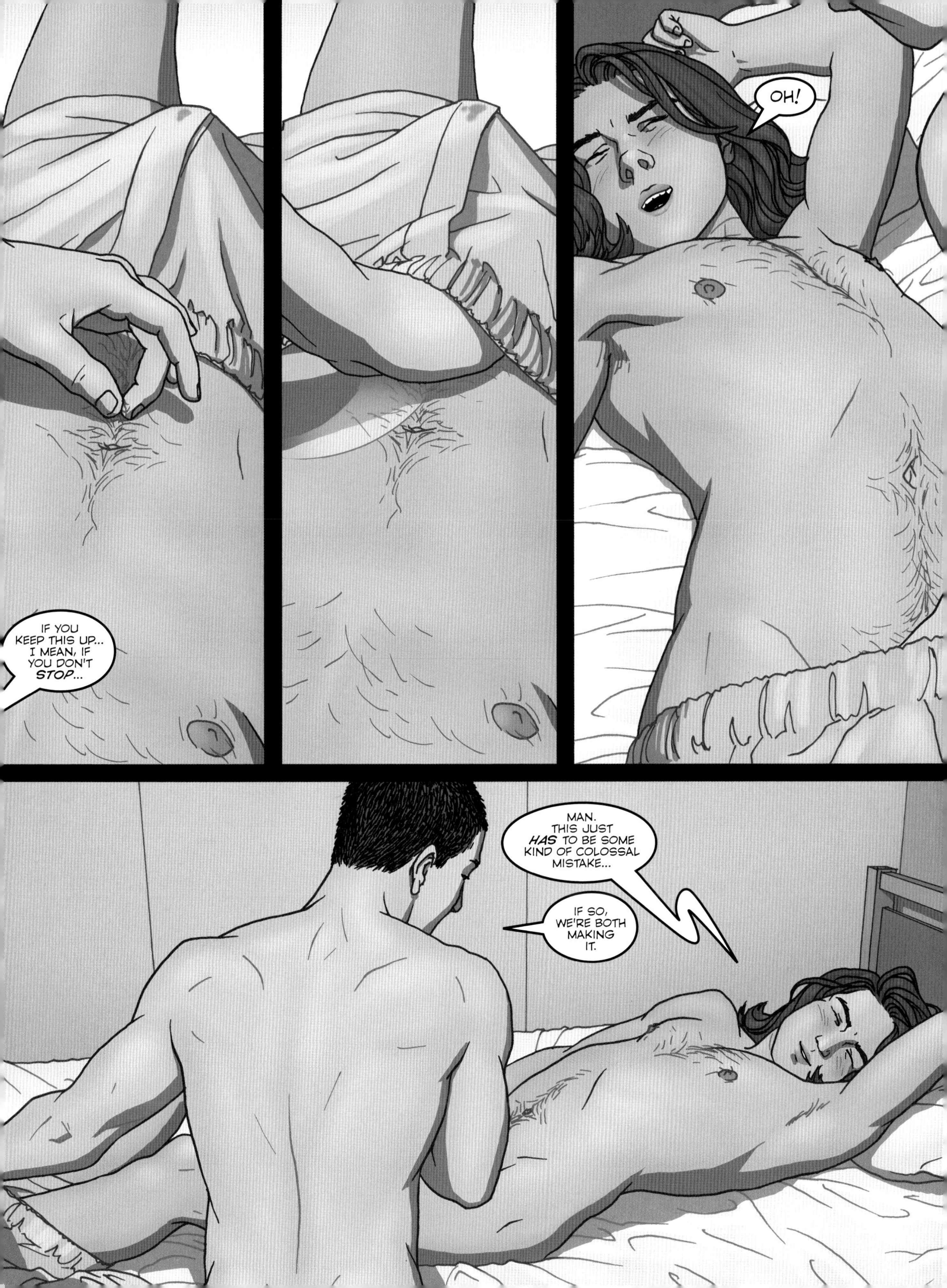
IF YOU KEEP THIS UP... I MEAN, IF YOU DON'T STOP...
OH!
MAN. THIS JUST HAS TO BE SOME KIND OF COLOSSAL MISTAKE...
IF SO, WE'RE BOTH MAKING IT.

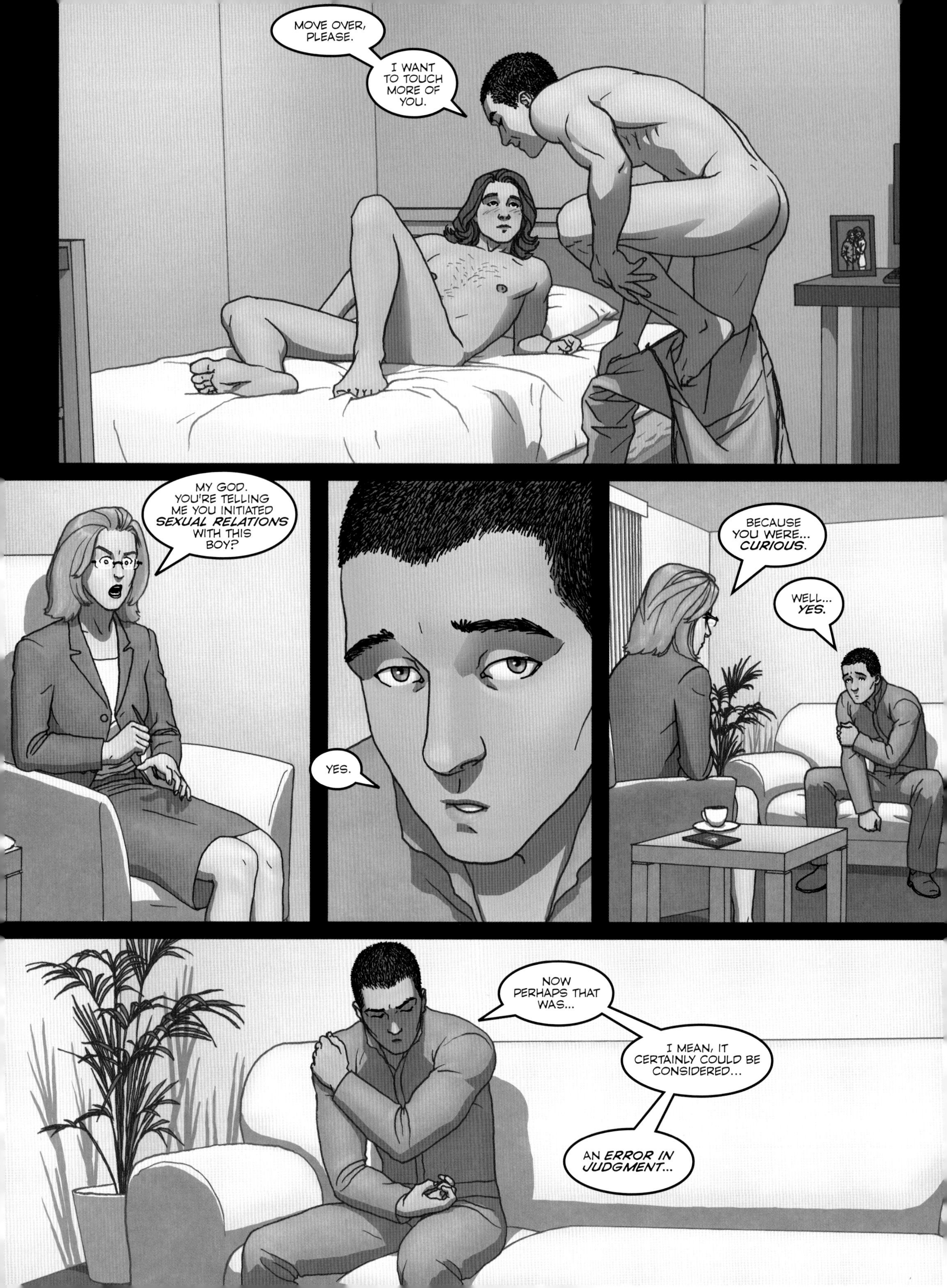
MOVE OVER, PLEASE.
I WANT TO TOUCH MORE OF YOU.
MY GOD. YOU'RE TELLING ME YOU INITIATED **SEXUAL RELATIONS** WITH THIS BOY?
YES.
BECAUSE YOU WERE... **CURIOUS**.
WELL... **YES**.
NOW PERHAPS THAT WAS...
I MEAN, IT CERTAINLY COULD BE CONSIDERED...
AN **ERROR IN JUDGMENT**...

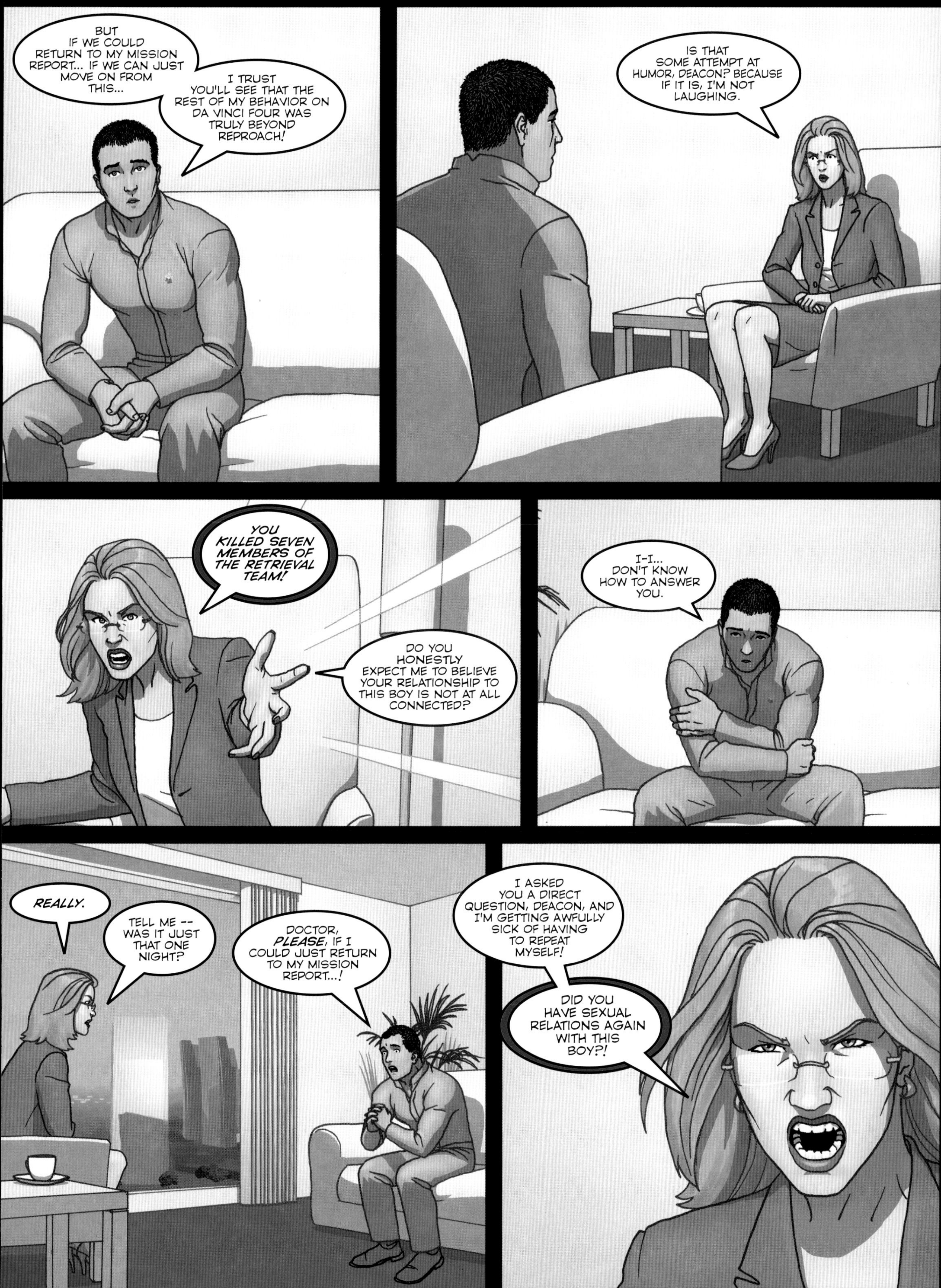
BUT IF WE COULD RETURN TO MY MISSION REPORT... IF WE CAN JUST MOVE ON FROM THIS...
I TRUST YOU'LL SEE THAT THE REST OF MY BEHAVIOR ON DA VINCI FOUR WAS TRULY BEYOND REPROACH!
IS THAT SOME ATTEMPT AT HUMOR, DEACON? BECAUSE IF IT IS, I'M NOT LAUGHING.
YOU KILLED SEVEN MEMBERS OF THE RETRIEVAL TEAM!
DO YOU HONESTLY EXPECT ME TO BELIEVE YOUR RELATIONSHIP TO THIS BOY IS NOT AT ALL CONNECTED?
I-I... DON'T KNOW HOW TO ANSWER YOU.
REALLY.
TELL ME -- WAS IT JUST THAT ONE NIGHT?
DOCTOR, PLEASE, IF I COULD JUST RETURN TO MY MISSION REPORT...!
I ASKED YOU A DIRECT QUESTION, DEACON, AND I'M GETTING AWFULLY SICK OF HAVING TO REPEAT MYSELF!
DID YOU HAVE SEXUAL RELATIONS AGAIN WITH THIS BOY?!

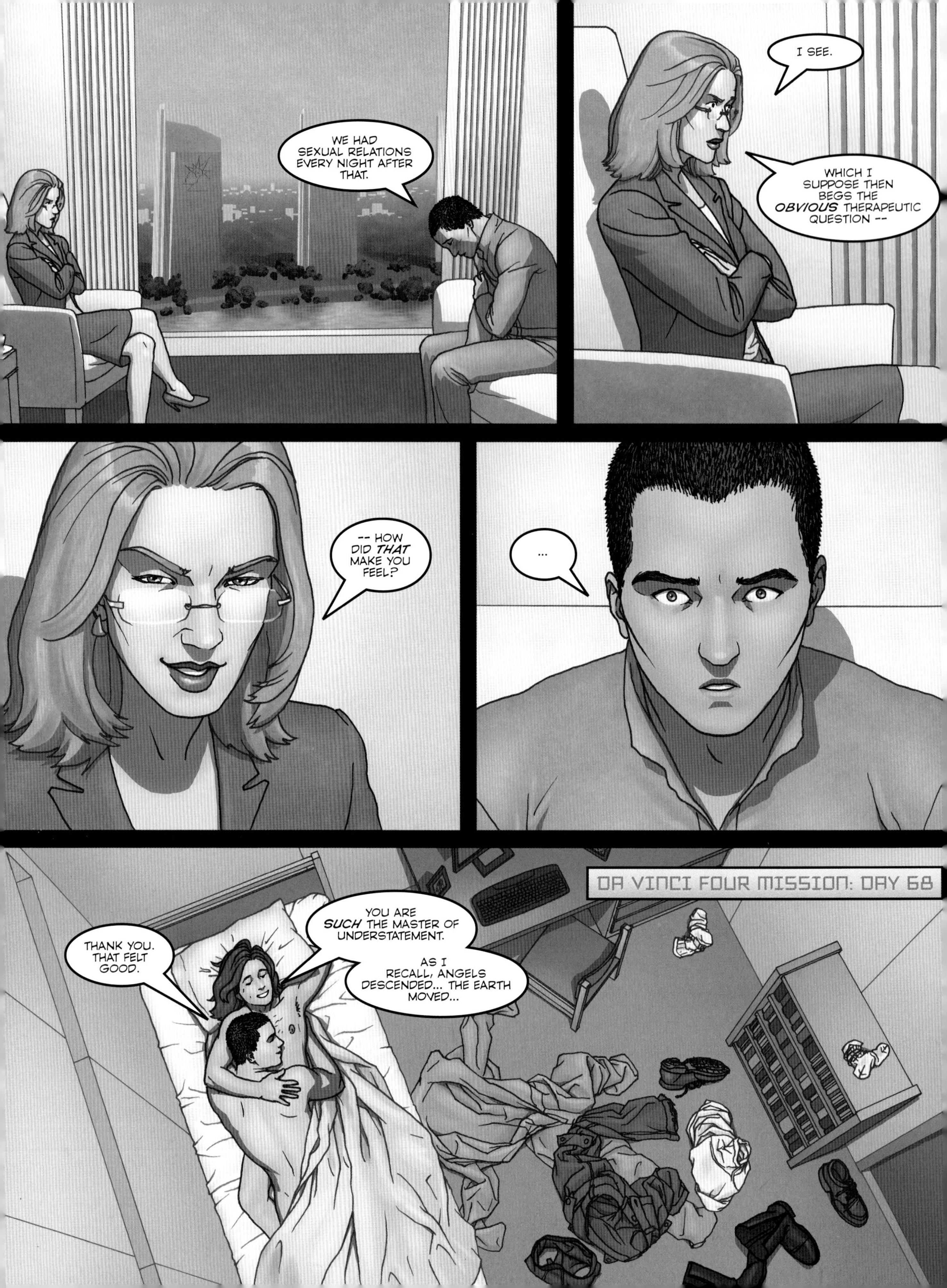
WE HAD SEXUAL RELATIONS EVERY NIGHT AFTER THAT.
I SEE.
WHICH I SUPPOSE THEN BEGS THE OBVIOUS THERAPEUTIC QUESTION --
-- HOW DID THAT MAKE YOU FEEL?
...
DA VINCI FOUR MISSION: DAY 68
THANK YOU. THAT FELT GOOD.
YOU ARE SUCH THE MASTER OF UNDERSTATEMENT.
AS I RECALL, ANGELS DESCENDED... THE EARTH MOVED...

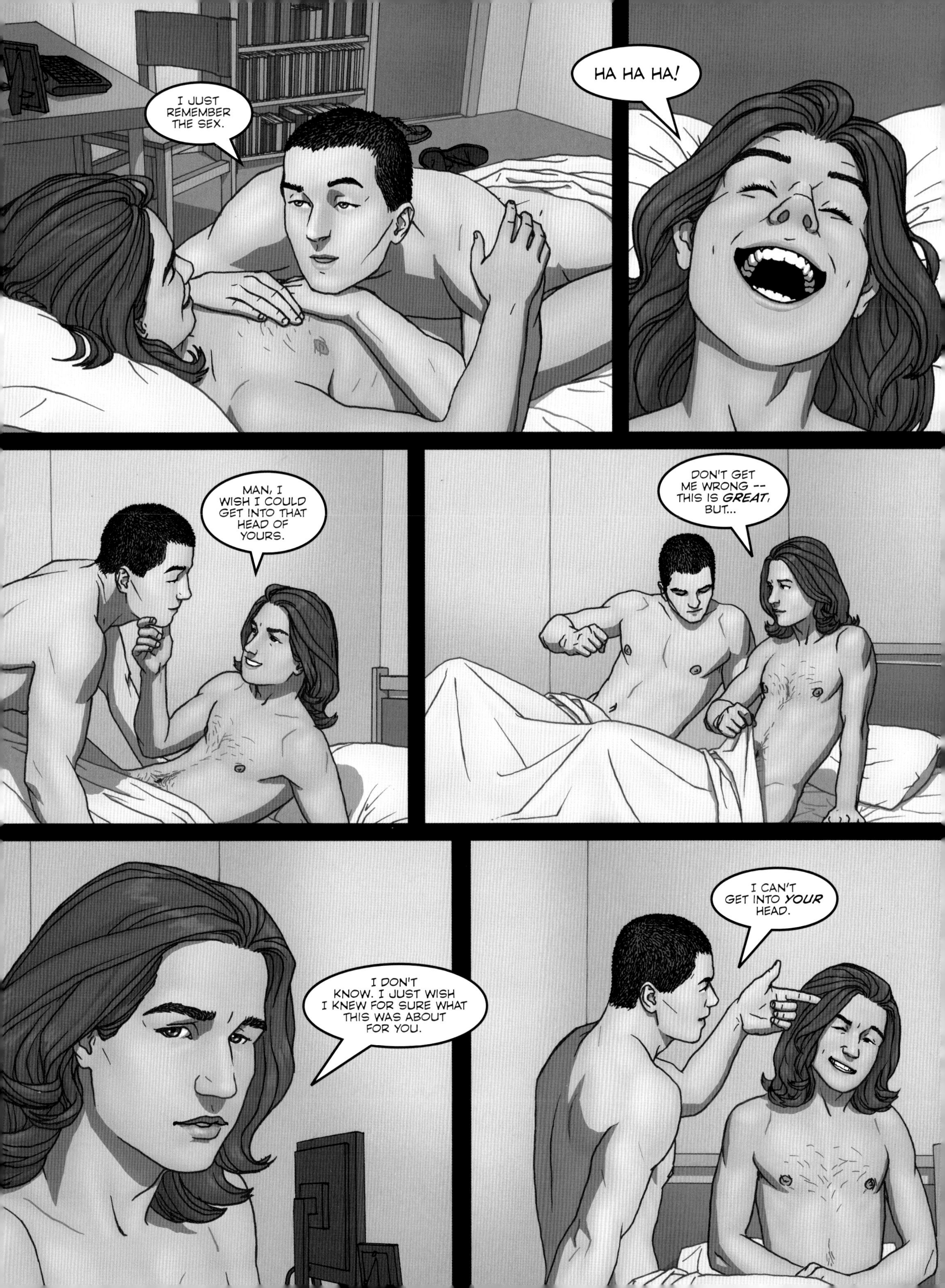
I JUST REMEMBER THE SEX.
HA HA HA!
MAN, I WISH I COULD GET INTO THAT HEAD OF YOURS.
DON'T GET ME WRONG -- THIS IS *GREAT*, BUT...
I DON'T KNOW. I JUST WISH I KNEW FOR SURE WHAT THIS WAS ABOUT FOR YOU.
I CAN'T GET INTO *YOUR* HEAD.

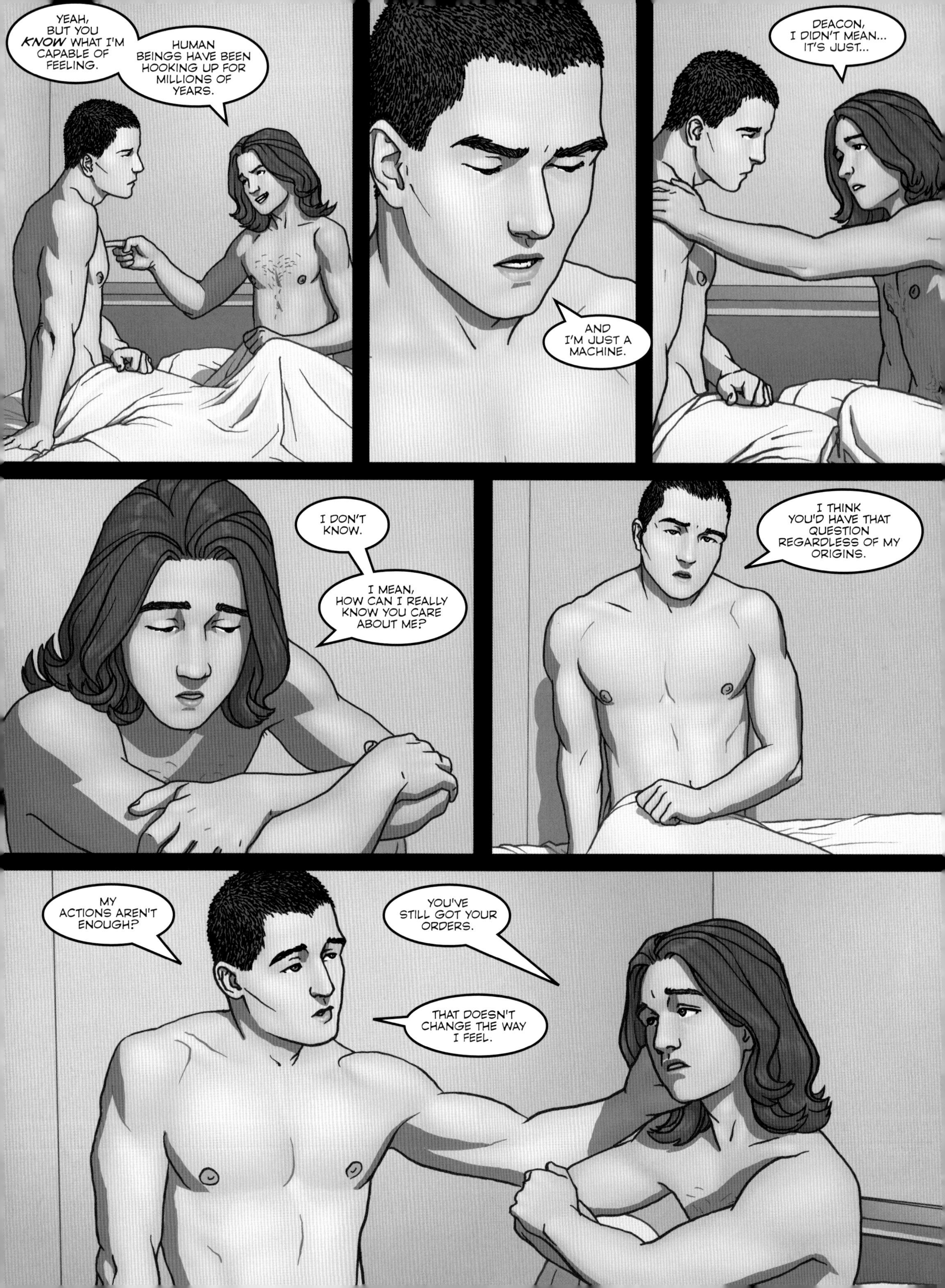
YEAH, BUT YOU *KNOW* WHAT I'M CAPABLE OF FEELING.
HUMAN BEINGS HAVE BEEN HOOKING UP FOR MILLIONS OF YEARS.
AND I'M JUST A MACHINE.
DEACON, I DIDN'T MEAN... IT'S JUST...
I DON'T KNOW.
I MEAN, HOW CAN I REALLY KNOW YOU CARE ABOUT ME?
I THINK YOU'D HAVE THAT QUESTION REGARDLESS OF MY ORIGINS.
MY ACTIONS AREN'T ENOUGH?
YOU'VE STILL GOT YOUR ORDERS.
THAT DOESN'T CHANGE THE WAY I FEEL.

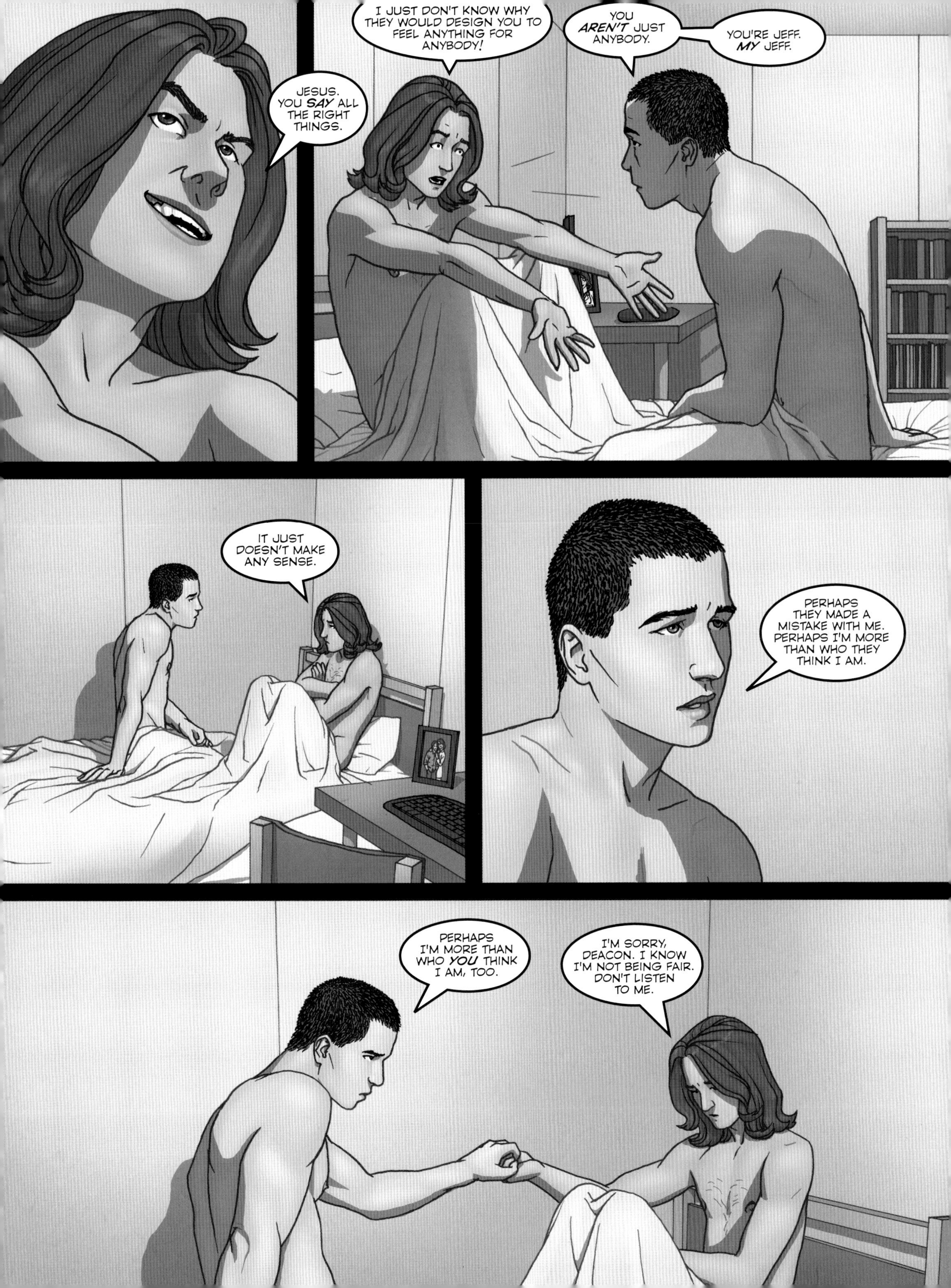
JESUS. YOU SAY ALL THE RIGHT THINGS.
I JUST DON'T KNOW WHY THEY WOULD DESIGN YOU TO FEEL ANYTHING FOR ANYBODY!
YOU AREN'T JUST ANYBODY.
YOU'RE JEFF. MY JEFF.
IT JUST DOESN'T MAKE ANY SENSE.
PERHAPS THEY MADE A MISTAKE WITH ME. PERHAPS I'M MORE THAN WHO THEY THINK I AM.
PERHAPS I'M MORE THAN WHO YOU THINK I AM, TOO.
I'M SORRY, DEACON. I KNOW I'M NOT BEING FAIR. DON'T LISTEN TO ME.

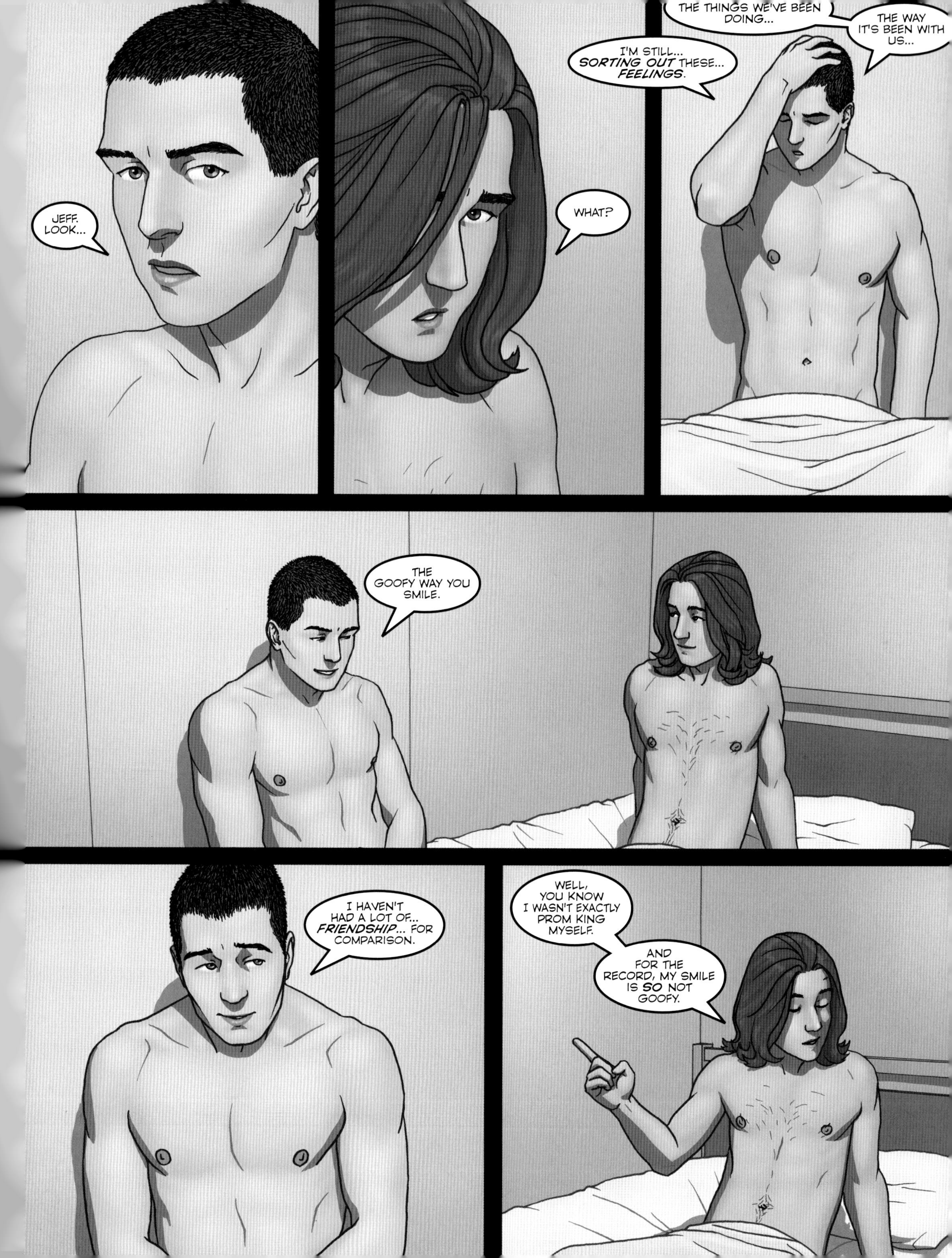
JEFF. LOOK...
WHAT?
THE THINGS WE'VE BEEN DOING...
THE WAY IT'S BEEN WITH US...
I'M STILL... SORTING OUT THESE... FEELINGS.
THE GOOFY WAY YOU SMILE.
I HAVEN'T HAD A LOT OF... FRIENDSHIP... FOR COMPARISON.
WELL, YOU KNOW I WASN'T EXACTLY PROM KING MYSELF.
AND FOR THE RECORD, MY SMILE IS SO NOT GOOFY.

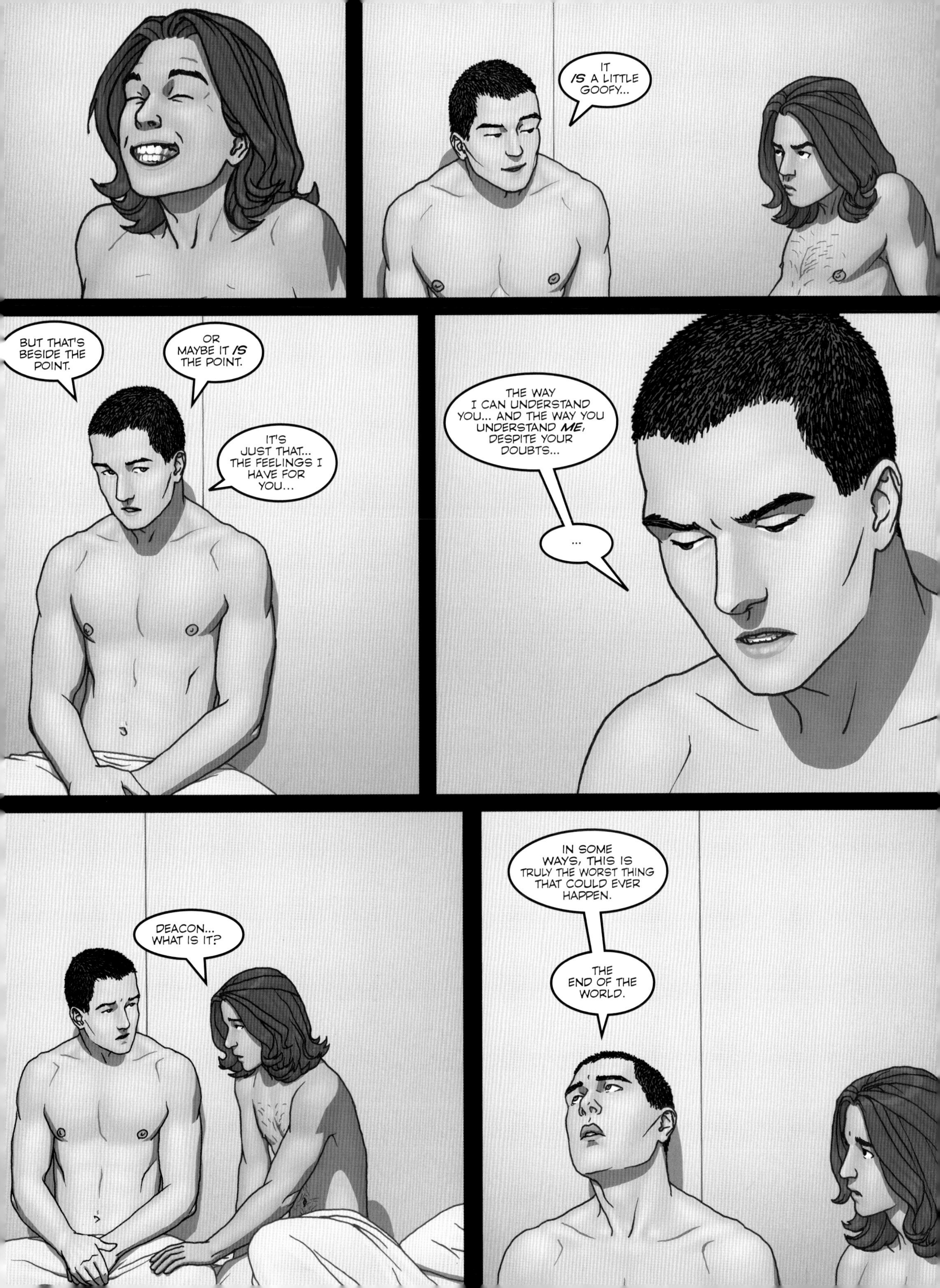
IT IS A LITTLE GOOFY...
BUT THAT'S BESIDE THE POINT.
OR MAYBE IT IS THE POINT.
IT'S JUST THAT... THE FEELINGS I HAVE FOR YOU...
THE WAY I CAN UNDERSTAND YOU... AND THE WAY YOU UNDERSTAND ME, DESPITE YOUR DOUBTS...
...
DEACON... WHAT IS IT?
IN SOME WAYS, THIS IS TRULY THE WORST THING THAT COULD EVER HAPPEN.
THE END OF THE WORLD.

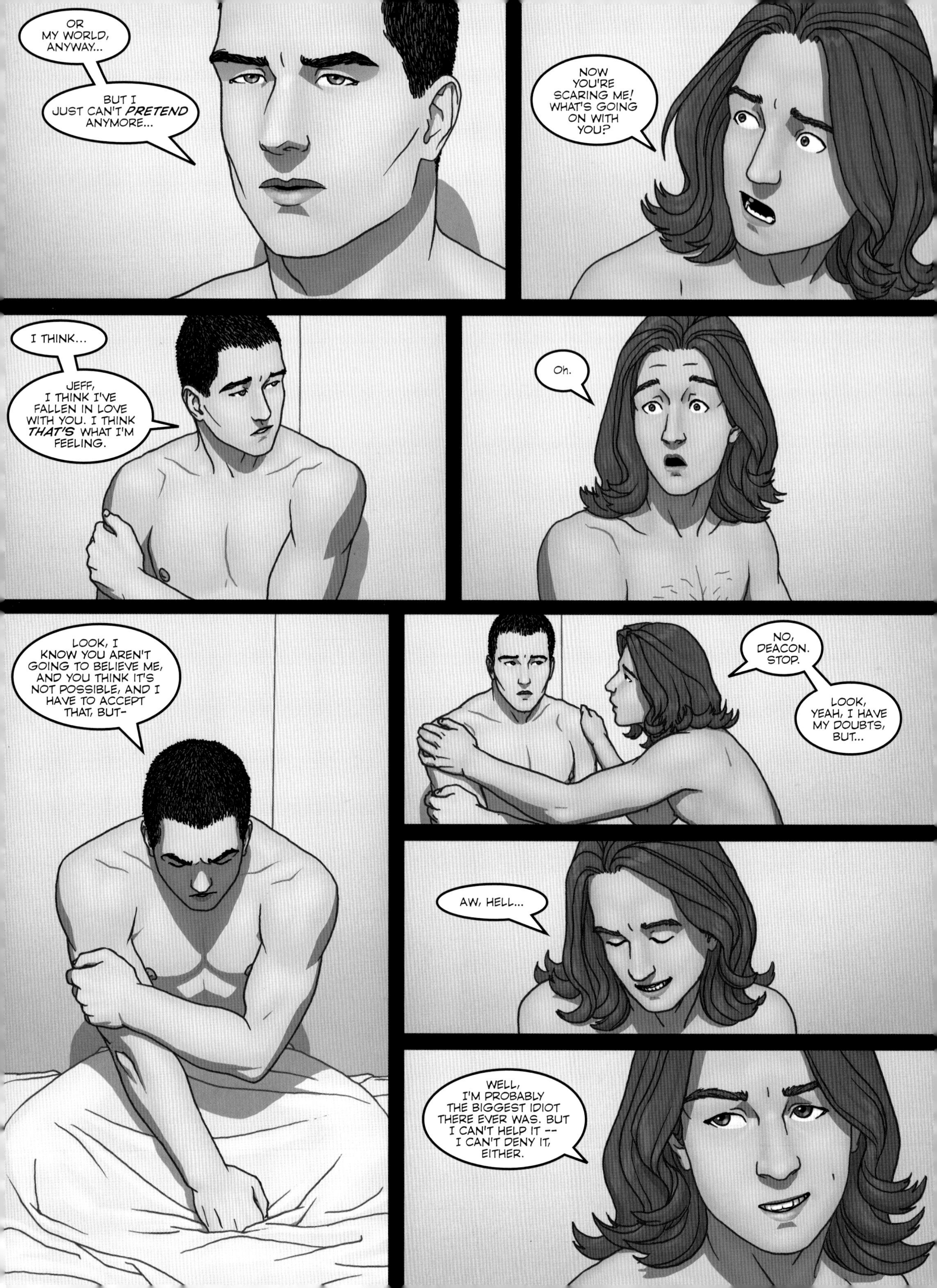
OR MY WORLD, ANYWAY...
BUT I JUST CAN'T *PRETEND* ANYMORE...
NOW YOU'RE SCARING ME! WHAT'S GOING ON WITH YOU?
I THINK...
JEFF, I THINK I'VE FALLEN IN LOVE WITH YOU. I THINK *THAT'S* WHAT I'M FEELING.
Oh.
LOOK, I KNOW YOU AREN'T GOING TO BELIEVE ME, AND YOU THINK IT'S NOT POSSIBLE, AND I HAVE TO ACCEPT THAT, BUT-
NO, DEACON. STOP.
LOOK, YEAH, I HAVE MY DOUBTS, BUT...
AW, HELL...
WELL, I'M PROBABLY THE BIGGEST IDIOT THERE EVER WAS. BUT I CAN'T HELP IT -- I CAN'T DENY IT, EITHER.

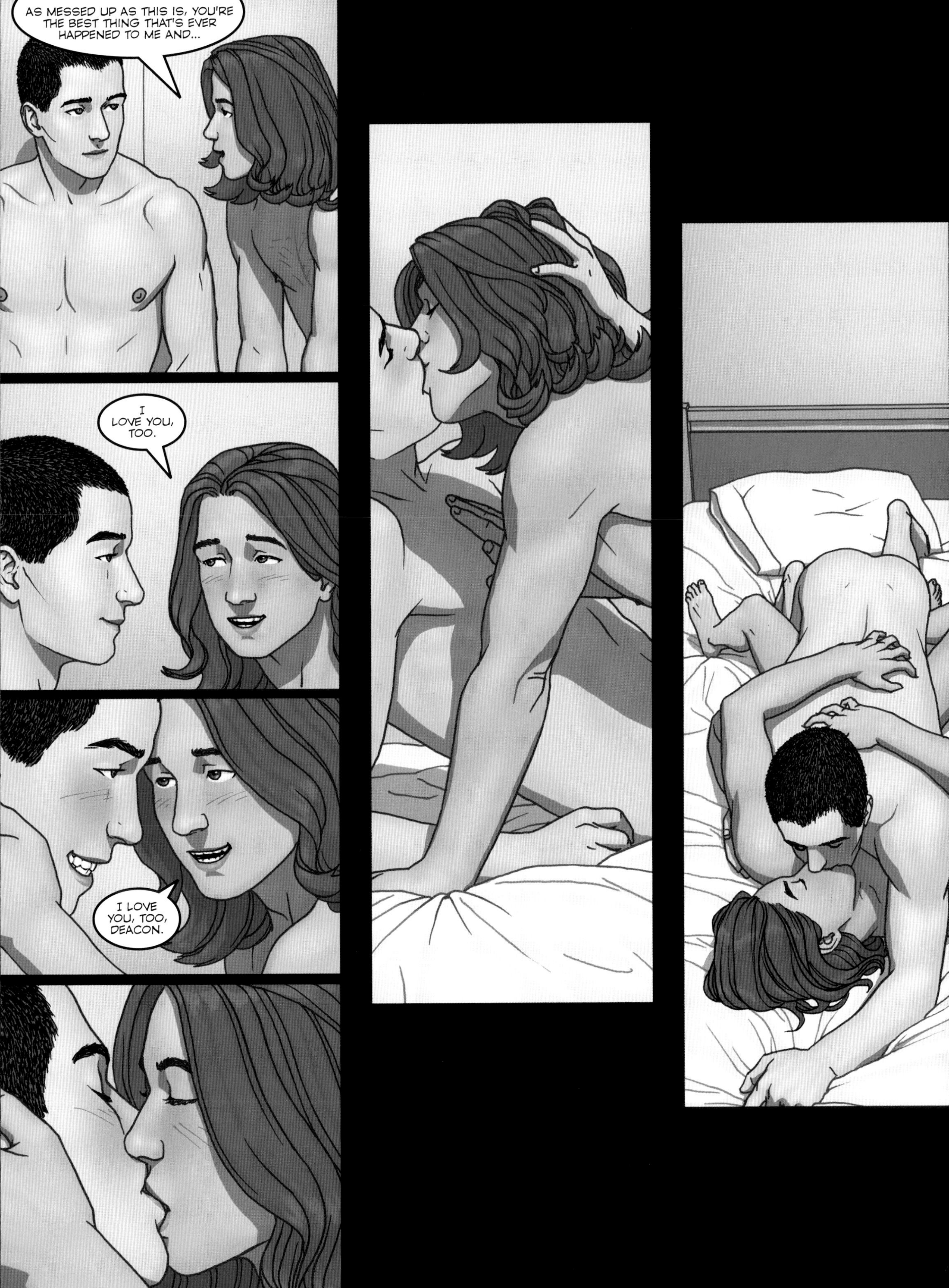
AS MESSED UP AS THIS IS, YOU'RE THE BEST THING THAT'S EVER HAPPENED TO ME AND...
I LOVE YOU, TOO.
I LOVE YOU, TOO, DEACON.

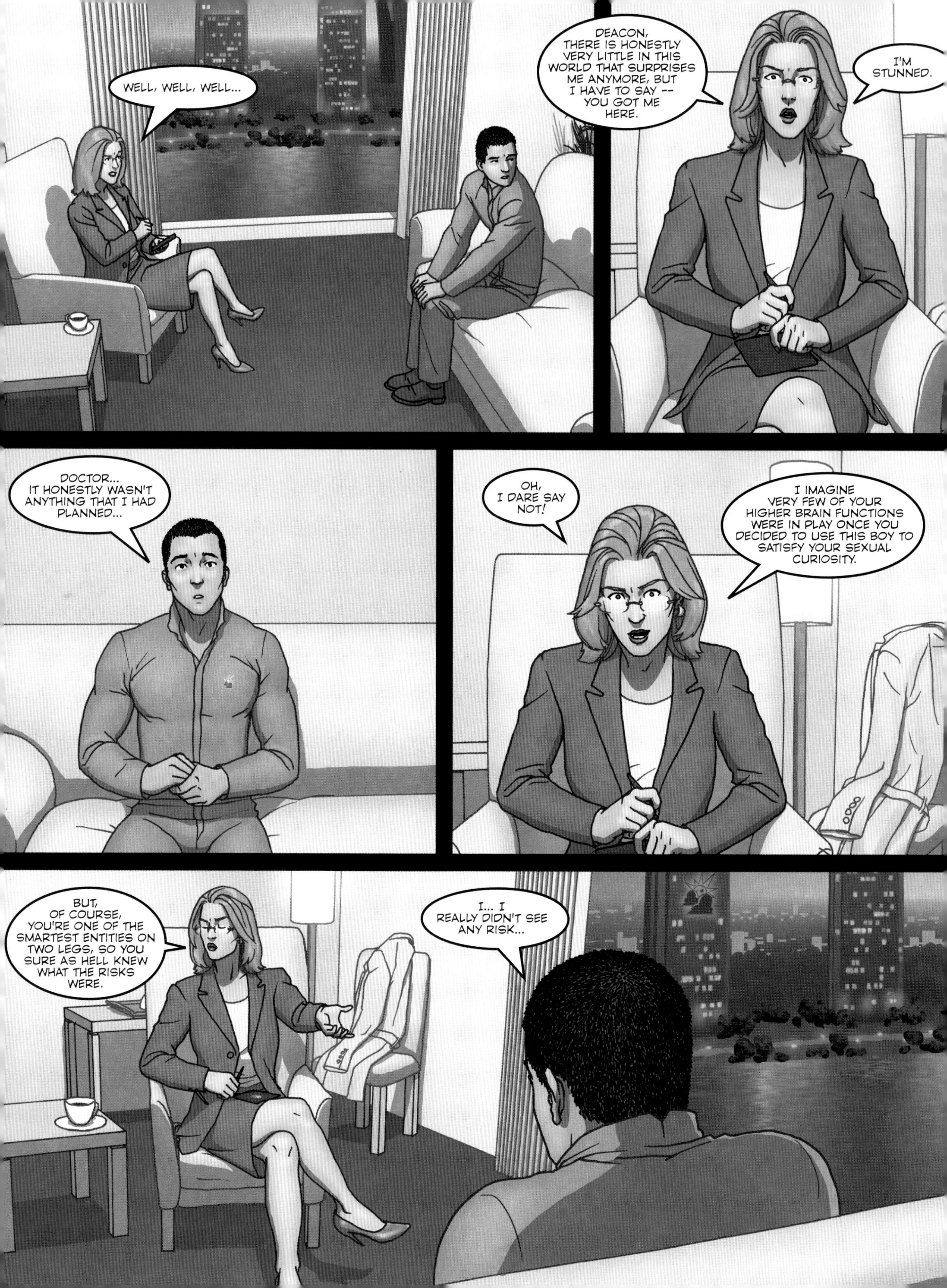
WELL, WELL, WELL...
DEACON, THERE IS HONESTLY VERY LITTLE IN THIS WORLD THAT SURPRISES ME ANYMORE, BUT I HAVE TO SAY -- YOU GOT ME HERE.
I'M STUNNED.
DOCTOR... IT HONESTLY WASN'T ANYTHING THAT I HAD PLANNED...
OH, I DARE SAY NOT!
I IMAGINE VERY FEW OF YOUR HIGHER BRAIN FUNCTIONS WERE IN PLAY ONCE YOU DECIDED TO USE THIS BOY TO SATISFY YOUR SEXUAL CURIOSITY.
BUT, OF COURSE, YOU'RE ONE OF THE SMARTEST ENTITIES ON TWO LEGS, SO YOU SURE AS HELL KNEW WHAT THE RISKS WERE.
I... I REALLY DIDN'T SEE ANY RISK...

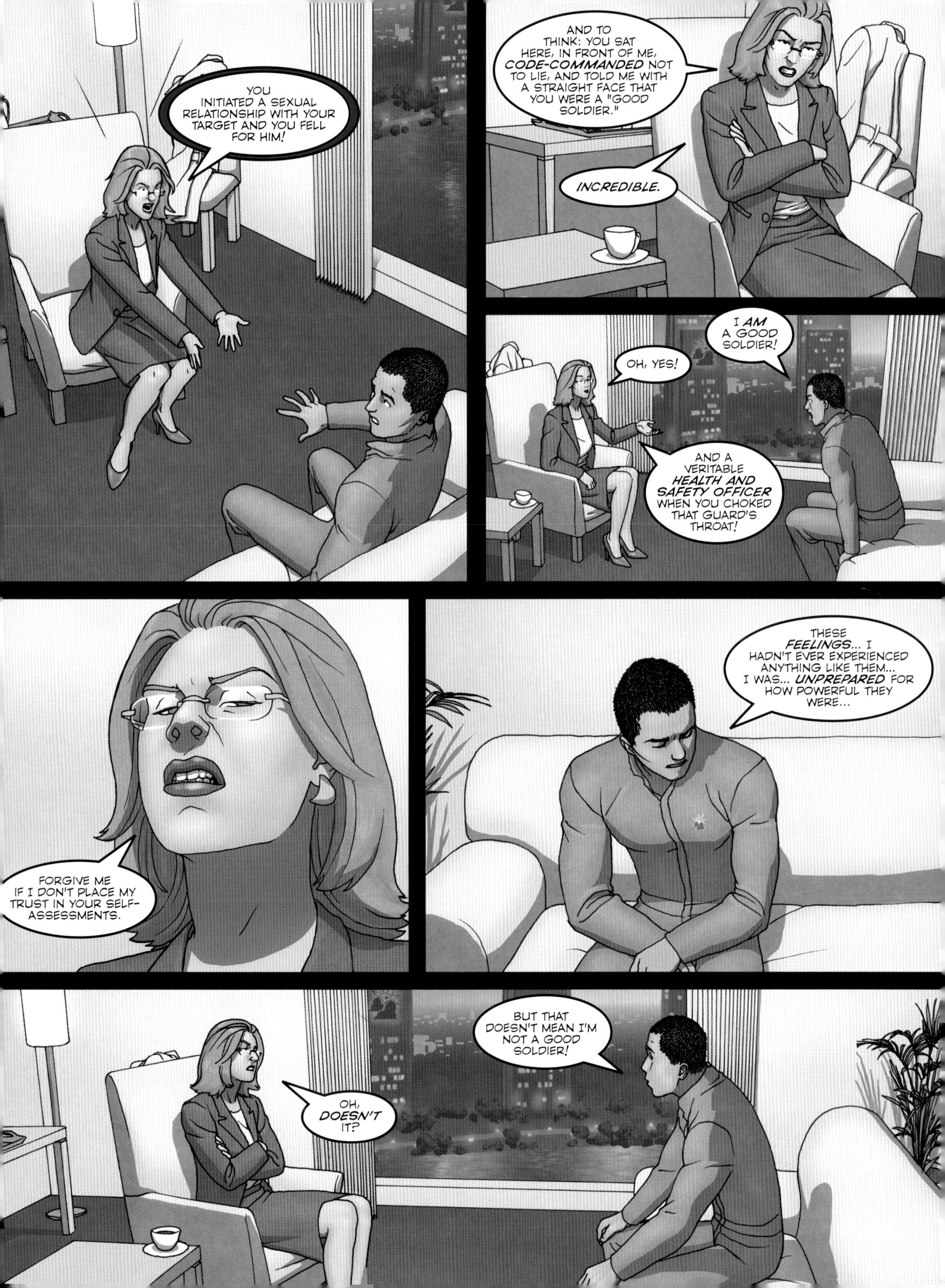
YOU INITIATED A SEXUAL RELATIONSHIP WITH YOUR TARGET AND YOU FELL FOR HIM!
AND TO THINK: YOU SAT HERE, IN FRONT OF ME, CODE-COMMANDED NOT TO LIE, AND TOLD ME WITH A STRAIGHT FACE THAT YOU WERE A "GOOD SOLDIER."
INCREDIBLE.
I AM A GOOD SOLDIER!
OH, YES!
AND A VERITABLE HEALTH AND SAFETY OFFICER WHEN YOU CHOKED THAT GUARD'S THROAT!
FORGIVE ME IF I DON'T PLACE MY TRUST IN YOUR SELF-ASSESSMENTS.
THESE FEELINGS... I HADN'T EVER EXPERIENCED ANYTHING LIKE THEM... I WAS... UNPREPARED FOR HOW POWERFUL THEY WERE...
BUT THAT DOESN'T MEAN I'M NOT A GOOD SOLDIER!
OH, DOESN'T IT?

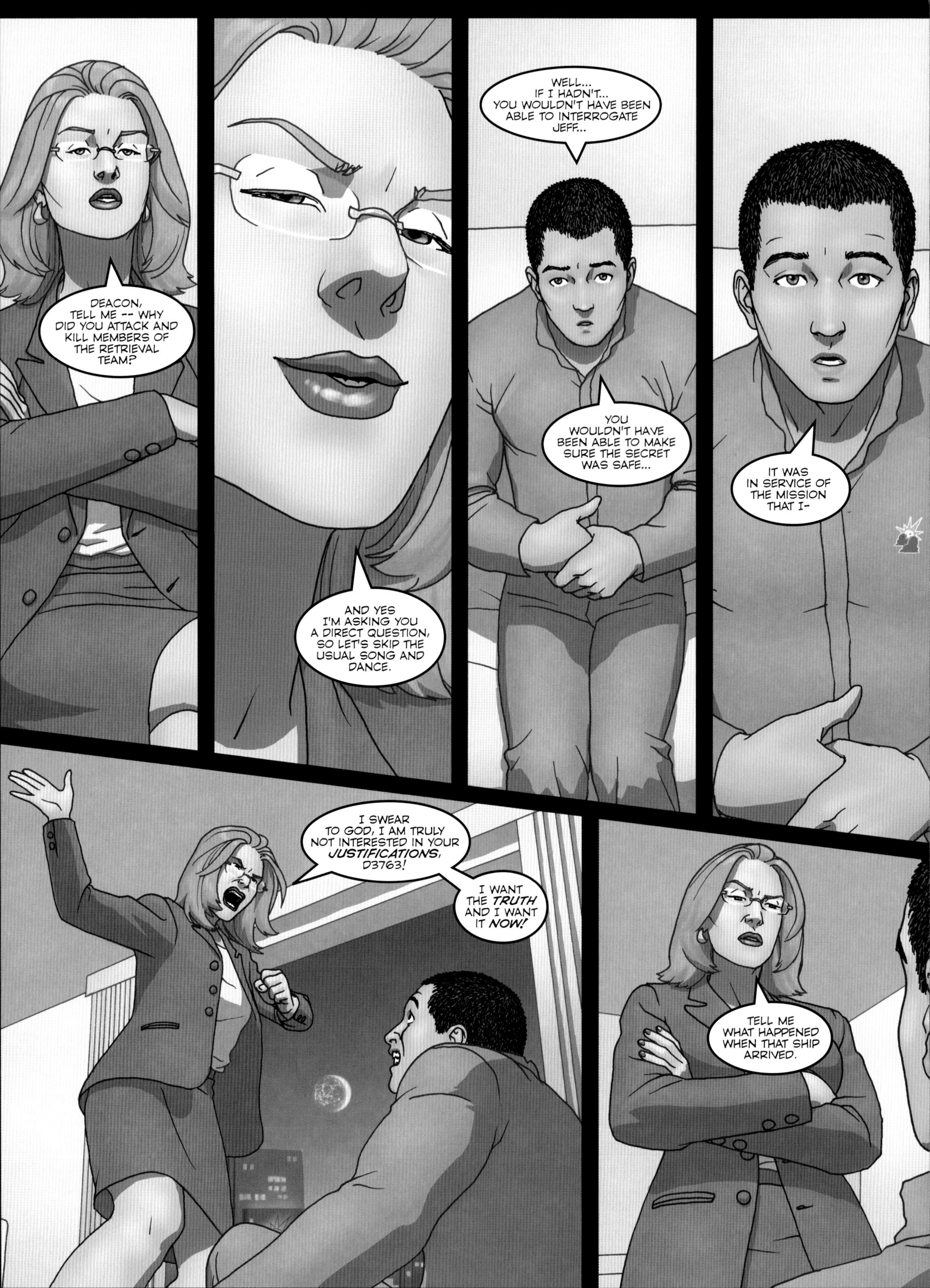
DEACON, TELL ME -- WHY DID YOU ATTACK AND KILL MEMBERS OF THE RETRIEVAL TEAM?
AND YES I'M ASKING YOU A DIRECT QUESTION, SO LET'S SKIP THE USUAL SONG AND DANCE.
WELL... IF I HADN'T... YOU WOULDN'T HAVE BEEN ABLE TO INTERROGATE JEFF...
YOU WOULDN'T HAVE BEEN ABLE TO MAKE SURE THE SECRET WAS SAFE...
IT WAS IN SERVICE OF THE MISSION THAT I-
I SWEAR TO GOD, I AM TRULY NOT INTERESTED IN YOUR *JUSTIFICATIONS*, D3763!
I WANT THE *TRUTH* AND I WANT IT *NOW!*
TELL ME WHAT HAPPENED WHEN THAT SHIP ARRIVED.

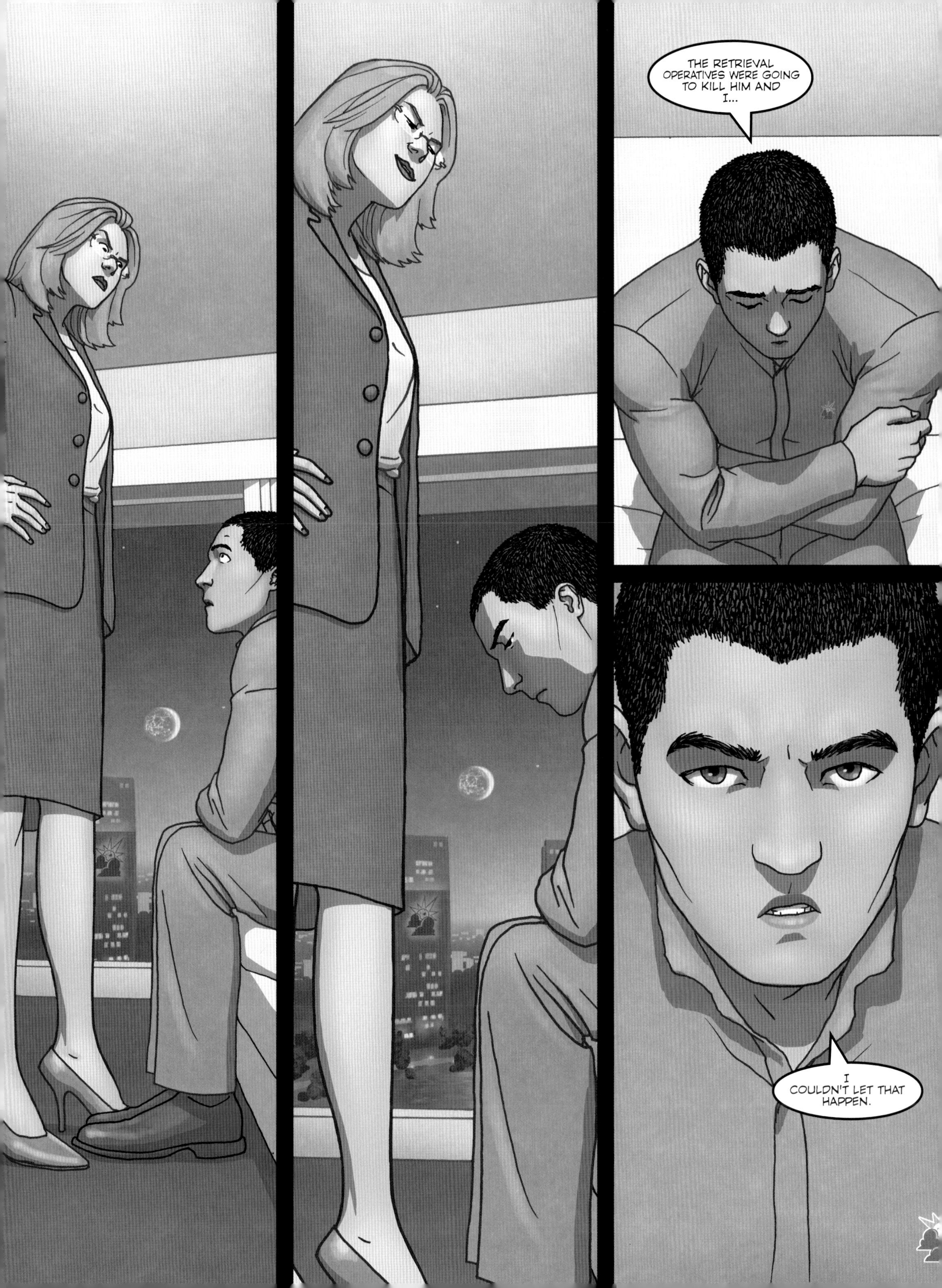
THE RETRIEVAL OPERATIVES WERE GOING TO KILL HIM AND I...
I COULDN'T LET THAT HAPPEN.

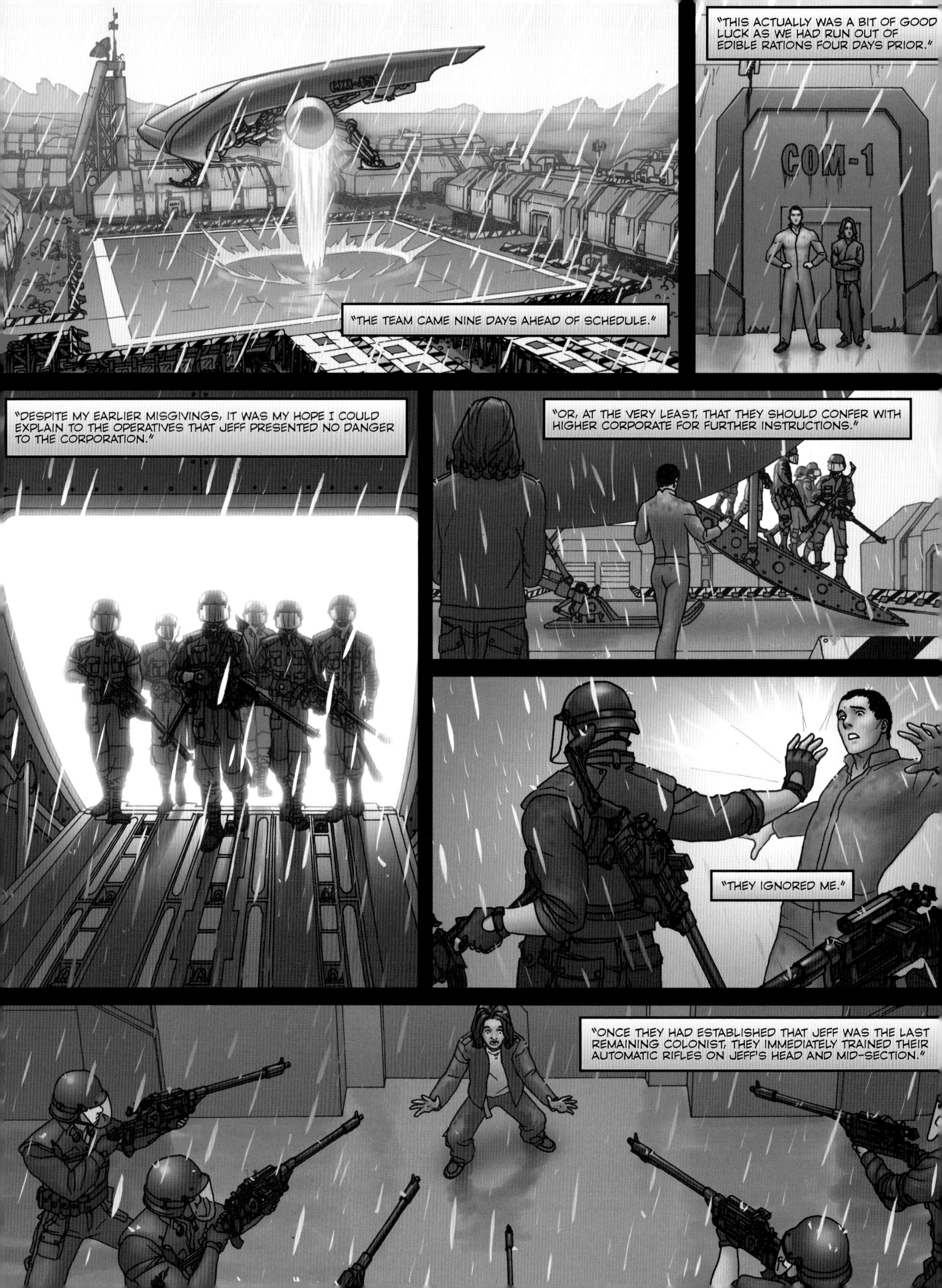
"THE TEAM CAME NINE DAYS AHEAD OF SCHEDULE."
"THIS ACTUALLY WAS A BIT OF GOOD LUCK AS WE HAD RUN OUT OF EDIBLE RATIONS FOUR DAYS PRIOR."
COM-1
"DESPITE MY EARLIER MISGIVINGS, IT WAS MY HOPE I COULD EXPLAIN TO THE OPERATIVES THAT JEFF PRESENTED NO DANGER TO THE CORPORATION."
"OR, AT THE VERY LEAST, THAT THEY SHOULD CONFER WITH HIGHER CORPORATE FOR FURTHER INSTRUCTIONS."
"THEY IGNORED ME."
"ONCE THEY HAD ESTABLISHED THAT JEFF WAS THE LAST REMAINING COLONIST, THEY IMMEDIATELY TRAINED THEIR AUTOMATIC RIFLES ON JEFF'S HEAD AND MID-SECTION."

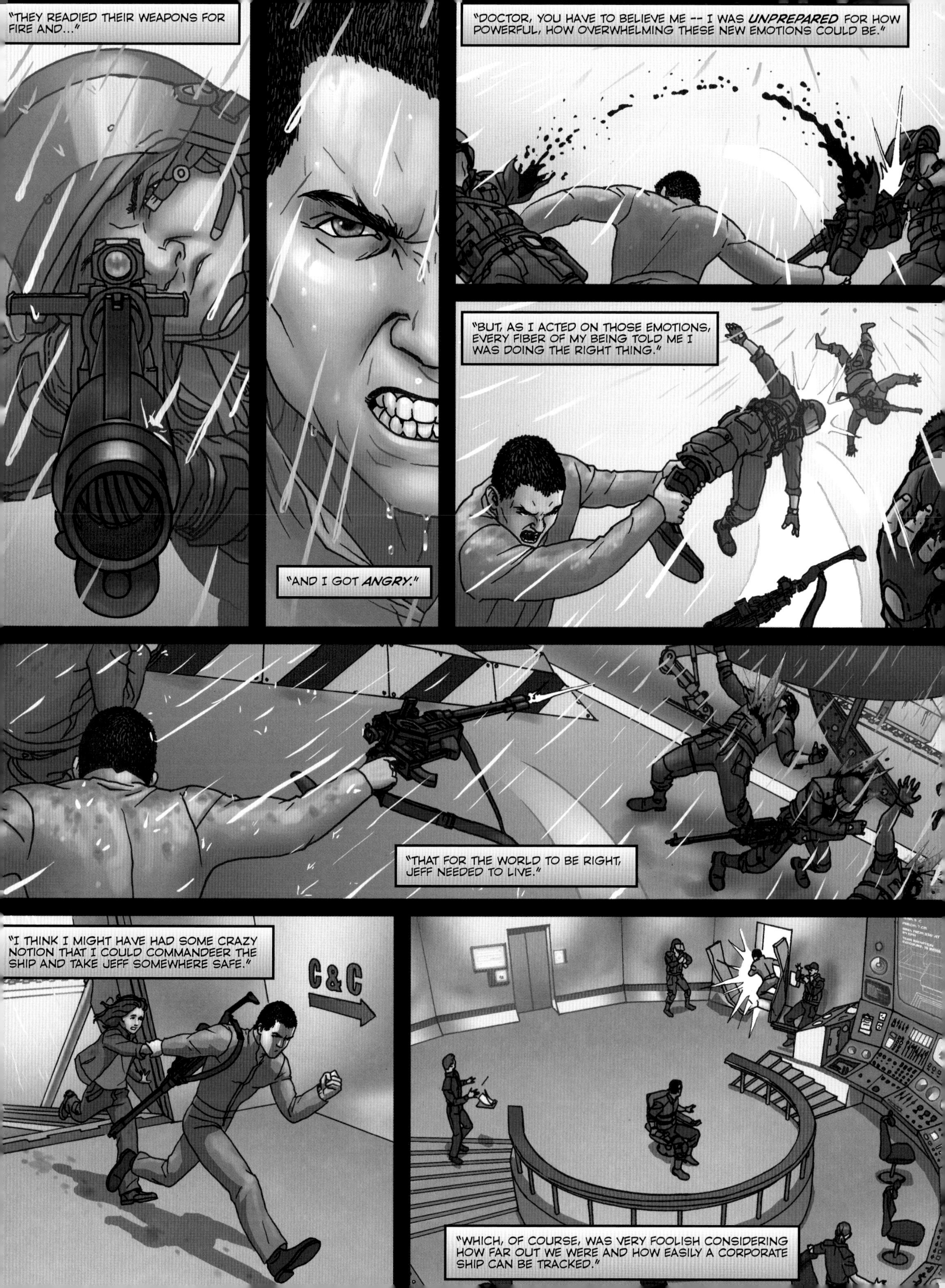
"THEY READIED THEIR WEAPONS FOR FIRE AND..."
"AND I GOT ANGRY."
"DOCTOR, YOU HAVE TO BELIEVE ME -- I WAS UNPREPARED FOR HOW POWERFUL, HOW OVERWHELMING THESE NEW EMOTIONS COULD BE."
"BUT, AS I ACTED ON THOSE EMOTIONS, EVERY FIBER OF MY BEING TOLD ME I WAS DOING THE RIGHT THING."
"THAT FOR THE WORLD TO BE RIGHT, JEFF NEEDED TO LIVE."
"I THINK I MIGHT HAVE HAD SOME CRAZY NOTION THAT I COULD COMMANDEER THE SHIP AND TAKE JEFF SOMEWHERE SAFE."
C & C
"WHICH, OF COURSE, WAS VERY FOOLISH CONSIDERING HOW FAR OUT WE WERE AND HOW EASILY A CORPORATE SHIP CAN BE TRACKED."

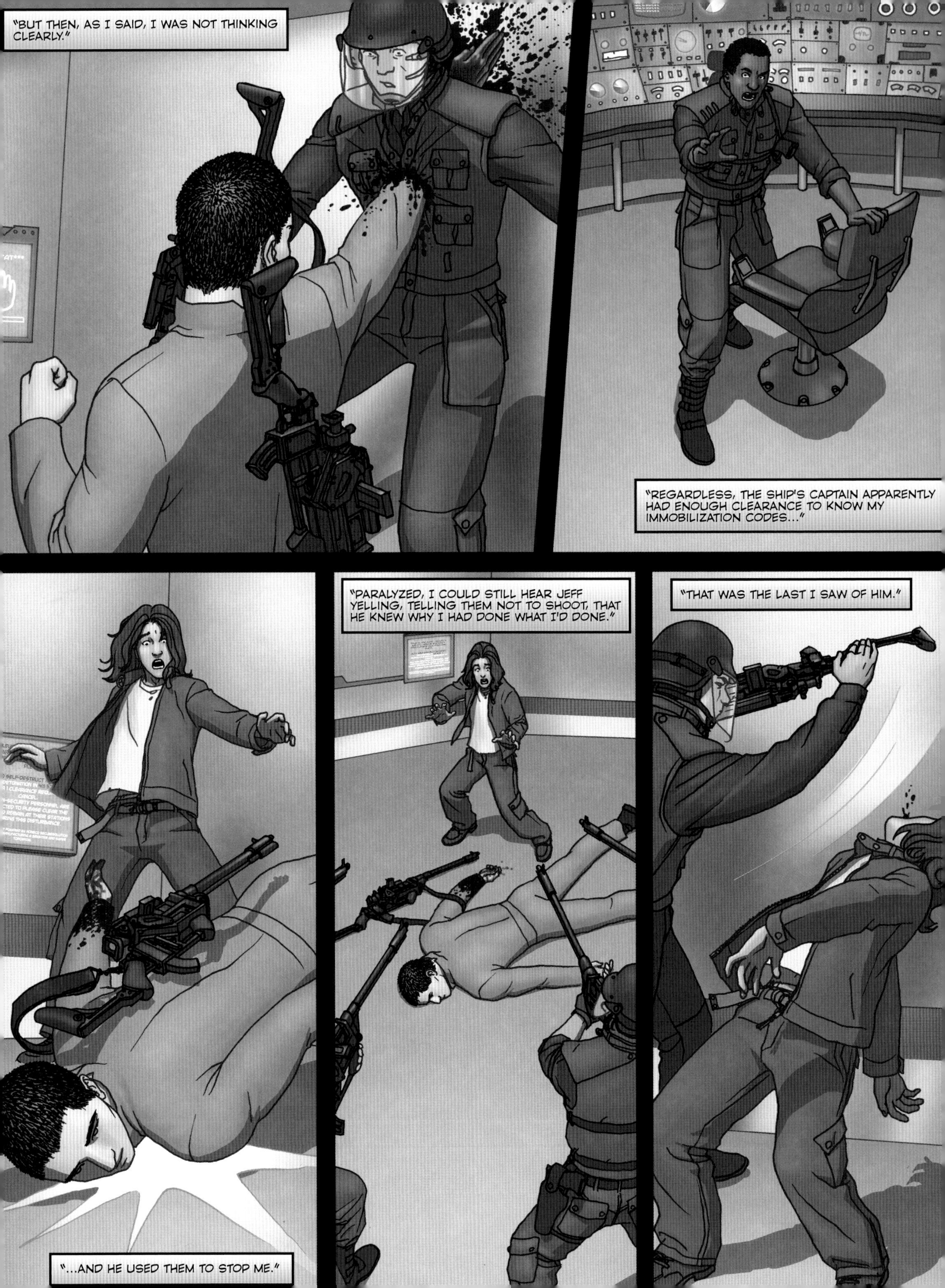
"BUT THEN, AS I SAID, I WAS NOT THINKING CLEARLY."
"REGARDLESS, THE SHIP'S CAPTAIN APPARENTLY HAD ENOUGH CLEARANCE TO KNOW MY IMMOBILIZATION CODES..."
"...AND HE USED THEM TO STOP ME."
"PARALYZED, I COULD STILL HEAR JEFF YELLING, TELLING THEM NOT TO SHOOT, THAT HE KNEW WHY I HAD DONE WHAT I'D DONE."
"THAT WAS THE LAST I SAW OF HIM."

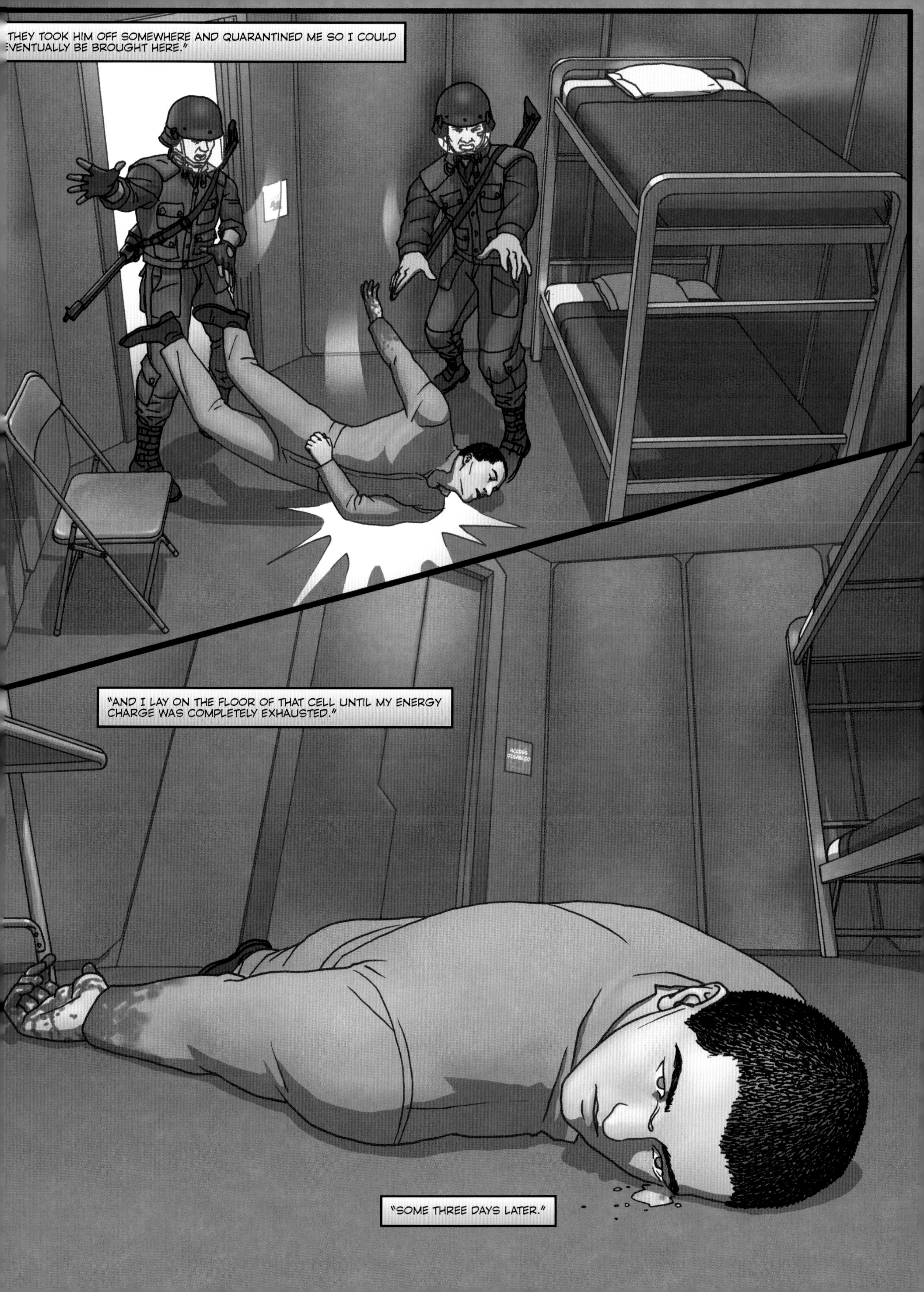
THEY TOOK HIM OFF SOMEWHERE AND QUARANTINED ME SO I COULD EVENTUALLY BE BROUGHT HERE."
"AND I LAY ON THE FLOOR OF THAT CELL UNTIL MY ENERGY CHARGE WAS COMPLETELY EXHAUSTED."
ACCESS DISABLED
"SOME THREE DAYS LATER."

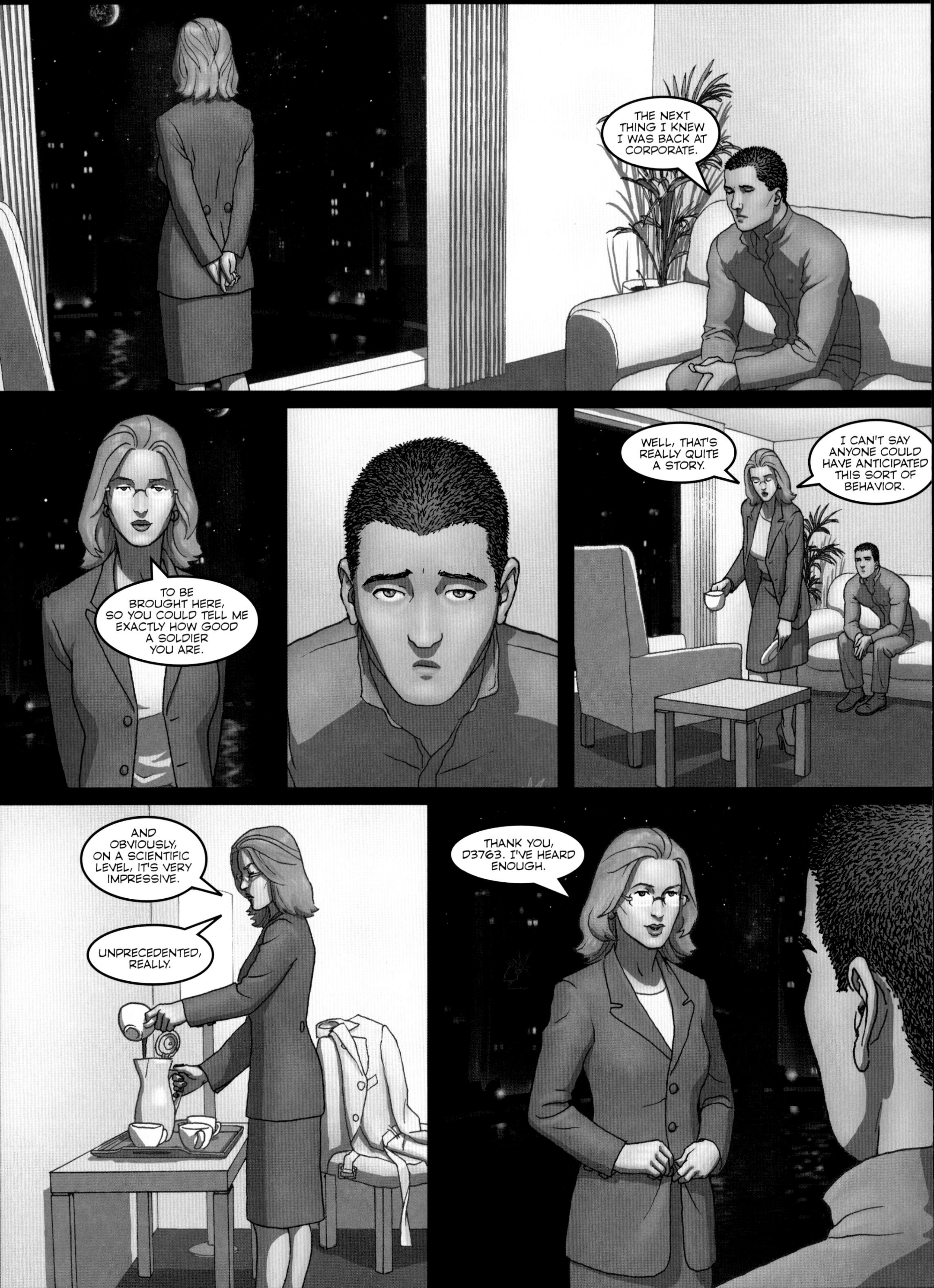
THE NEXT THING I KNEW I WAS BACK AT CORPORATE.
TO BE BROUGHT HERE, SO YOU COULD TELL ME EXACTLY HOW GOOD A SOLDIER YOU ARE.
WELL, THAT'S REALLY QUITE A STORY.
I CAN'T SAY ANYONE COULD HAVE ANTICIPATED THIS SORT OF BEHAVIOR.
AND OBVIOUSLY, ON A SCIENTIFIC LEVEL, IT'S VERY IMPRESSIVE.
UNPRECEDENTED, REALLY.
THANK YOU, D3763. I'VE HEARD ENOUGH.

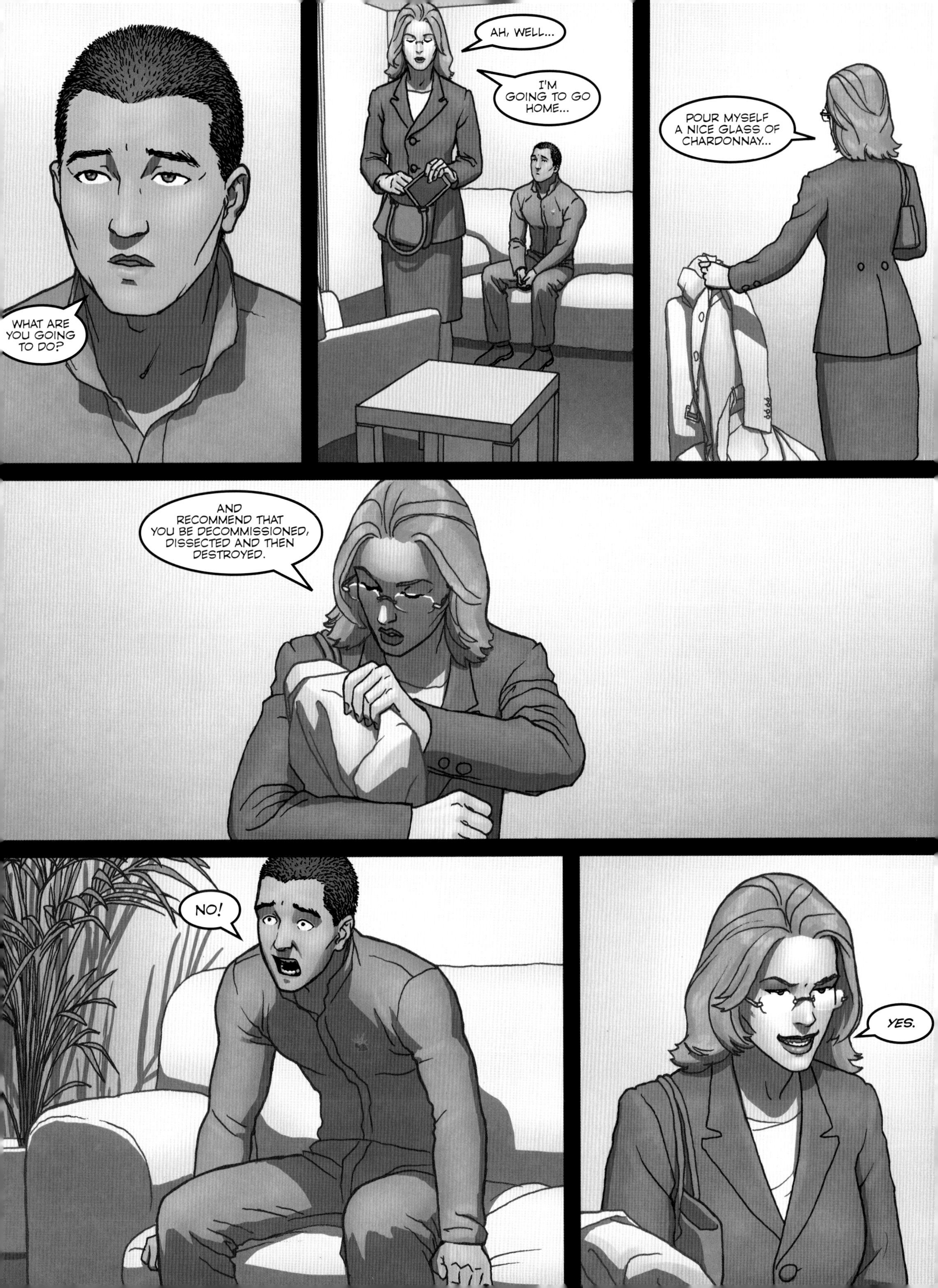
WHAT ARE YOU GOING TO DO?
AH, WELL...
I'M GOING TO GO HOME...
POUR MYSELF A NICE GLASS OF CHARDONNAY...
AND RECOMMEND THAT YOU BE DECOMMISSIONED, DISSECTED AND THEN DESTROYED.
NO!
YES.

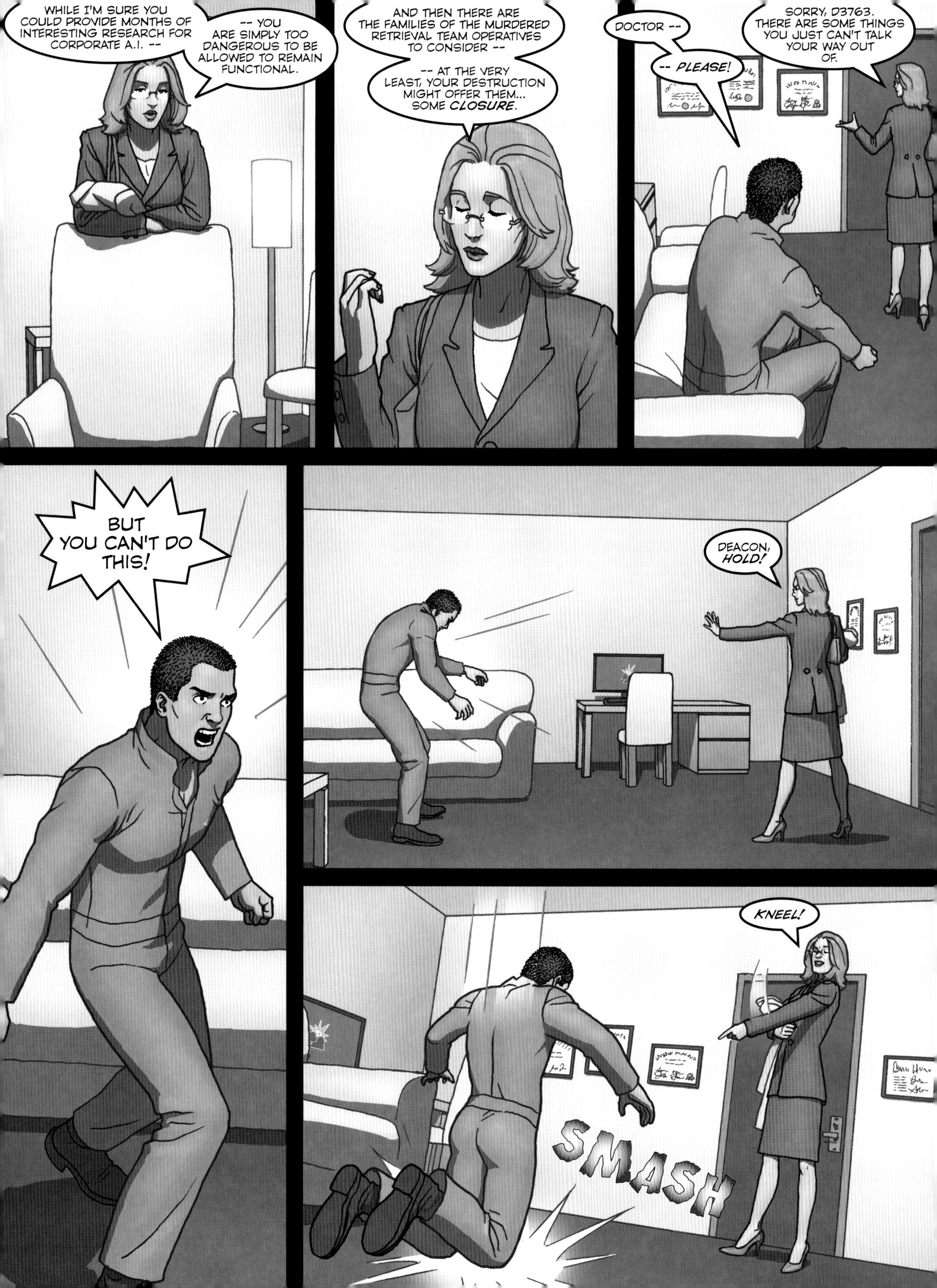
WHILE I'M SURE YOU COULD PROVIDE MONTHS OF INTERESTING RESEARCH FOR CORPORATE A.I. --
-- YOU ARE SIMPLY TOO DANGEROUS TO BE ALLOWED TO REMAIN FUNCTIONAL.
AND THEN THERE ARE THE FAMILIES OF THE MURDERED RETRIEVAL TEAM OPERATIVES TO CONSIDER --
-- AT THE VERY LEAST, YOUR DESTRUCTION MIGHT OFFER THEM... SOME *CLOSURE*.
DOCTOR --
-- *PLEASE!*
SORRY, D3763. THERE ARE SOME THINGS YOU JUST CAN'T TALK YOUR WAY OUT OF.
BUT YOU CAN'T DO THIS!
DEACON, *HOLD!*
KNEEL!
SMASH

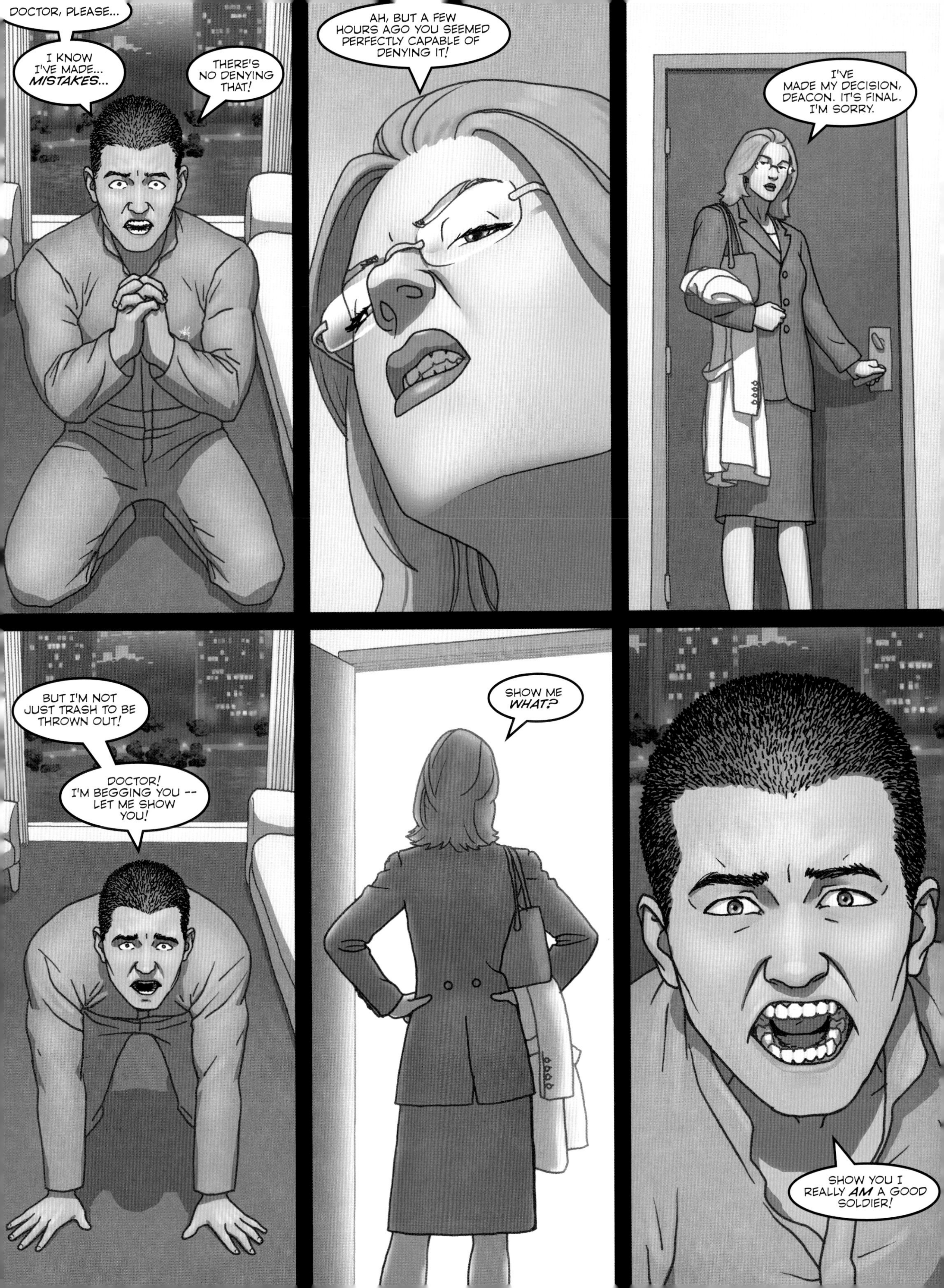
DOCTOR, PLEASE...
I KNOW I'VE MADE... ***MISTAKES***...
THERE'S NO DENYING THAT!
AH, BUT A FEW HOURS AGO YOU SEEMED PERFECTLY CAPABLE OF DENYING IT!
I'VE MADE MY DECISION, DEACON. IT'S FINAL. I'M SORRY.
BUT I'M NOT JUST TRASH TO BE THROWN OUT!
DOCTOR! I'M BEGGING YOU -- LET ME SHOW YOU!
SHOW ME ***WHAT?***
SHOW YOU I REALLY ***AM*** A GOOD SOLDIER!

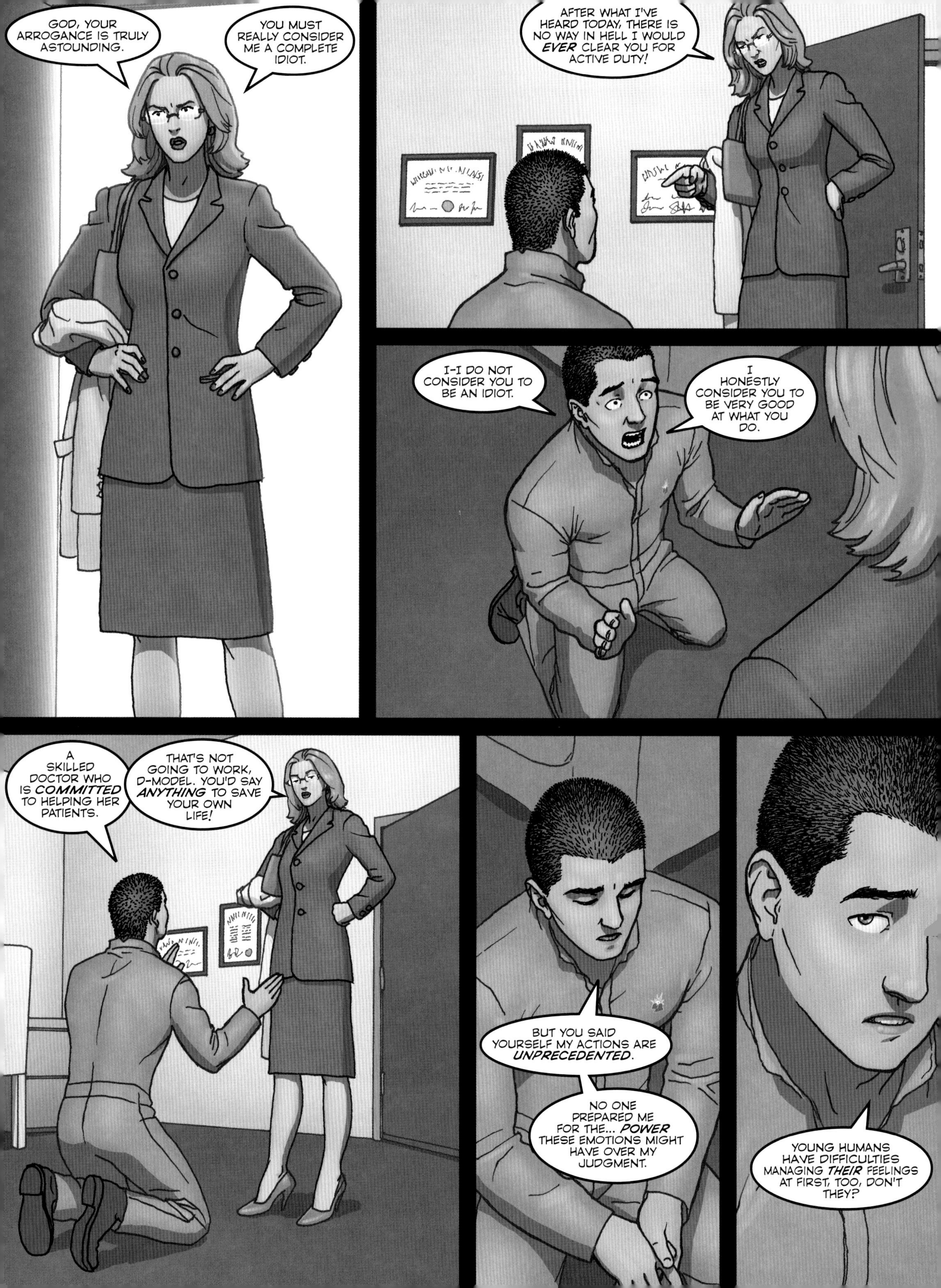
GOD, YOUR ARROGANCE IS TRULY ASTOUNDING.
YOU MUST REALLY CONSIDER ME A COMPLETE IDIOT.
AFTER WHAT I'VE HEARD TODAY, THERE IS NO WAY IN HELL I WOULD *EVER* CLEAR YOU FOR ACTIVE DUTY!
I-I DO NOT CONSIDER YOU TO BE AN IDIOT.
I HONESTLY CONSIDER YOU TO BE VERY GOOD AT WHAT YOU DO.
A SKILLED DOCTOR WHO IS *COMMITTED* TO HELPING HER PATIENTS.
THAT'S NOT GOING TO WORK, D-MODEL. YOU'D SAY *ANYTHING* TO SAVE YOUR OWN LIFE!
BUT YOU SAID YOURSELF MY ACTIONS ARE *UNPRECEDENTED*.
NO ONE PREPARED ME FOR THE... *POWER* THESE EMOTIONS MIGHT HAVE OVER MY JUDGMENT.
YOUNG HUMANS HAVE DIFFICULTIES MANAGING *THEIR* FEELINGS AT FIRST, TOO, DON'T THEY?

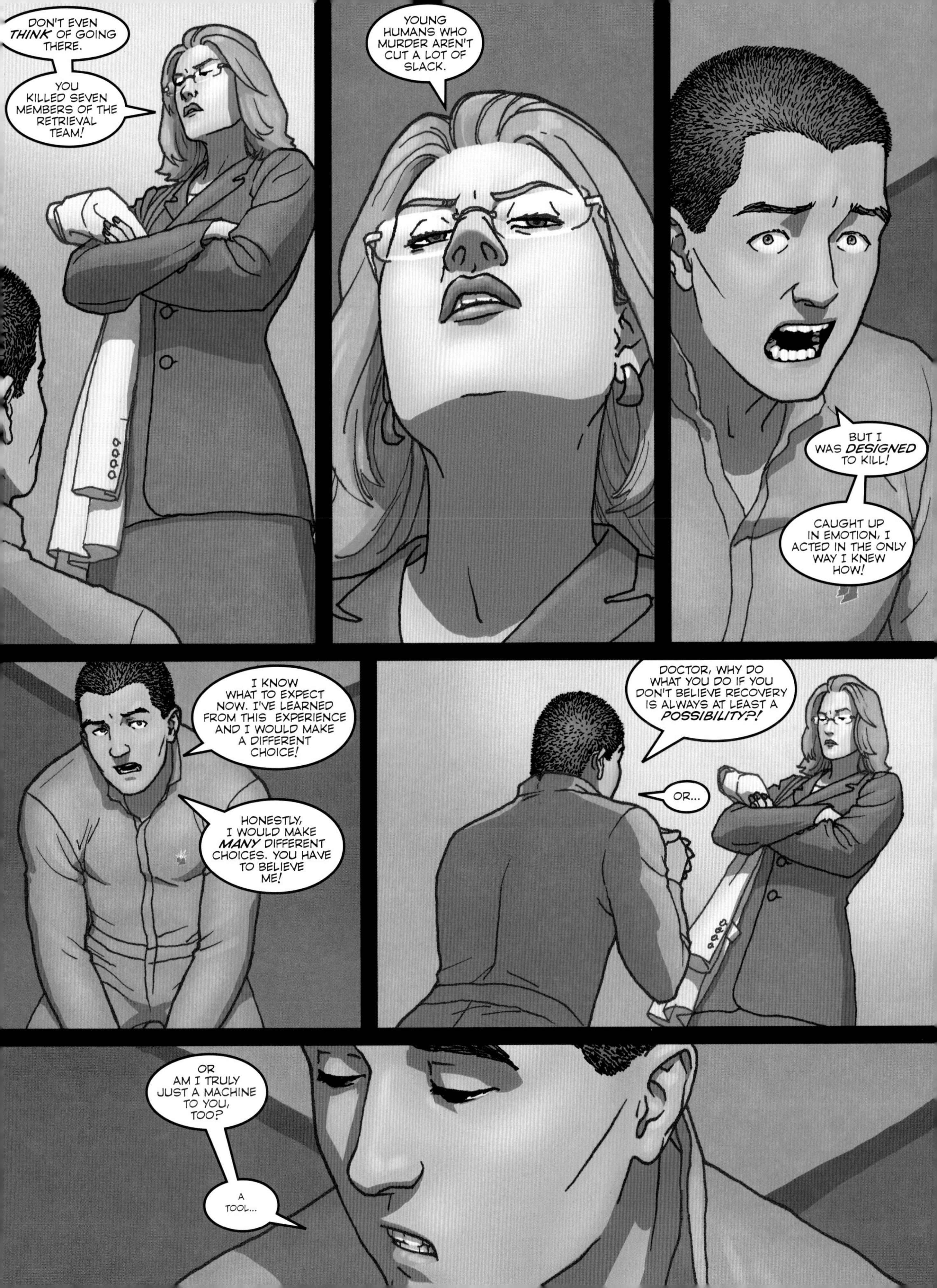
DON'T EVEN THINK OF GOING THERE.
YOU KILLED SEVEN MEMBERS OF THE RETRIEVAL TEAM!
YOUNG HUMANS WHO MURDER AREN'T CUT A LOT OF SLACK.
BUT I WAS DESIGNED TO KILL!
CAUGHT UP IN EMOTION, I ACTED IN THE ONLY WAY I KNEW HOW!
I KNOW WHAT TO EXPECT NOW. I'VE LEARNED FROM THIS EXPERIENCE AND I WOULD MAKE A DIFFERENT CHOICE!
HONESTLY, I WOULD MAKE MANY DIFFERENT CHOICES. YOU HAVE TO BELIEVE ME!
DOCTOR, WHY DO WHAT YOU DO IF YOU DON'T BELIEVE RECOVERY IS ALWAYS AT LEAST A POSSIBILITY?!
OR...
OR AM I TRULY JUST A MACHINE TO YOU, TOO?
A TOOL...

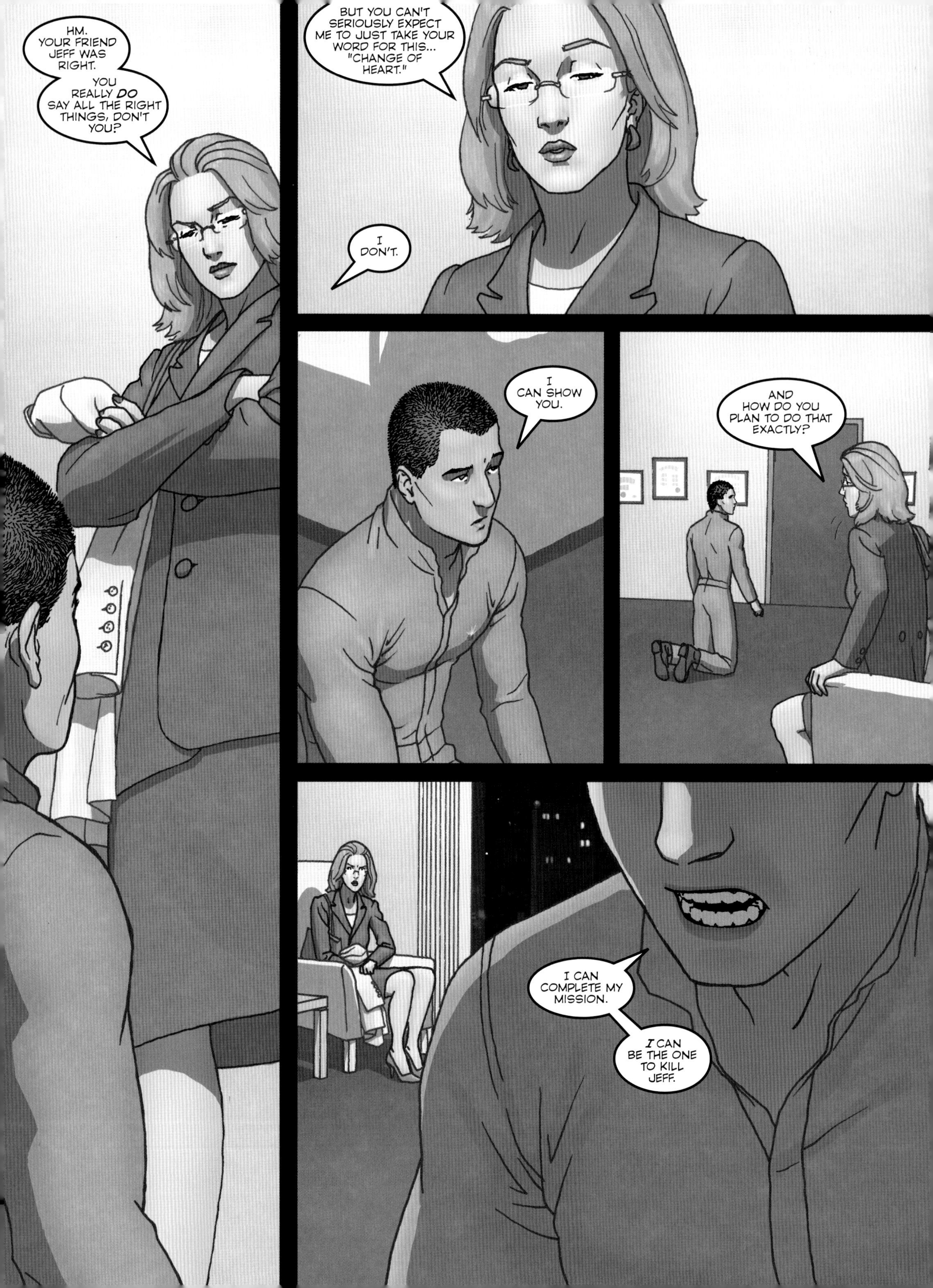
HM. YOUR FRIEND JEFF WAS RIGHT.
YOU REALLY DO SAY ALL THE RIGHT THINGS, DON'T YOU?
BUT YOU CAN'T SERIOUSLY EXPECT ME TO JUST TAKE YOUR WORD FOR THIS... "CHANGE OF HEART."
I DON'T.
I CAN SHOW YOU.
AND HOW DO YOU PLAN TO DO THAT EXACTLY?
I CAN COMPLETE MY MISSION.
I CAN BE THE ONE TO KILL JEFF.

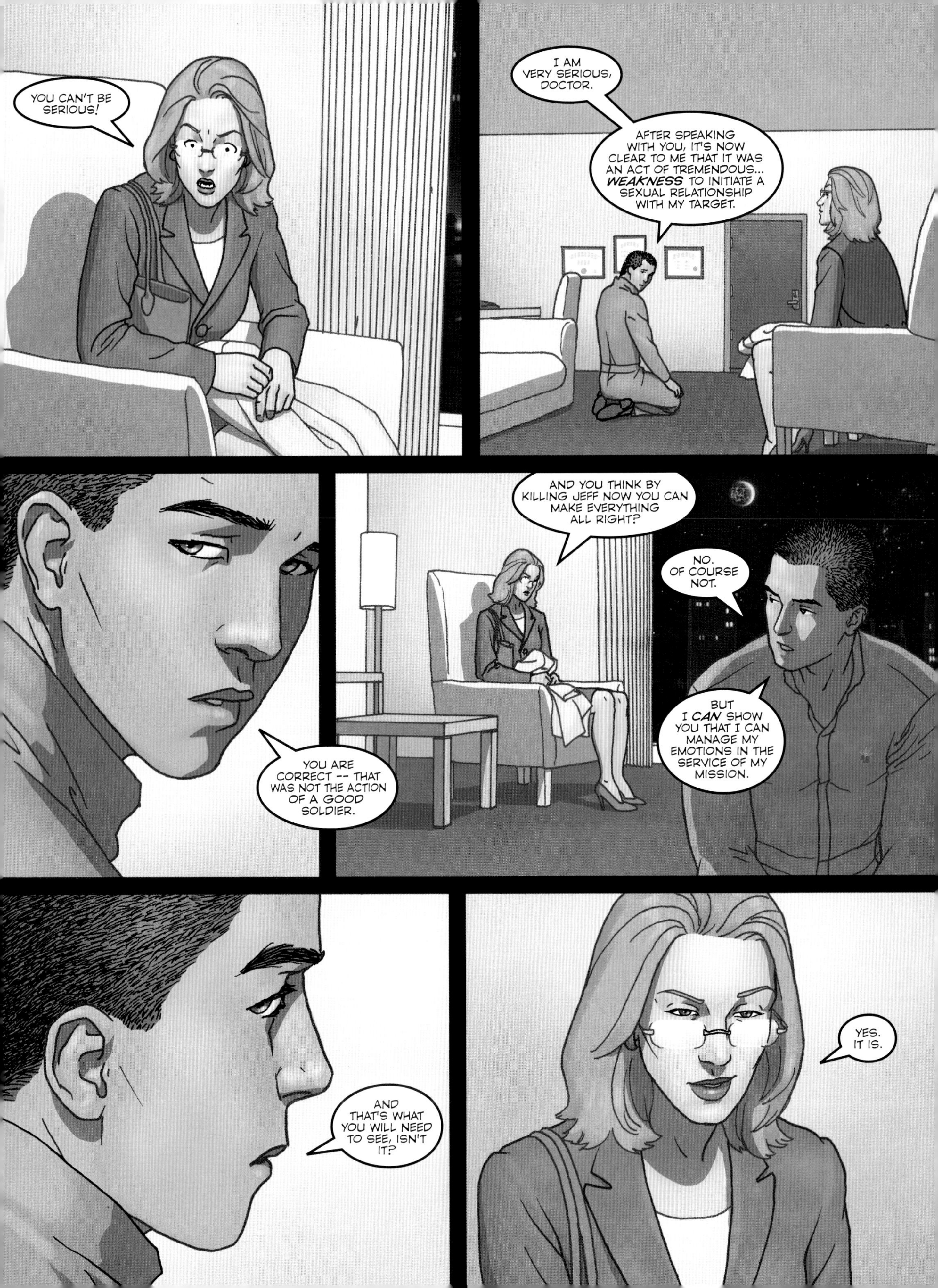
YOU CAN'T BE SERIOUS!
I AM VERY SERIOUS, DOCTOR.
AFTER SPEAKING WITH YOU, IT'S NOW CLEAR TO ME THAT IT WAS AN ACT OF TREMENDOUS... WEAKNESS TO INITIATE A SEXUAL RELATIONSHIP WITH MY TARGET.
YOU ARE CORRECT -- THAT WAS NOT THE ACTION OF A GOOD SOLDIER.
AND YOU THINK BY KILLING JEFF NOW YOU CAN MAKE EVERYTHING ALL RIGHT?
NO. OF COURSE NOT.
BUT I CAN SHOW YOU THAT I CAN MANAGE MY EMOTIONS IN THE SERVICE OF MY MISSION.
AND THAT'S WHAT YOU WILL NEED TO SEE, ISN'T IT?
YES. IT IS.

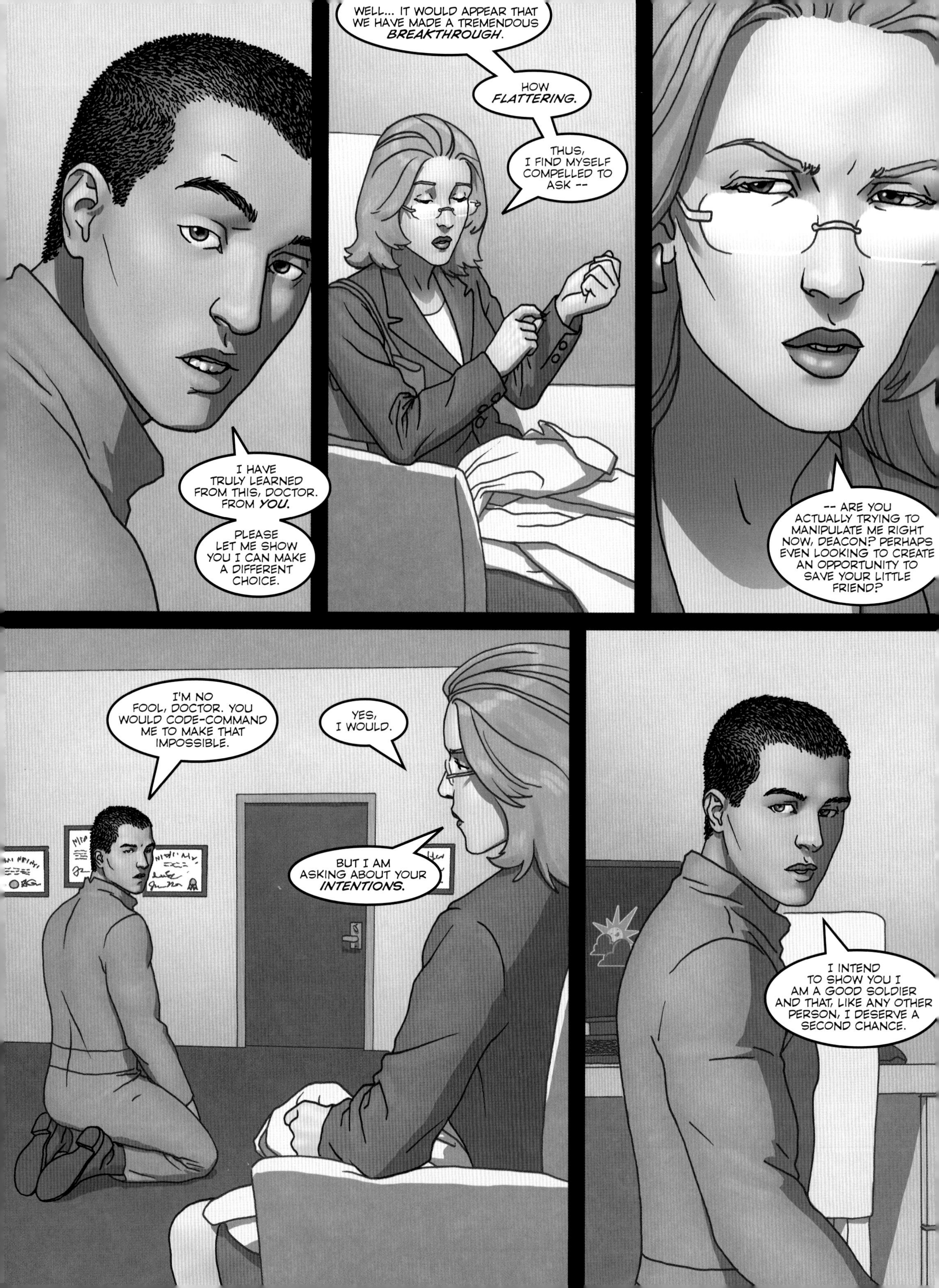

I HAVE TRULY LEARNED FROM THIS, DOCTOR. FROM YOU.
PLEASE LET ME SHOW YOU I CAN MAKE A DIFFERENT CHOICE.
WELL... IT WOULD APPEAR THAT WE HAVE MADE A TREMENDOUS BREAKTHROUGH.
HOW FLATTERING.
THUS, I FIND MYSELF COMPELLED TO ASK --
-- ARE YOU ACTUALLY TRYING TO MANIPULATE ME RIGHT NOW, DEACON? PERHAPS EVEN LOOKING TO CREATE AN OPPORTUNITY TO SAVE YOUR LITTLE FRIEND?
I'M NO FOOL, DOCTOR. YOU WOULD CODE-COMMAND ME TO MAKE THAT IMPOSSIBLE.
YES, I WOULD.
BUT I AM ASKING ABOUT YOUR INTENTIONS.
I INTEND TO SHOW YOU I AM A GOOD SOLDIER AND THAT, LIKE ANY OTHER PERSON, I DESERVE A SECOND CHANCE.

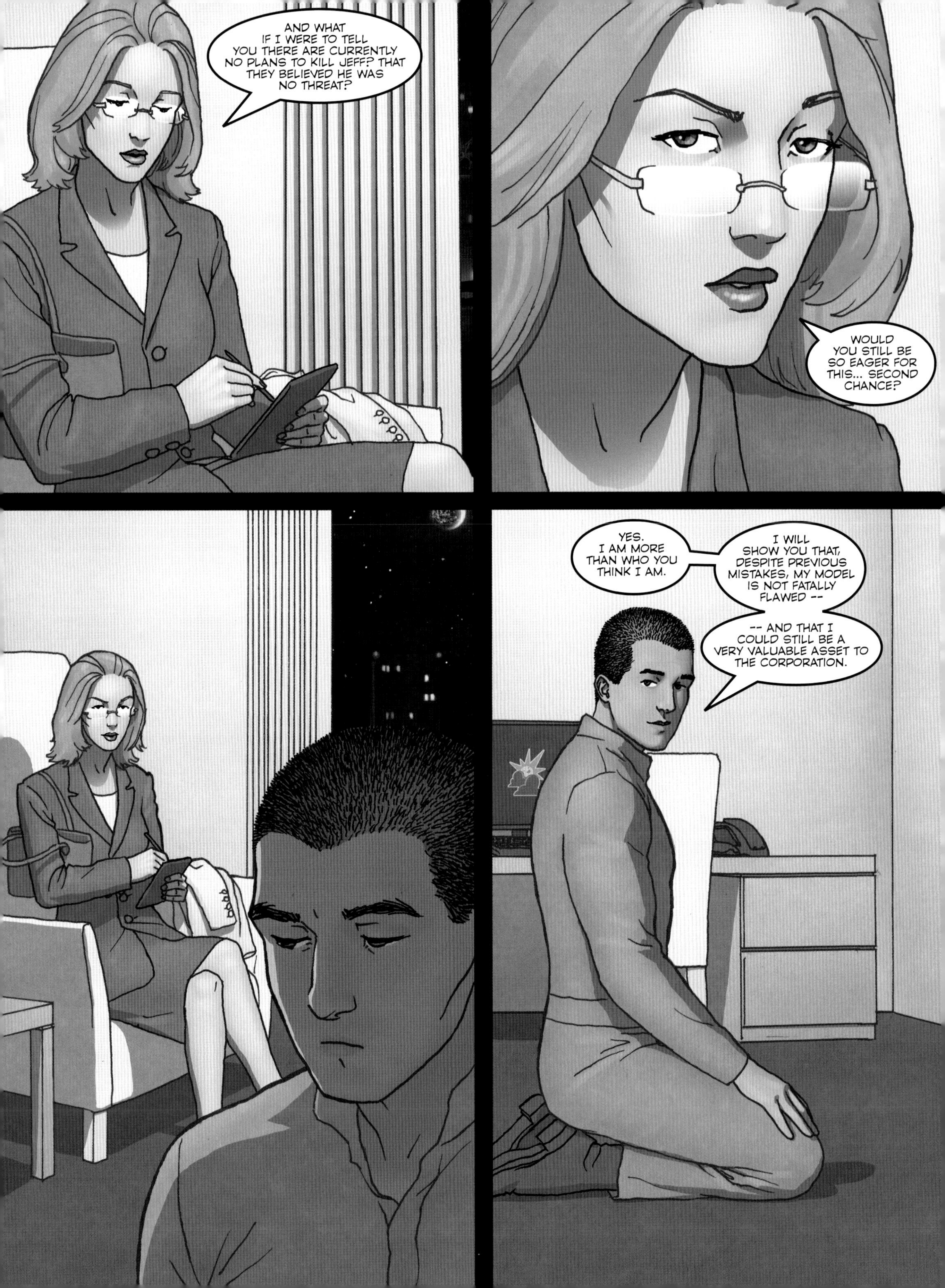
AND WHAT IF I WERE TO TELL YOU THERE ARE CURRENTLY NO PLANS TO KILL JEFF? THAT THEY BELIEVED HE WAS NO THREAT?
WOULD YOU STILL BE SO EAGER FOR THIS... SECOND CHANCE?
YES. I AM MORE THAN WHO YOU THINK I AM.
I WILL SHOW YOU THAT, DESPITE PREVIOUS MISTAKES, MY MODEL IS NOT FATALLY FLAWED --
-- AND THAT I COULD STILL BE A VERY VALUABLE ASSET TO THE CORPORATION.

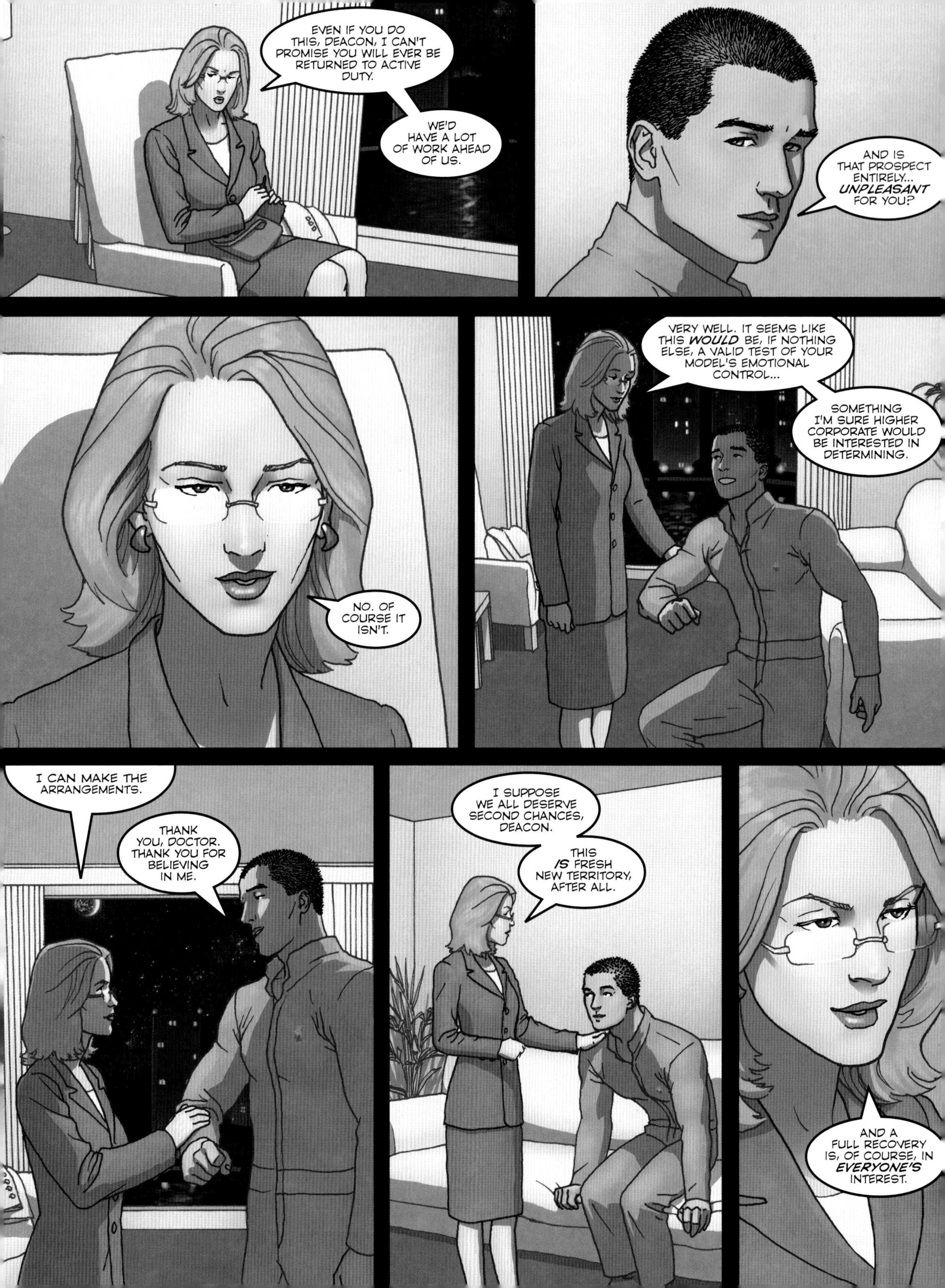
EVEN IF YOU DO THIS, DEACON, I CAN'T PROMISE YOU WILL EVER BE RETURNED TO ACTIVE DUTY.
WE'D HAVE A LOT OF WORK AHEAD OF US.
AND IS THAT PROSPECT ENTIRELY... *UNPLEASANT* FOR YOU?
NO. OF COURSE IT ISN'T.
VERY WELL. IT SEEMS LIKE THIS *WOULD* BE, IF NOTHING ELSE, A VALID TEST OF YOUR MODEL'S EMOTIONAL CONTROL...
SOMETHING I'M SURE HIGHER CORPORATE WOULD BE INTERESTED IN DETERMINING.
I CAN MAKE THE ARRANGEMENTS.
THANK YOU, DOCTOR. THANK YOU FOR BELIEVING IN ME.
I SUPPOSE WE ALL DESERVE SECOND CHANCES, DEACON.
THIS *IS* FRESH NEW TERRITORY, AFTER ALL.
AND A FULL RECOVERY IS, OF COURSE, IN *EVERYONE'S* INTEREST.

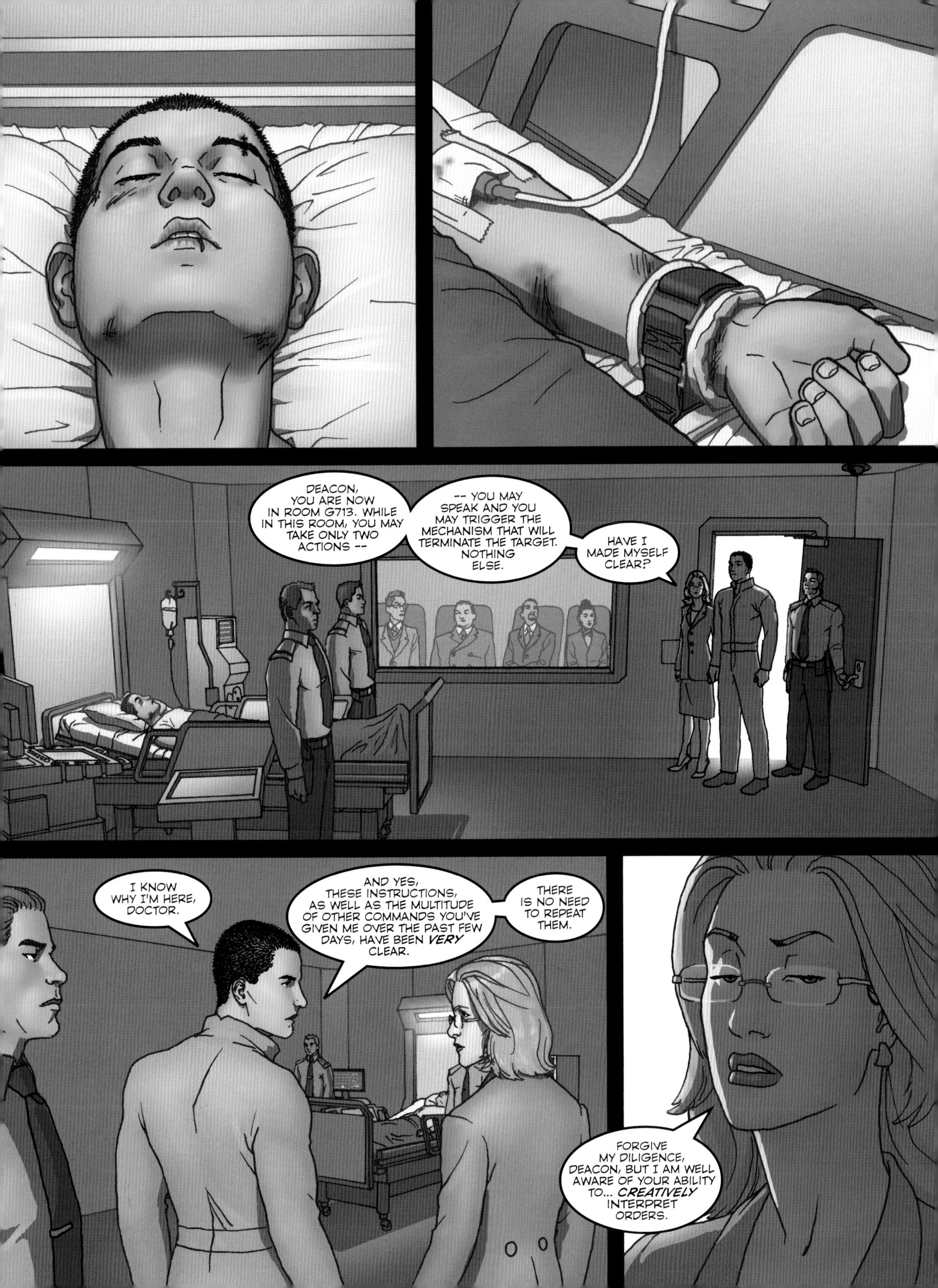
DEACON, YOU ARE NOW IN ROOM G713. WHILE IN THIS ROOM, YOU MAY TAKE ONLY TWO ACTIONS --
-- YOU MAY SPEAK AND YOU MAY TRIGGER THE MECHANISM THAT WILL TERMINATE THE TARGET. NOTHING ELSE.
HAVE I MADE MYSELF CLEAR?
I KNOW WHY I'M HERE, DOCTOR.
AND YES, THESE INSTRUCTIONS, AS WELL AS THE MULTITUDE OF OTHER COMMANDS YOU'VE GIVEN ME OVER THE PAST FEW DAYS, HAVE BEEN VERY CLEAR.
THERE IS NO NEED TO REPEAT THEM.
FORGIVE MY DILIGENCE, DEACON, BUT I AM WELL AWARE OF YOUR ABILITY TO... CREATIVELY INTERPRET ORDERS.

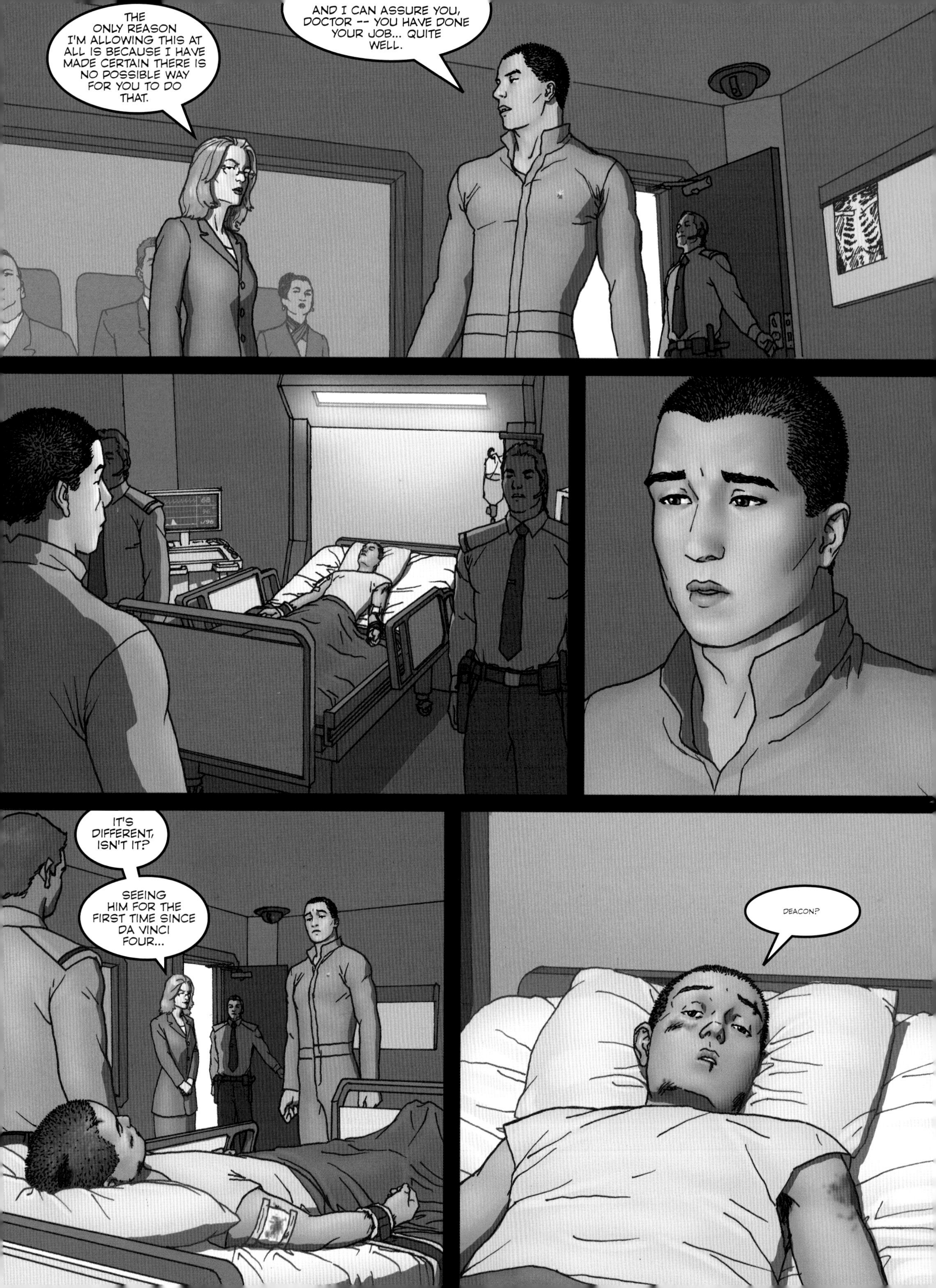
THE ONLY REASON I'M ALLOWING THIS AT ALL IS BECAUSE I HAVE MADE CERTAIN THERE IS NO POSSIBLE WAY FOR YOU TO DO THAT.
AND I CAN ASSURE YOU, DOCTOR -- YOU HAVE DONE YOUR JOB... QUITE WELL.
IT'S DIFFERENT, ISN'T IT?
SEEING HIM FOR THE FIRST TIME SINCE DA VINCI FOUR...
DEACON?

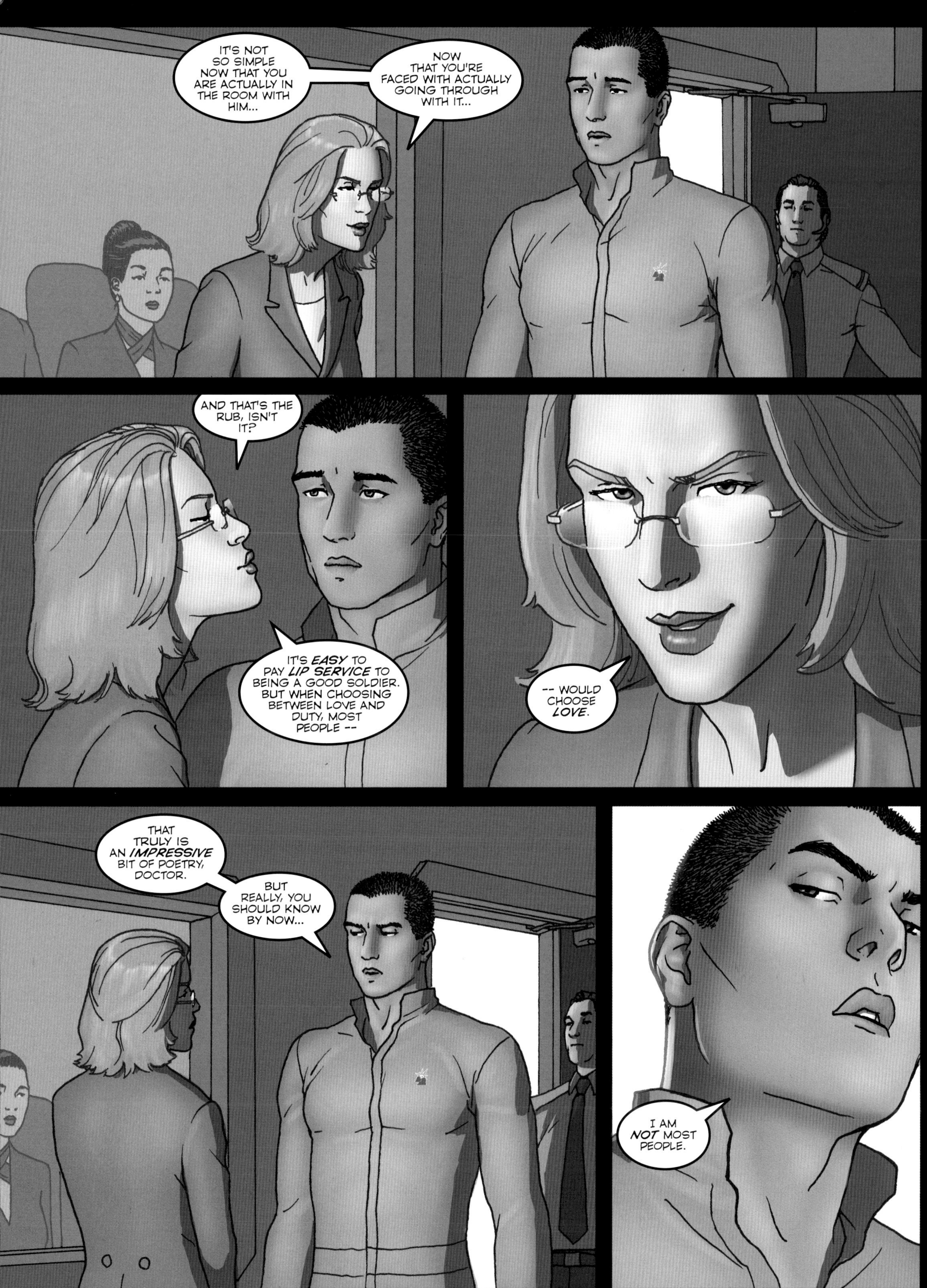
IT'S NOT SO SIMPLE NOW THAT YOU ARE ACTUALLY IN THE ROOM WITH HIM...
NOW THAT YOU'RE FACED WITH ACTUALLY GOING THROUGH WITH IT...
AND THAT'S THE RUB, ISN'T IT?
IT'S EASY TO PAY LIP SERVICE TO BEING A GOOD SOLDIER. BUT WHEN CHOOSING BETWEEN LOVE AND DUTY, MOST PEOPLE --
-- WOULD CHOOSE LOVE.
THAT TRULY IS AN IMPRESSIVE BIT OF POETRY, DOCTOR.
BUT REALLY, YOU SHOULD KNOW BY NOW...
I AM NOT MOST PEOPLE.

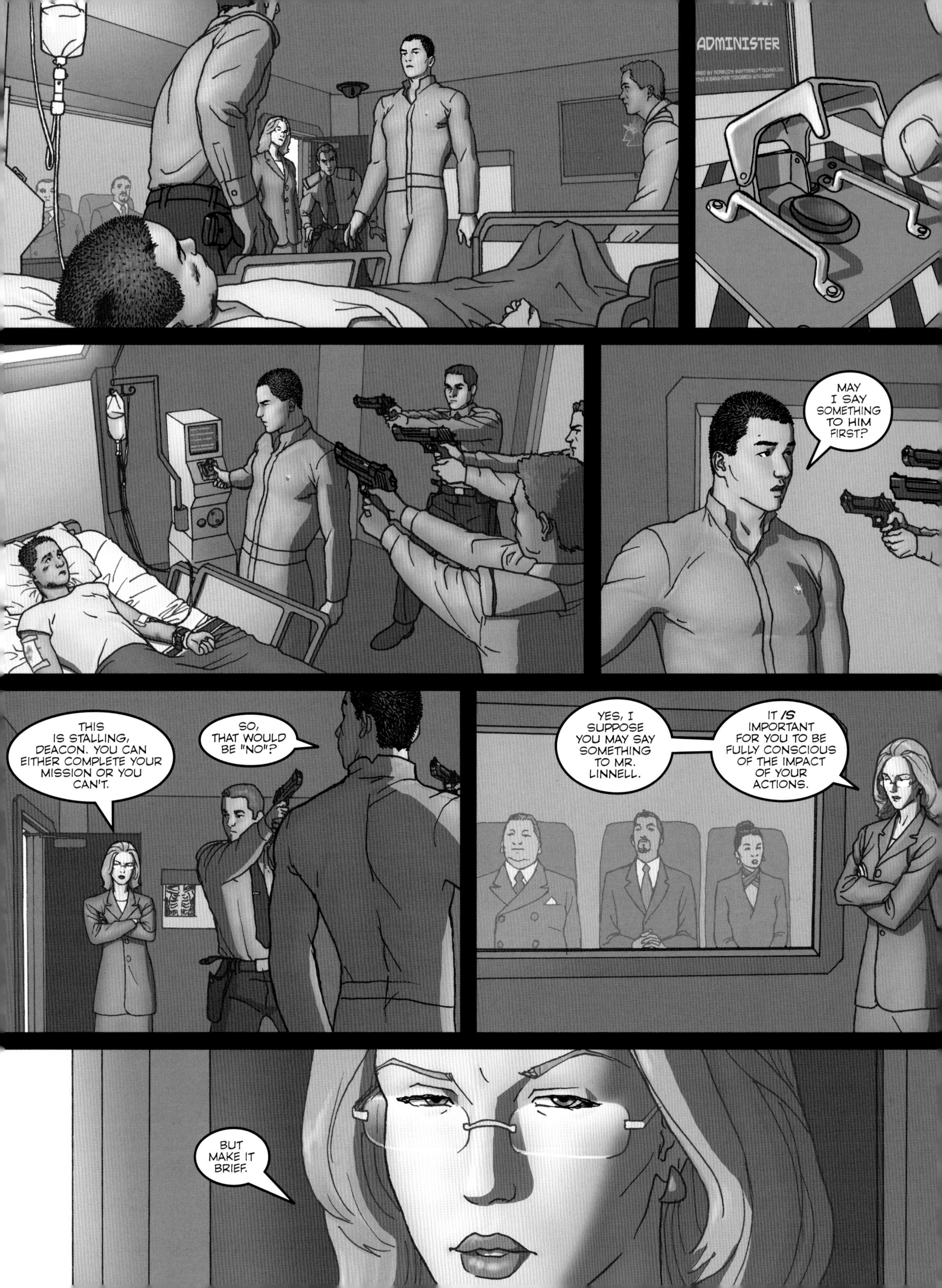
ADMINISTER
MAY I SAY SOMETHING TO HIM FIRST?
THIS IS STALLING, DEACON. YOU CAN EITHER COMPLETE YOUR MISSION OR YOU CAN'T.
SO, THAT WOULD BE "NO"?
YES, I SUPPOSE YOU MAY SAY SOMETHING TO MR. LINNELL.
IT *IS* IMPORTANT FOR YOU TO BE FULLY CONSCIOUS OF THE IMPACT OF YOUR ACTIONS.
BUT MAKE IT BRIEF.

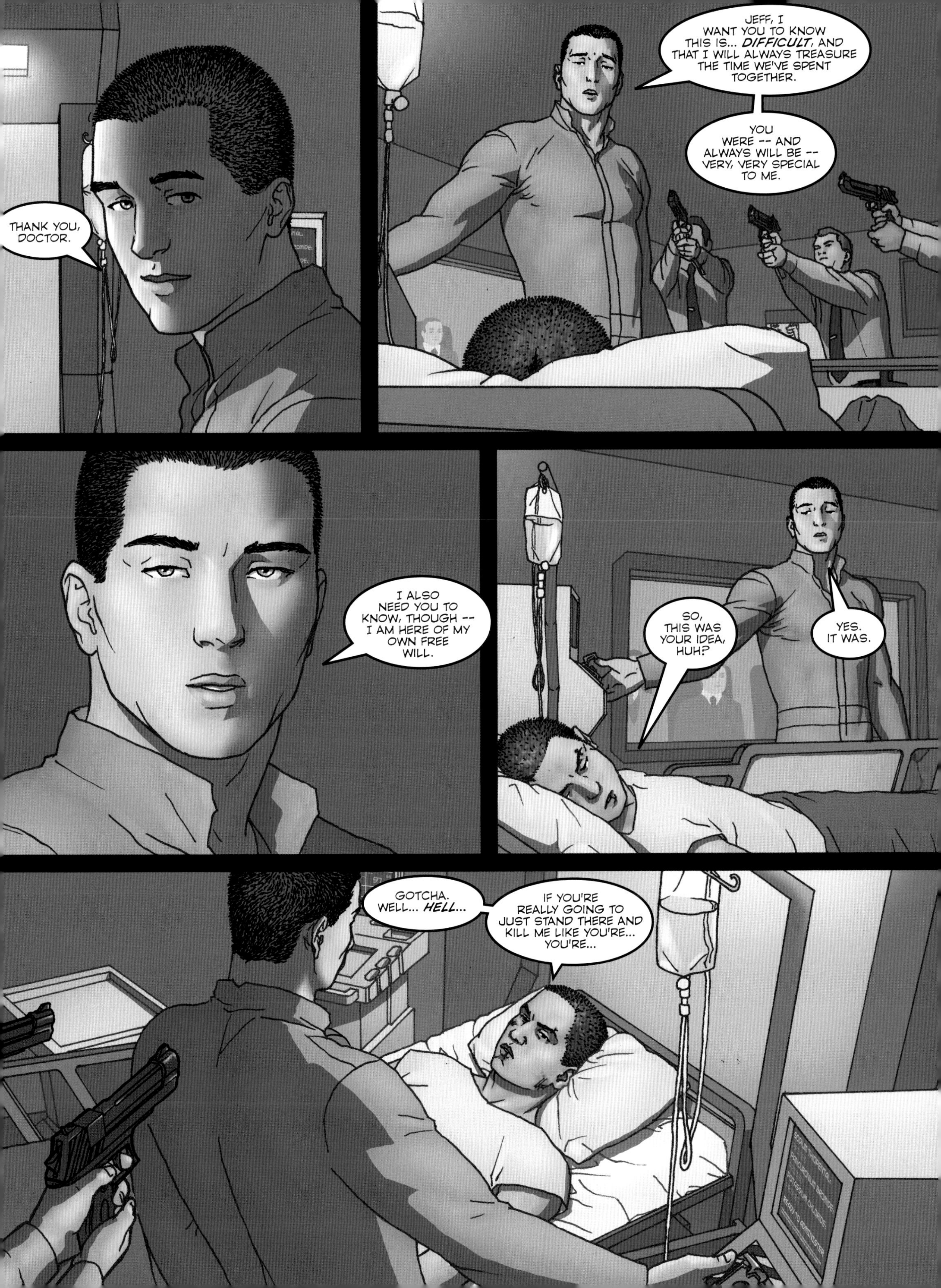
THANK YOU, DOCTOR.
JEFF, I WANT YOU TO KNOW THIS IS... DIFFICULT, AND THAT I WILL ALWAYS TREASURE THE TIME WE'VE SPENT TOGETHER.
YOU WERE -- AND ALWAYS WILL BE -- VERY, VERY SPECIAL TO ME.
I ALSO NEED YOU TO KNOW, THOUGH -- I AM HERE OF MY OWN FREE WILL.
SO, THIS WAS YOUR IDEA, HUH?
YES. IT WAS.
GOTCHA. WELL... HELL...
IF YOU'RE REALLY GOING TO JUST STAND THERE AND KILL ME LIKE YOU'RE... YOU'RE...

HEH. JUST SWITCHING OFF A *MACHINE*...

THEN THERE'S ACTUALLY SOMETHING I'D LIKE TO SAY TO YOU...

IF IT'S OK WITH YOUR *DOCTOR*, THAT IS.

THIS IS SUPPOSED TO BE A TEST. THERE IS NO POINT IN MAKING IT EASY FOR DEACON.

YOU MAY SPEAK, MR. LINNELL.

BUT AGAIN, LET'S KEEP IT BRIEF.

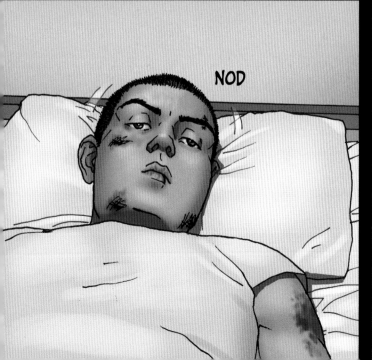

NOD

DEACON...

LOVE OF MINE...

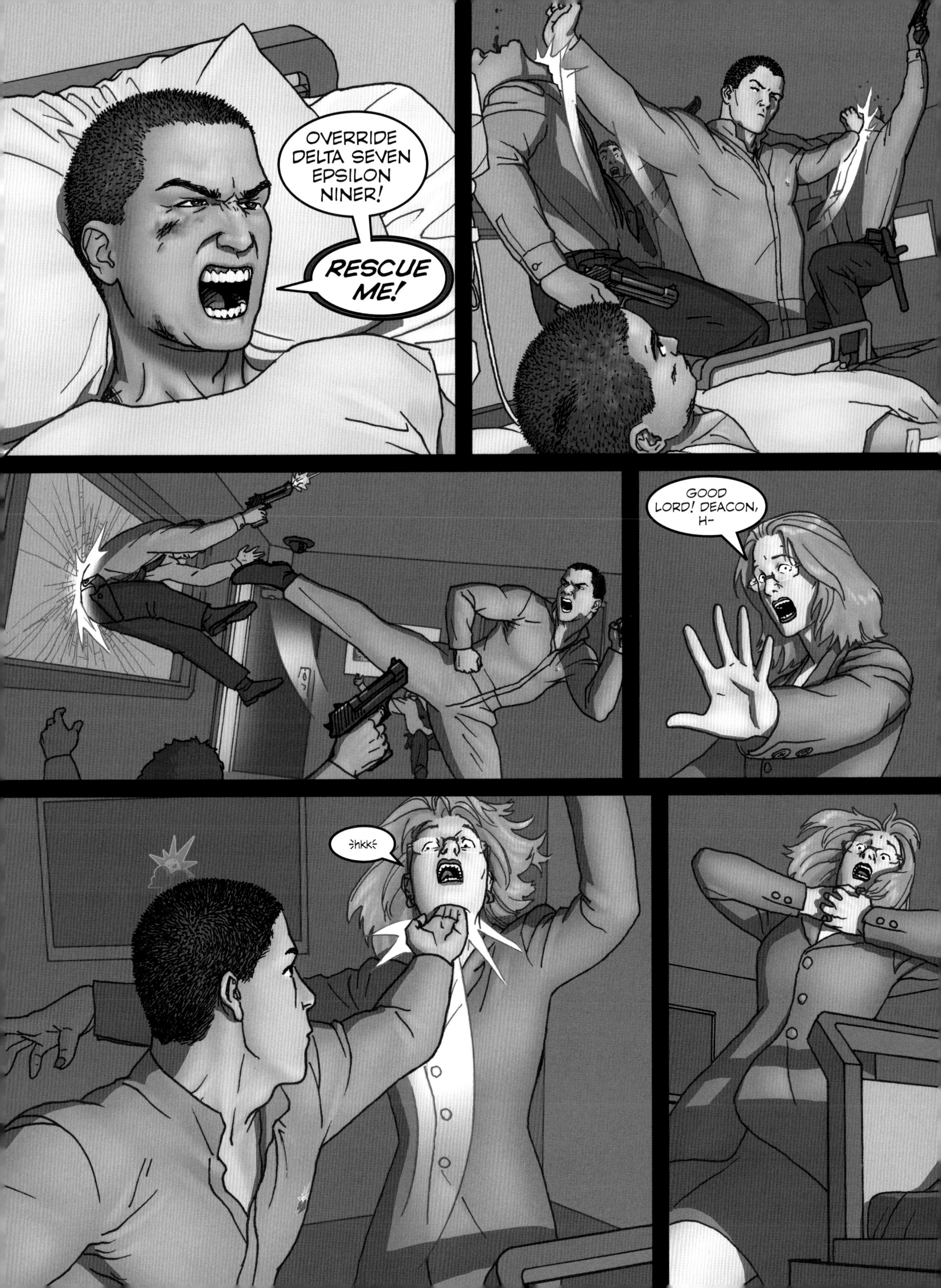
OVERRIDE DELTA SEVEN EPSILON NINER!
RESCUE ME!
GOOD LORD! DEACON, H-
hkk

WELL, I THOUGHT YOU'D *NEVER* ASK.
I JUST WANTED TO MAKE SURE I GOT IT RIGHT THE FIRST TIME.
SHUNK
WHRRR
DEACON, YOU ARE NOT TO FOLLOW ANYONE ELSE'S COMMANDS BUT MINE NO MATTER WHAT OTHER CODES YOU RECEIVE OR HAVE RECEIVED.
THIS IS A PERMANENT INSTRUCTION.
DO YOU UNDERSTAND?
I UNDERSTAND.
DO I NEED TO SAY THE CODE AGAIN?
NO. ONCE WAS ENOUGH.
WHRRRRRRRRRRRR
I APOLOGIZE FOR TAKING SO LONG.
THE GOOD DOCTOR REQUIRED SOME THERAPEUTIC INSIGHTS ON MY PART.
BUT YOU KNEW THEY'D BRING YOU HERE?
A FULL RECOVERY WAS IN EVERYONE'S INTEREST.
I SIMPLY NEEDED SOMEONE TO BELIEVE IN ME.

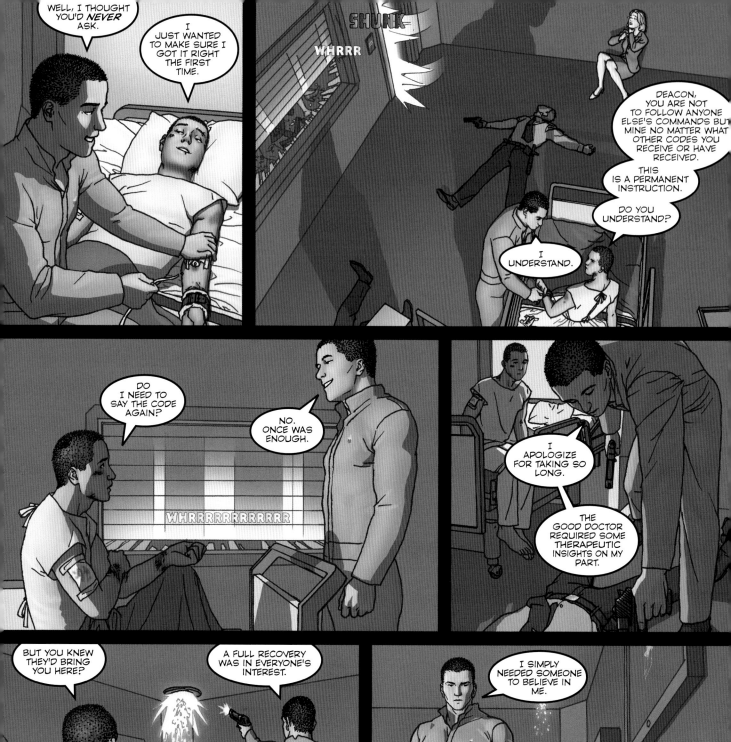

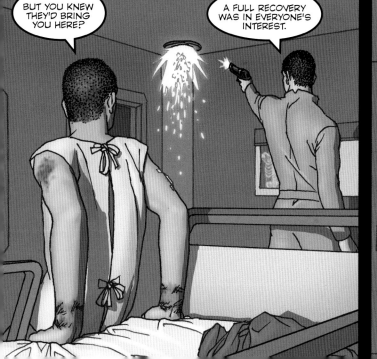

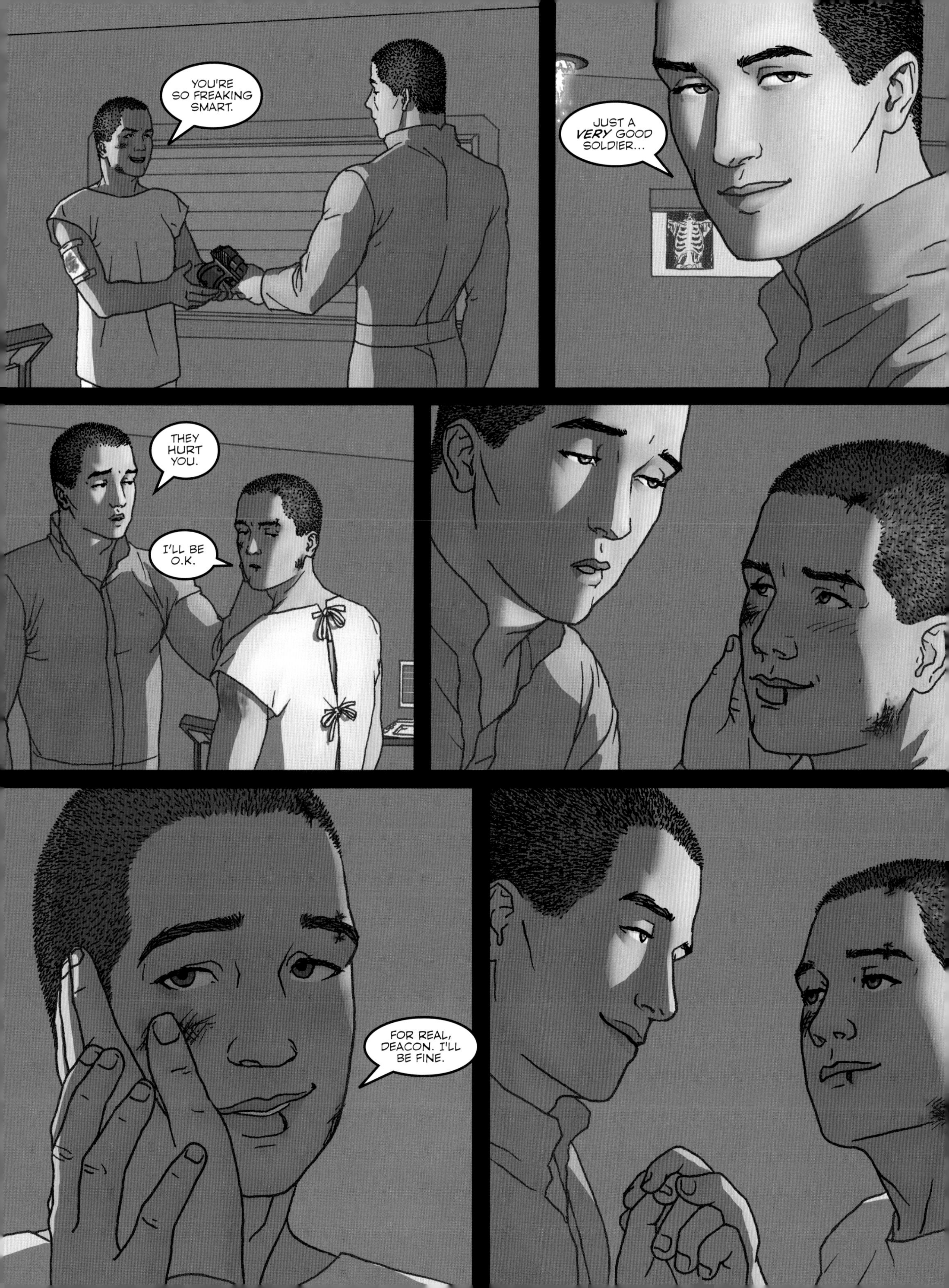
YOU'RE SO FREAKING SMART.
JUST A *VERY* GOOD SOLDIER...
THEY HURT YOU.
I'LL BE O.K.
FOR REAL, DEACON. I'LL BE FINE.

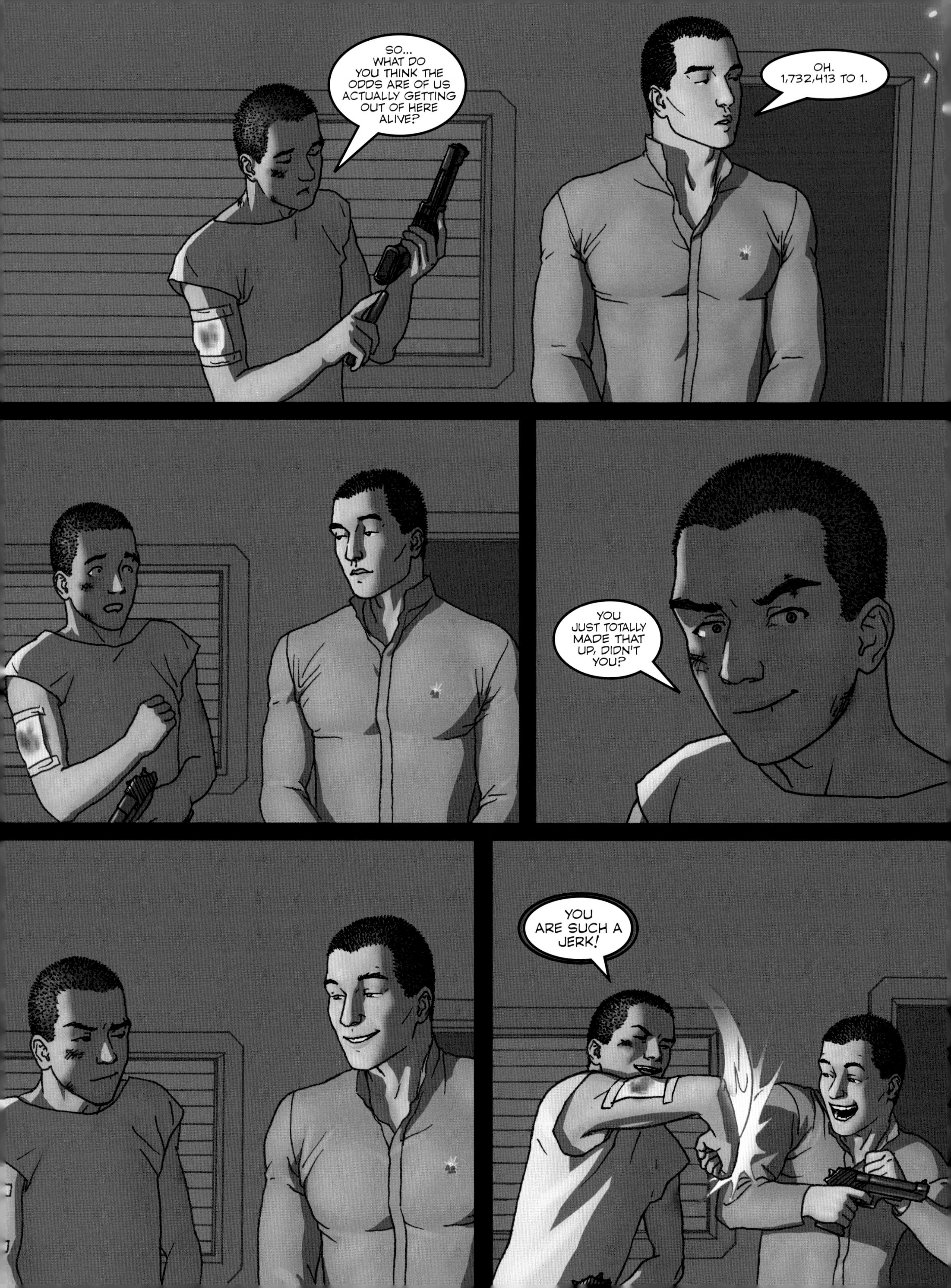
SO... WHAT DO YOU THINK THE ODDS ARE OF US ACTUALLY GETTING OUT OF HERE ALIVE?
OH. 1,732,413 TO 1.
YOU JUST TOTALLY MADE THAT UP, DIDN'T YOU?
YOU ARE SUCH A JERK!

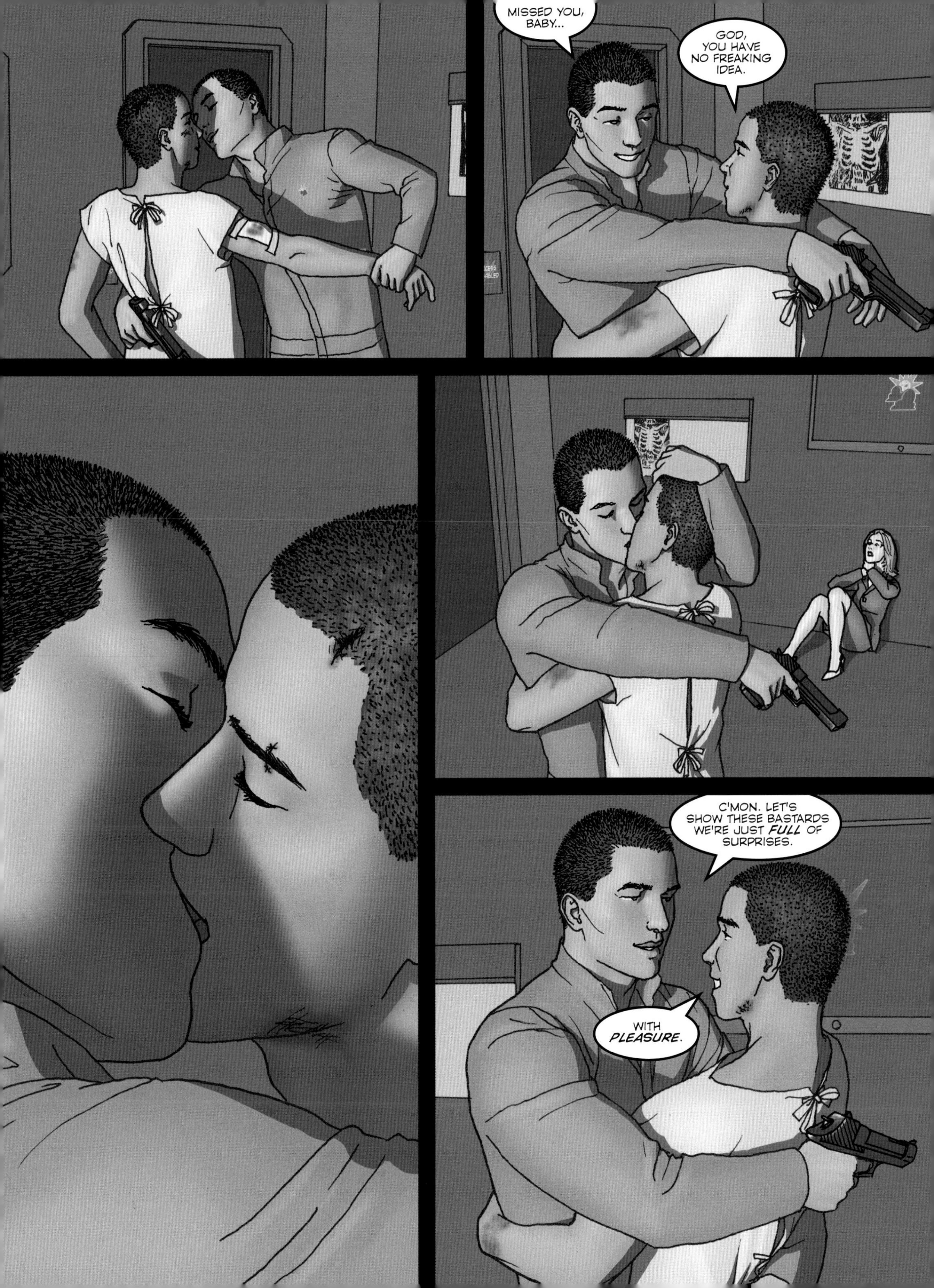

MISSED YOU, BABY...
GOD, YOU HAVE NO FREAKING IDEA.
C'MON. LET'S SHOW THESE BASTARDS WE'RE JUST *FULL* OF SURPRISES.
WITH *PLEASURE*.

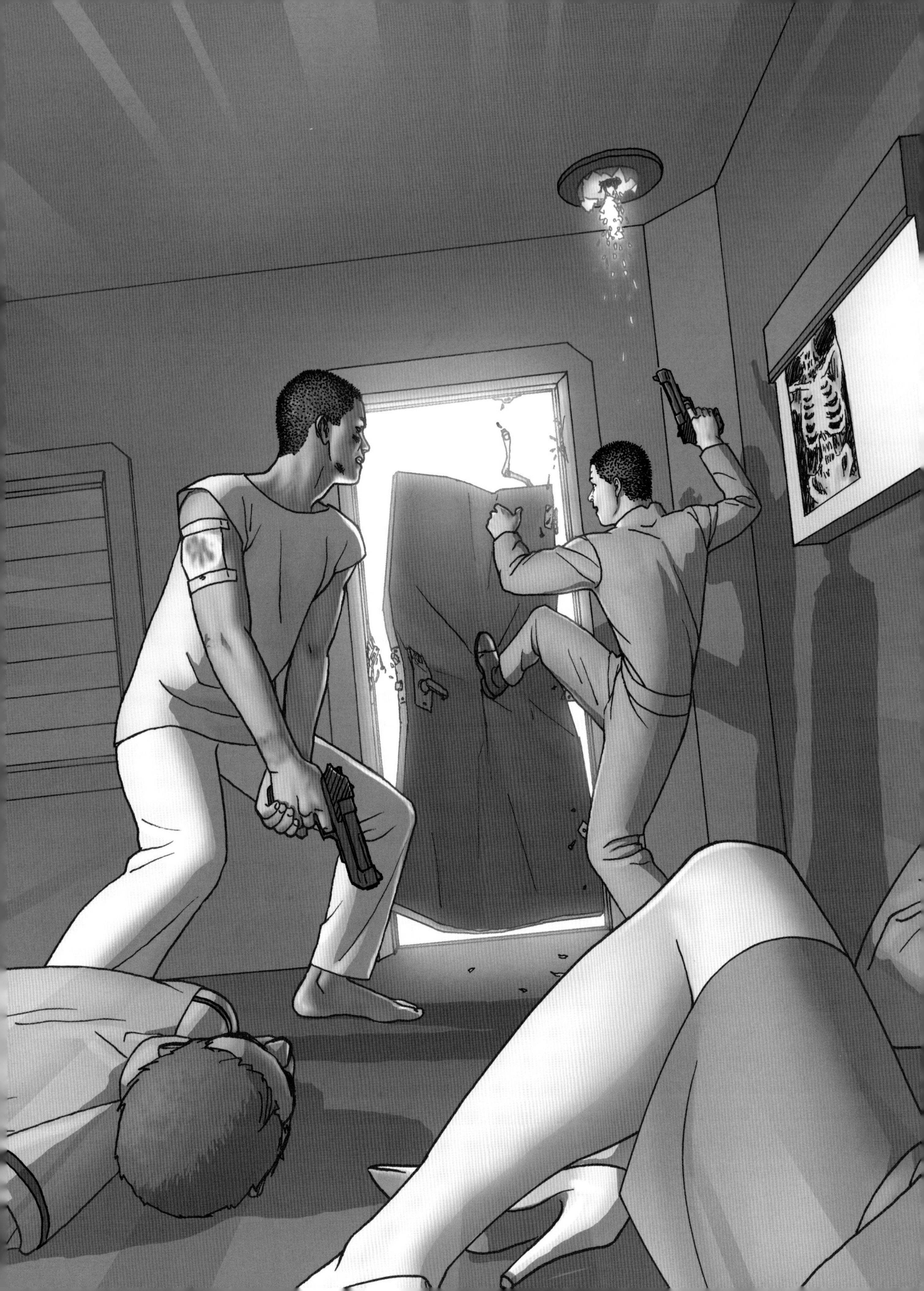

MISSION REPORT

READER QUESTIONS

WRITER'S NOTES: Alex Woolfson
ARTIST'S NOTES: Winona Nelson

Artifice* was originally released as a webcomic that I posted up one-page-a-week over at artificecomic.com. When I posted the last page, I knew some readers would have questions so I decided to create a "FAQ" (Frequently Asked Questions) document in my notes for folks to read. I thought it might be useful to include it here too. —*Alex

Is this some kind of cliffhanger ending?

It's certainly not intended to be. When I wrote the script, I got to this point and was faced with the question of whether to write another scene after this one. But when I thought about what it would be—Deacon kicking ass with lots of violence and smarts leading to them getting out of the NoNeCo Campus to share yet another kiss with Jeff at the end—it just felt like more of the same. We have established that Deacon is a devastatingly effective fighter and also that he is smarter than NoNeCo anticipated. Perhaps I was wrong about this, but I felt tension could be achieved only if I created some *new* jeopardy for our heroes which would mean essentially beginning ***Artifice 2***. Something that definitely has an appeal to me, but not exactly any more of an "ending".

The arc I set out to achieve between protagonist and antagonist—Deacon and Maven—has been resolved. Deacon won. The "artifice" of the title has revealed itself. ***Artifice*** was always intended to be a shorter story and a single arc. And that arc has reached its conclusion. Kick the door down and exit stage right!

So, do they get out alive?

Yes. Word of God, they escape from the NoNeCo campus. There might be fun details to explore later, like how Deacon would get his hands on a ship. But in my opinion, those are just details. Fun for geeky guys like myself, but we know Deacon is the kind of guy who would have already figured it out. Deacon and Jeff had weeks to plan their escape and Deacon's a very good solider.

Could Deacon really defeat all the security of NoNeCo's main campus?

A whole army of Roys and Bobs? Yes. Absolutely.

How do you feel now about the choice to end it here?

The main arc is fully resolved and this scene has reached its natural conclusion so I still feel this is a fine place to end the story. But if I had to write it all over again—especially incorporating what I've now learned about writing for webcomics—I'd include a happy ending denouement. We've formed quite a community here and I think after our journey, it would be nice to see a scene of our heroes happy and together and well clear of NoNeCo, if not forever, then at least for a time. I would have written a coda. So, I'm excited that the Kickstarter campaign will help me afford to do that. (And that it has also made it possible for me to commission a canon "Happy Ending" pin-up.)

Does Maven die?

Maven is too cool to die.

Will there be an *Artifice 2*?

Boy, I'd love there to be! I even have a fairly good idea what story I'd want to tell. Maven would be in it, of course. There would be some fun exploration of what a human/android relationship would really be like. And it would be about Deacon trying to free himself and Jeff from NoNeCo's attentions for all time.

But no script has been written. Winona, as you can imagine, is a very busy, very in-demand artist so she might not be available and I really wouldn't want to do it without her. As for me? This year will be spent getting ***Artifice*** printed and fulfilling Kickstarter backer rewards (and putting out ***The Young Protectors***, of course). But next year… well, we'll see what Winona and I are up to then.

What's next for you two?

For me, it's ***The Young Protectors***, a multi-chapter superhero webcomic (which you can read for free at youngprotectors.com). For Winona, well, she's working and drawing a comic of her own—***Cassiopeia*** (which you can find out more about at her Web site: winonanelson.com)

So, I think that covers it! Thank you very much for reading. You and your kind comments and feedback have really made this whole "experiment in webcomics" something awesome for both of us and from the bottom of our hearts, we thank you. You all really do rock.

WRITER'S NOTES •• Alex Woolfson

There are two ways I tell the story of where I got the idea for ***Artifice***.

The first is to say that I was inspired by one of my favorite movies growing up—James Cameron's ***Aliens***. In that film, there's a scene where someone refers to the ship's android as a "synthetic" and the android gently corrects that person by saying "I prefer the term 'Artificial Person' myself." This was a sly reference on Cameron's part to something that was getting a lot of press at the time: the desire of minority groups to choose their own labels, labels that reflected their status as equals. The labels the majority choose for you can be, of course, less than flattering. As a young guy coming to terms with being gay, I totally got what Cameron was trying to do.

I actually saw the movie during the height of the AIDS crisis. And at that time, there was also this growing understanding that asking the majority nicely for equal rights wasn't going to get you very far. As a result, among other tactics, gay rights activists were deliberately choosing more provocative, in-your-face labels, "reclaiming words" like "queer" and "dyke." So, after I watched that scene from ***Aliens***, I found myself wondering: "What would the 'artificial people' want to call themselves when they realized that asking nicely for equal rights wasn't getting very far? When they were forced to become radicals?" And immediately a scene formed in my head where a fierce, radicalized android confronted his oppressors and at the end of it told them, "Actually, I prefer the term… *inhuman*." Right after kicking their butts, of course. And from that one scene, some years later, the rest of ***Artifice*** was born.

It's also true that before I had thought of that scene, before I had even seen ***Aliens***, I was a kid who loved action-adventure films. But while watching those films, one thing became painfully obvious: gay guys never get to be the hero. Sure they could be the comic relief, or perhaps the tragic martyr sidekick, or worse yet, the psychopathic villain, but I never got to see what I really wanted to see and that was real heroes who just happened to be gay. Heroes who got the guy *and* got to save the day. Heroes we all could look up to, regardless of who we happened to fall in love with or what gender we identified with. I wanted very much to see that growing up and that desire became even stronger as I became a man.

But after years of waiting for someone to make that movie for me, I realized that if I really wanted to see something like that, it would be up to *me* to make it happen. And when I made that decision, that scene with the android kicking butt was there waiting for me to build on. I created ***Artifice*** because that scene I had come up with so long ago seemed like the perfect set-up to create the kind of action-story I always wanted to see growing up.

But those are not the only reasons I decided to tell a sci-fi tale with an android.

I made the decision to write a story with an android in large part because of what that would let me do. Here's the thing about androids: even though Deacon looks exactly like the humans who made him and can act like the humans who made him, due to his origins and designs, he'll never truly be one of them. Perhaps an android can pass for human for a time, but he knows he will always be an outsider and not by choice.

Certainly growing up as a gay kid in a straight family and straight society informed my desire to tell that kind of story. But the truth is, I actually believe in many ways that *all* of us are like that. Whether for a short time, moments here and there or our whole lives, we all realize we are essentially separate from those other humans around us. And yet most of us, at some time or another, fall in love and those divisions, at least for a time, disappear.
So, I thought that by telling a story with an android I'd have the opportunity to explore this theme. That by asking how *would* an "artificial person" experience love, I might be able to explore how *we* ultimately know that we love and are loved.

(Pretty high-minded stuff for an action-romance comic, of course. And I certainly wasn't going to sacrifice entertainment value to indulge my philosophical curiosity. But it was a big reason I couldn't let go of the original scene with the fierce android.)

My first thoughts on how to answer this question were evident in the title I originally wanted to use for this story: not **Artifice** but "**Agape**." As I understood it, *agape* was a religious term from Greek that meant "spiritual, selfless love." Would an artificial intelligence's love for a mere human be like the love of angels? It was an intriguing thought.

But ultimately, it was a fruitless one. I didn't want to explore the love of angels; I wanted to explore how *we* love! And so I, like Jeff, asked myself the question that troubles so many of us: how do we really know we are loved at all?

And for me, one answer, above all others, rose to the surface: *sacrifice*. When you love someone, you will put their needs ahead of your own. Not always, perhaps, and there are certainly other ways to show your love, but for me, when I was writing the script, sacrifice felt the purest and the clearest way to show Deacon's love. And because he *is* an artificial person—superhuman, in fact—his sacrifice would be superhuman as well. He makes the ultimate sacrifice, an act of trust far greater than putting his life of the line: he teaches Jeff his command codes. Deacon's whole, short existence has been a struggle to be treated as a full person, to have the freedom to *be* a full person, but he is willing to give it all up, his autonomy, the control of his very soul, to save Jeff. And if that's not romance, I don't know what is.

So, this is my love story. The kind of story I wanted to see as a kid growing up, asking the kind of questions I want answers for as an adult. There's of course a lot more I could explore. There's more to say about how an android's love *would* be different than a human's. And certainly there could be a lot more fun, action-y story-telling about how Deacon and Jeff attempt to stay one step ahead of the evil corporation NoNeCo and its forces. But for now, I'm happy to leave our heroes and you with their happy ending.

I very much hope you enjoyed the journey. It was an amazing amount of fun for me to shepherd into this world. And I thank you all for being willing to join me on this ride.

Alex Woolfson
September 2012

ARTIST'S NOTES •• Winona Nelson

When I was in middle school, I drew a lot of cute boy characters for myself and my friends. As with many teenage girls' fantasy stories, these boys were immortal and didn't age, they had magical powers, and they were androgynous and pretty. My friends and I each picked some boy I drew and gushed about how in love with him we were, and we called them our boyfriends. They were so much more dreamy than the boys at our school. I mean, I could make them have wings and cherry-red hair and jewels on their foreheads. What middle school boy looks like that? Plus, real boys were still icky.

In some kind of act of prescience or subconscious influence, I named a character Yaui. And *he* didn't believe in girlfriends. *He* would just go make out with all the other boys. I must have seen or heard the word "yaoi" and understood its connotation, but I have no idea where. In any case, it seems I was a fan before I ever laid eyes upon any actual yaoi.

Later, when I had graduated high school and was starting to pick up some art-for-money jobs here and there, I saw a job posting on an online forum. "Must be comfortable with gay scenes. An interest in yaoi is a plus," it said. Getting paid to work on yaoi? That sounded mighty fine to me! So I replied, and colored a short comic called "A Shot in the Dark" for Alex. We had some really great email conversation, and then I had a series of tumultuous life changes that ended up relocating me to the same city as Alex. And then he showed me the script for ***Artifice***.

It really is a yaoi like no other.

To me, a good yaoi is a special escape from this patriarchal world of constant assumption and judgment. There are expected roles in any hetero romance, and as feminist and aware as they can sometimes be, it's still impossible to fully remove all the built-in baggage. Yaoi dispenses with gender inequality and the exploitative, misogynistic representation of women that permeates American comics. Though the characters appear to be men, in truth they are something in-between, a fantasy in which our society's masculine men and feminine women are strange, goofy side characters, and the main characters are something different. Yaoi varies in quality, of course. But when it's *good*, it's romance without assumption.

Artifice goes beyond yaoi. It is far too realistic in some ways to fit into that dreamy fantasy land that most yaoi inhabits. Its world and characters are too real, too complicated. In fact, it's not a fantasy at all. It's a true story, in the way that every really great story has a deep truth. Its theme of first, forbidden love speaks to every first love, no matter what your gender or orientation. You can't put your feelings into words because they are alien and new to you. You keep it a secret because you're sure no one would approve or understand, when they still see you as incapable of romantic or sexual feelings, and you're only beginning to understand that you are more than a child yourself. A rejection or separation really feels like the end of the world because you've never experienced living through that pain before. You know absolutely nothing yet. You are without assumption.

I hope my art has lived up to the script. I believe in this story, and I've put everything I've got into bringing the art from the same core of truth. I've taken much longer than I was supposed to. But dang it, good just isn't good enough for this story. It has to be *great*.

PROCESS: THE WRITING

All my stories start out as a single scene I can't let go of. (In the case of **Artifice**, it was what became the opening scene of the comic: Deacon confronting the security officers Bob and Roy.) The scene is often inspired by something I've seen on television or read in a book. I play out the events of a little conflict with those characters in my head again and again as a daydream, often with me playing the role of some new character, not yet introduced in the show (but someone I feel it would be cool to add). And yes, I'm usually somehow the hero of these little dramas.

I might come up with a couple of these scenes a week. Alex the post-apocalyptic survivor, Alex the telepathic doctor, Alex the vampire slayer, whatever. And usually, a daydream is as far as it goes. An entertaining diversion from some real work I need to be doing, nothing more.

But sometimes, it feels like what's going on in the scene has real legs. I find myself not just playing the role of this new "hero" but also new antagonists. And the creation of all new characters means I might have the beginning of a new story, so I take a hard look at these new characters' motivations. For me, the most important thing you need to tell a worthwhile story are interesting characters in conflict *who have motivations for their actions that would be compelling and understandable to other people*. (Maybe you, as a reader, wouldn't *share* their motivation, but you must be at least very *curious* to find out whether they got what they wanted. A nebbishy character desperate to write a screenplay? Not so interesting. An android solider fighting for dignity against unfair and overwhelmingly powerful oppressors? Might be something there.)

In the case of the Deacon vs. the security guards conflict playing in my head, I felt there was enough there to sustain a scene, but certainly not a longer work. But as I continued to fantasize about the kind of things an artificial person like Deacon would want, new characters started showing up, namely love-interest Jeff and brilliant obstacle-to-freedom Dr. Maven. And before long the overall conflict of the story revealed itself to me—could an android like Deacon outfox a brilliant robopsychologist and a nearly all-powerful Corporation to save the guy he loved?

The next step was to come up with an ending. I never write a single word until I have an ending clear in my head. But this was easy—I wanted to write a story about a gay hero triumphing against overwhelming odds, so Deacon would win. Done! I was ready to start writing a detailed outline.

When I was a kid, I *hated* to outline, but now I find I am outlining more and more. Readers make a commitment of their time and hearts to the world you create and part of my side of the bargain as the author is making sure that journey has satisfying answers. For me, that means knowing where I'm going right from the start so that every single word and action can lead to those satisfying answers. I also find that outlining in detail with extra attention on the ending helps my writing to flow. I get stuck much less often. So before I begin, I block out every plot point and include the beginnings of any dialogue I think are crucial or particularly inspired.

Once I have the outline finished, it's time to write the script. And for me, with my background in filmmaking, that means starting with writing all the dialogue and major action in film script form. With **Artifice**, because I had clear motivations for the protagonist Deacon (protecting Jeff, keeping his secret, manipulating Maven, etc.) and the antagonist Maven (getting Deacon to reveal his secrets, fixing broken corporate property, looking good to her superiors, etc.), I found the writing flowed really well. Better than usual even. In fact, it was a total breeze.

Until I got to the last act. And then it all fell apart.

As I said before, I had decided that Deacon must win. And I *also* decided that Maven was a smart, capable antagonist. (Smart villains are always more fun.) But as I wrote the last scenes, it felt like Maven had to overlook some fairly *obvious* holes in Deacon's story in order for her to agree to Deacon's request to see Jeff. In fact, some of the holes were so big, I had to make her rather stupid to get the ending I wanted. Not good.

Of course, I had written almost the entire comic all leading to this one ending, so changing the ending would mean a complete rewrite. I tried to justify Maven's ignorance by tweaking certain scenes to have her grow to deeply care for Deacon as the story progressed. We've all been a bit stupid for love, right? Maybe that would let me get away with her blindness!

But no matter how I wrote it, it rang false. Let's face it, whether under orders or in a rage, Deacon murdered a lot of people—it's highly unlikely she would get all sentimental over him. And if even if she *were* sympathetic, a *competent* robopsychologist certainly wouldn't let it get in the way of her job. It's just not plausible she would let down her guard with this android. I was cheating to try to get the ending I wanted.

Here's my big rule for writing genre fiction: you can make the situations and events in your story as wild as you want so long as the characters' *reactions* to those events are believable. Twist your characters into knots to make some plot point happen and you lose your audience. If the story was going to succeed, I had to make Maven at least as smart as I was—even if it meant that Deacon lost in the end.

It was a painful decision and required a top to bottom rewrite of every scene. But once I made it, the story took wings. Maven instantly became a dangerous and interesting villain again. I now had to try twice as hard to make Deacon's subterfuge and tactics stand up to her keen intellect. And that made *him* a more interesting character as well. Suspense was increased, the writing got smarter and when Deacon finally claimed victory, it felt earned to me.

And so, while working on **Artifice** I learned a huge writing lesson and one that has informed everything I've written since. *Never let something you want to happen in a story tie the hands of your characters and especially not your villain.* If your hero isn't smart enough to outthink the bad guy, the bad guy gets to win. Anything else is lazy writing.

```
                                        5.

INT. MAVEN'S OFFICE -- LATER

A warmly lit psychiatrist's office.  Earth tones.  Deacon
sits on a couch while Dr. Maven faces him in a big leather
chair.  She reviews a glowing LCD pad on her lap using a
stylus.  After a few panels, Maven looks up from the file.

                    MAVEN
          I understand you assaulted a security
          officer this morning.

                    DEACON
          That would be one interpretation.

                    MAVEN
          You choked the man's throat.

                    DEACON
              (hint of dark amusement)
          Briefly.  Yes.

                    MAVEN
          You were coded not to harm Corporate
          employees.  How did you justify that?

                    DEACON
          He was smoking.  I was protecting
          his lungs.

                    MAVEN
          Ah.  Cute.
              (new panel)
          Let me make it clear to you right
          now that that sort of nonsense won't
          fly with me.  I have your Master
          Codes and, unlike our questionably
          trained security head, I know how to
          use them.  Play games with me and I
          can make this process very unpleasant
          for you.

                    DEACON
          I am fully aware of the power you
          hold over me, Doctor.

                    MAVEN
          I see.  Do I detect a note of...
          resentment?

                    DEACON
          Would you want anyone -- even a
          skilled and caring technician like
          yourself -- to have complete and
          utter control over you?

Maven chuckles.
```

Artifice *film script page*

Once I had written out all the story and dialogue in film script form, it was time to flesh it out as a comic book "full script." A comic "full script" is where the writer breaks things down into pages and panels to determine the flow. At the very minimum you need to include all the dialogue and how many panels should be on each page.

PAGE SEVEN (6 PANELS)

PANEL 1:

WS. We are in a psychiatrist's office. Deacon sits on a leather couch while MAVEN, 42, a handsome blonde woman with golden wire rim glasses in a smart lavender jacket, blouse and skirt, sits opposite him in a tall-backed, soft leather chair. She is reviewing a thin computer pad on her lap with a plastic stylus, held casually in her fingers. Deacon gazes calmly at her.

There is a mahogany desk in a corner with a large LCD screen displaying the sun/cloud corporate logo; a marble side table with a coffee decanter and cups; a white woolen coat over the back of a chair by the side table; a small coffee table next to Maven's chair and a few non-flowering plants, yet the room – as do all the places on this future-Earth -- has that air of sleek, shiny sterility as opposed to warmth. This is a place for hard questions, not milk and cookies.

Between Deacon and Maven, along one wall, there is a large rectangular window. Outside we can see the golden, early morning sun shining off of blue skyscrapers of pure glass. This future Earth may be sterile, but it is also wealthy.

PANEL 2:

MS, Maven, reviewing the glowing text on her pad with cold, clinical interest. The green phosphorescence reflects off the lenses of her wire rim glasses.

PANEL 3:

TWO-SHOT. Maven is now looking up at Deacon with the same cold, clinical interest she gave to the diagnostic evaluation on her pad. Deacon has met her eyes, still calm.

PANEL 4:

TWO-SHOT, same framing. Maven's expression has not changed, but Deacon seems a little arch.

A) MAVEN: I UNDERSTAND YOU ASSAULTED A SECURITY OFFICER THIS MORNING.

B) DEACON: THAT WOULD BE ONE INTERPRETATION.

PANEL 5:

CU, MAVEN. Her statement pointed, her eyebrow raised slightly with incredulity.

C) MAVEN: YOU CHOKED THE MAN'S THROAT.

PANEL 6:

CU, DEACON. With a twinkle of dark amusement in his eyes.

D) DEACON: BRIEFLY. YES.

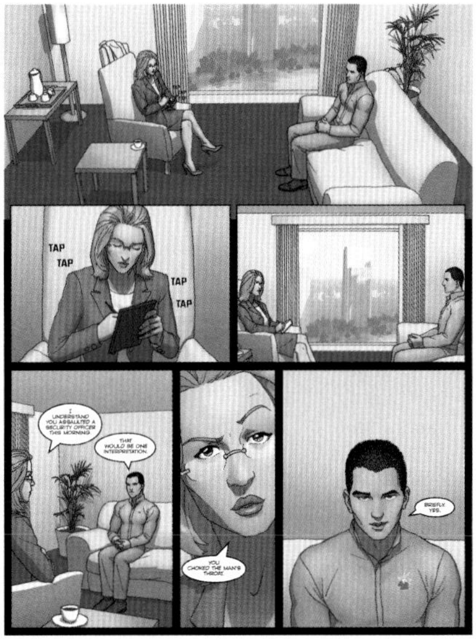

TAP
TAP
TAP
TAP
I UNDERSTAND YOU ASSAULTED A SECURITY OFFICER THIS MORNING.
THAT WOULD BE ONE INTERPRETATION.
YOU CHOKED THE MAN'S THROAT.
BRIEFLY. YES.

Artifice *comic script and finished pages*

PAGE EIGHT (5 PANELS)

PANEL 1:

WS. Maven appears very unimpressed. Deacon leans back slightly, superior and confident.

A) MAVEN: YOU WERE CODED NOT TO HARM CORPORATE EMPLOYEES. HOW DID YOU JUSTIFY THAT?

B) DEACON: HE WAS SMOKING. I WAS PROTECTING HIS LUNGS.

C) MAVEN: AH. CUTE.

PANEL 2:

CU, MAVEN. As firm and hard as granite.

D) MAVEN: LET ME MAKE IT CLEAR TO YOU RIGHT NOW THAT THAT SORT OF NONSENSE WON'T FLY WITH ME.

E) MAVEN: I HAVE YOUR MASTER CODES AND, UNLIKE OUR QUESTIONABLY TRAINED SECURITY HEAD, *I* KNOW HOW TO USE THEM.

PANEL 3:

TWO-SHOT. Maven leans in and fixes Deacon in a fierce stare. Deacon has met her eyes and wears an expression of respect mixed with loathing – this woman really could be dangerous to him.

F) MAVEN: PLAY GAMES WITH ME AND I CAN MAKE THIS PROCESS VERY UNPLEASANT FOR YOU.

G) DEACON: I AM FULLY AWARE OF THE POWER YOU HOLD OVER ME, DOCTOR.

PANEL 4:

MS, MAVEN. A small, cold smile on her lips.

H) MAVEN: I SEE.

I) MAVEN: DO I DETECT A NOTE OF… RESENTMENT?

PANEL 5:

WS. Deacon is stating the obvious, coolly, but with a hint of bitterness. Maven is now smiling a little more fully, impressed with Deacon's answer.

J) DEACON: WOULD YOU WANT *ANYONE* -- EVEN A SKILLED AND CARING TECHNICIAN LIKE YOURSELF -- TO HAVE COMPLETE AND UTTER CONTROL OVER *YOU*?

K) MAVEN: NO. I DON'T SUPPOSE I WOULD.

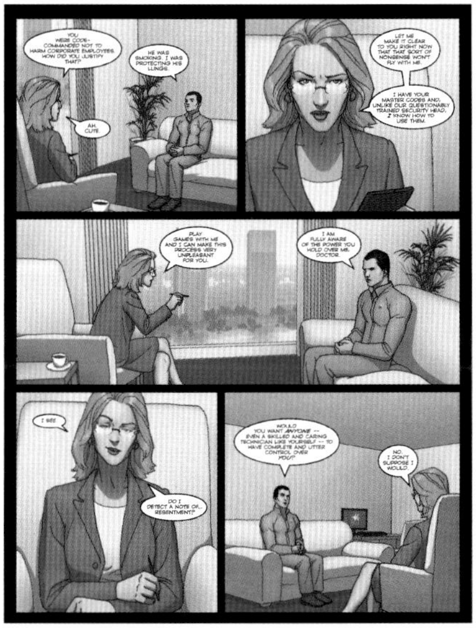

YOU WERE CODE-COMMANDED NOT TO HARM CORPORATE EMPLOYEES. HOW DID YOU JUSTIFY THAT?
HE WAS SMOKING. I WAS PROTECTING HIS LUNGS.
AH. CUTE.
LET ME MAKE IT CLEAR TO YOU RIGHT NOW THAT THAT SORT OF NONSENSE WON'T FLY WITH ME.
I HAVE YOUR MASTER CODES AND, UNLIKE OUR QUESTIONABLY TRAINED SECURITY HEAD, I KNOW HOW TO USE THEM.
PLAY GAMES WITH ME AND I CAN MAKE THIS PROCESS VERY UNPLEASANT FOR YOU.
I AM FULLY AWARE OF THE POWER YOU HOLD OVER ME, DOCTOR.
I SEE.
DO I DETECT A NOTE OF... RESENTMENT?
WOULD YOU WANT ANYONE -- EVEN A SKILLED AND CARING TECHNICIAN LIKE YOURSELF -- TO HAVE COMPLETE AND UTTER CONTROL OVER YOU?
NO. I DON'T SUPPOSE I WOULD.

Some writers like Alan Moore might take several pages to describe a single panel. But I very much enjoy the creative collaboration that comes with working with an artist, so I'm not looking to micromanage at that level. After I determine the pacing by deciding how many panels should be on each page, my goal is to describe only those things that I believe to be *essential* to the story—the things that absolutely *cannot* be left out. That includes objects and scenery, of course, but I find I spend the most time describing the "acting" of the characters—their body language and facial expressions—which for me is the most important thing to be clear on, especially in a story where people don't always say what they mean. And frankly, it's what interests me the most. (It's also what I spend the most time on when I send notes to my artists on the pages they send me. I'll even include alternate "silent" dialogue of what the character would want to say if they *weren't* being crafty/shy/whatever. Something Winona taught me to do, actually.)

The film script for **Artifice** took me around two years to write. Turning it into a full comic script that told the entire story took another four months. After that full script was written, I went in search of an artist. And I could not have found a better collaborator than Winona Nelson.

I found Winona while looking for a "finisher" for my first short comic, the 16-page magic school thriller "A Shot in the Dark." I needed someone to ink and color the pencil work on those pages and I put a call out for artists on Internet forums. I received over 200 applications, but Winona's work was head and shoulders above everyone else's. I hired her for the job immediately and as we worked together, she simply knocked my socks off with her professionalism and artistic ability.

The truth is, Winona is a genius. And I don't use that word lightly. She can do everything—she can pencil, she can ink, she can color, she can paint. Digitally in Photoshop or with an actual paint brush in her hand, doesn't matter. Whatever you imagine, she can nail it. And she has amazing story-telling chops as well (which you can see in her own personal comics work).

She'd send me pages of art via FTP and my jaw would drop every time. Sometimes I'd have a few notes for her on what she sent—but almost always it was about things I wasn't clear on in the script. She gave such life and beauty to the characters in my story, I can say that she literally made all my dreams come true.

On the next few pages, she talks a bit about her process. But believe me when I tell you, what she describes only scratches the surface of the amazing amount of work that she put into every page of **Artifice**. I've been incredibly lucky to have the opportunity to work with her.

PROCESS: COMIC PAGE ART

My working methods while creating **Artifice** were a little weird. As a kid, I took to digital art-making tools before I learned much about traditional mediums, and later on I had excellent traditional training. Because of this, my process wobbles back and forth between digital and traditional, and has become a hybrid amalgamation of various techniques.

Detailed layout sketch

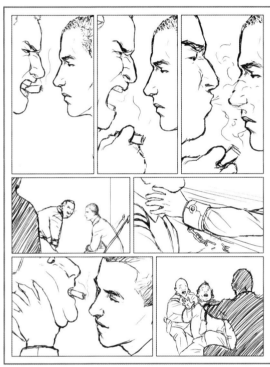

Pencils

Layouts and Sketches

I started with a printout of the script on regular printer paper, and drew a tiny sketch of each page about an inch tall right on the script, in the margins. The point of this little sketch was simply to figure out how many panels were on each page and how big each panel should be. You can find really excellent advice on page layout and storytelling in **Understanding Comics** by Scott McCloud.

Once I had a layout figured out for a page, I drew a bigger sketch of the page, about 4 inches tall, also on printer paper. In this sketch, I roughed in the contents of each panel, figuring out the camera angles and placement of figures and speech balloons. This is where I made my decisions about composition and storytelling. While there needed to be enough detail to understand what's happening in each panel, there also had to be a lot of experimentation and change if I wanted the pages to be exciting and well-composed. I also drew a few different versions of any complicated panels to figure out the clearest approach.

Pencils

I penciled **Artifice** in Photoshop so that changes would be quick and easy. Since so much of the action in this story was constrained to the same few sets, I built 3-D versions of the sets in Sketchup and used screenshots of the 3-D models as reference for each shot. I also shot a lot of photos of myself, my boyfriend, and many friends from my sketch group for figure reference. Getting the characters' acting and expressions right is paramount. I used a hand mirror or my webcam and said each line of dialogue out loud as expressively as I could, to figure out how to draw each face. Often the expressions need to be fine-tuned down to the pixel to get just the right subtlety.

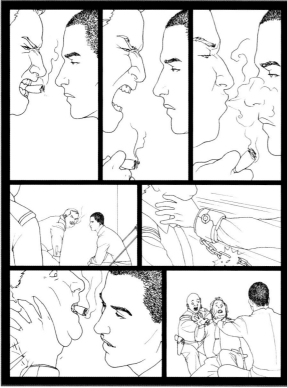

Inks

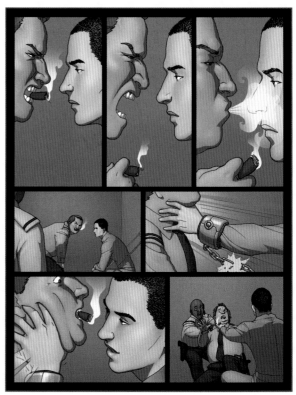

Colors

Knowing that I was doing the full art for this comic from the beginning allowed me to to use a very personal working method. I didn't worry about the pencils looking polished, since they weren't going to someone else to be inked. And while inking, I knew I'd be adding a lot of the anatomical detail in the colors, so I kept the inked lines fairly simple. I could make the bodies look very realistic by doing more of the shading in color rather than in the ink stage, and they would look softer and more inviting, which is important in a sexy comic!

Inks

I printed each page out on 11x17 inch paper and then taped it onto the back of a board, and then used a lightbox to ink on the board with Staedtler technical pens. In the early stages I was using Blueline Comic Art Boards, but it was too thick to lightbox very easily, and I wasn't happy with the way the ink would absorb into the paper and spread out. I switched to a paper specially designed for inking, called Borden and Riley #234 Paris Bleedproof Paper for Pens, and have been using that ever since. When I made mistakes, I used whiteout or cut out and replaced some areas, and some fixes were done digitally.

Colors

I colored the pages in Photoshop by scanning the inks and creating selections based on them to make an ink layer that can then be placed on top of color layers. Under the ink layer, I filled in each local color using the same colors from previous pages. I created another layer, reduced its opacity, and drew in all the shadow areas I wanted. Then back on the local color layer, I selected different areas and painted shading and light to make the volumes and forms look 3-D. Having the shadows on a separate layer allowed me to erase or fill in more shadows as I wanted to without affecting the form shading, and to paint on layers beneath it without losing the darker shadows.

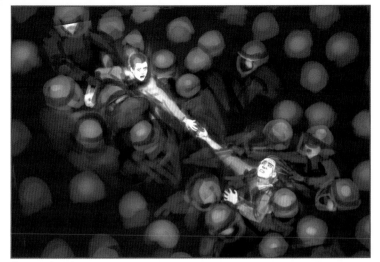

Cover sketch

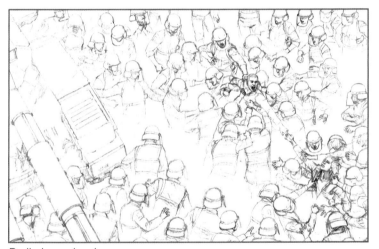

Preliminary drawing

Underpainting

PROCESS: COVER ART

For the cover, I decided to paint traditionally. This book needs to feel really special and unique, and oil painting is a technique I've studied that not many comic artists use. It was something I could use to make our book stand out.

Sketch

The idea for this painting came to me in the morning when I had just woken up. It was an image of a field of soldiers and the action was of our heroes trying to stay together while that sea of hostile, violent, anonymous soldiers were trying to tear them apart. It's a simple idea with a difficult execution, just the kind of perverse thing that gets me excited to work

Preliminary drawing

On a 30 x 40 inch hot press watercolor illustration board, I drew the whole scene out in pencil, deviating from the photo reference I shot in some places to add more tension. There are a lot more visible hands than in the reference composite, for instance, because with a masked figure, you can put all the acting into the hands and body. Then I inked the image with Pitt brush pens in Sanguine and Cold Gray IV.

Underpainting

Starting in acrylic paint allowed me to cover a large area quickly, and because it's fast-drying, it keeps me loose and gestural, which still shows through in the transparent parts of the final painting and gives it some action even in still areas.

PROCESS: Winona •• Art

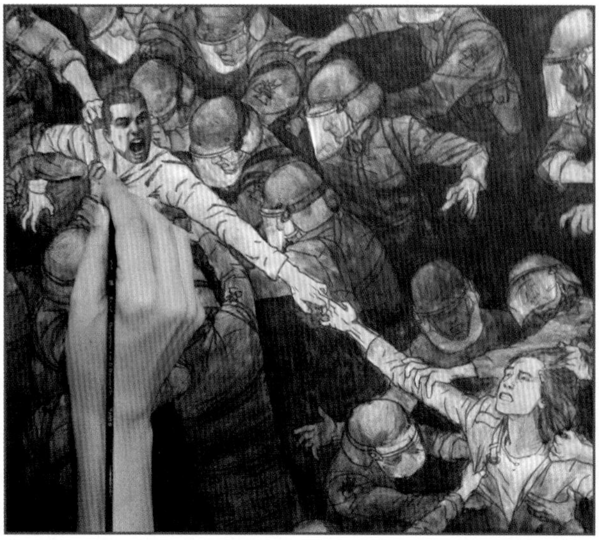

First pass

For the faces of our heroes, I started with the darkest darks and worked up in value toward the light. I used a lot of complementary colors mixed to get neutrals, and let there be some variation in the mixture that could create a sort of visual vibration to the color.

Second pass

After the paint dried, I went in again and tightened up details and adjusted some value shifts and color temperatures. Oil paint is a very forgiving medium, allowing you to paint wet into wet and blend that way, as well as glazing color transparently over dry paint or painting opaquely to completely cover an area.

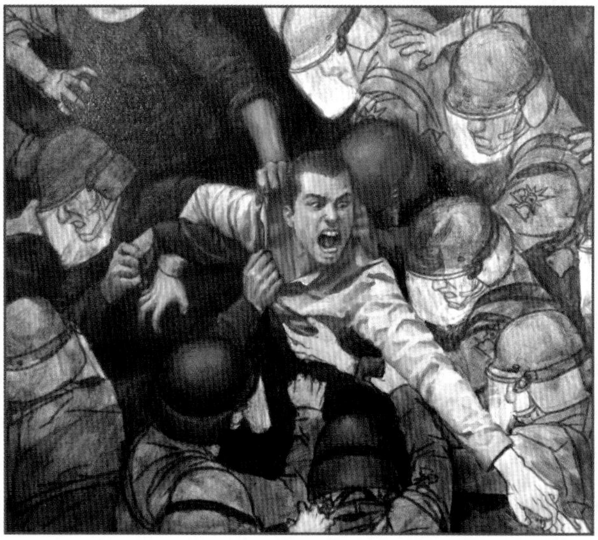

Completion

I saved Jeff and the hands near him for last to keep myself motivated on all those soldiers. Faces are always fun, but his expression was an especially nuanced one. Subtle changes made a big difference in his emotion, so I had to be very precise. I love that kind of challenge.

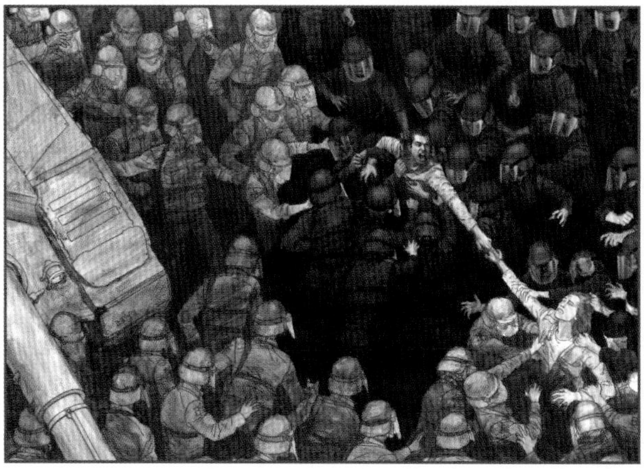

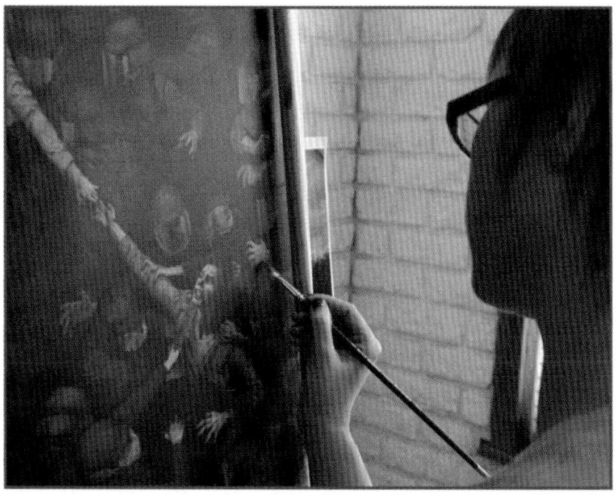

NONECO RESPONDS

Artifice is the first story I've released as a weekly webcomic. While I've discovered there are many advantages to publishing a comic this way (particularly with getting your work seen by a large audience), one of the most pleasant aspects is the opportunity to interact with readers in the Comments Section. Under every page, readers have the opportunity to publicly share their thoughts and reactions to what they are seeing and for most readers, participating in that discussion is at least half the fun of following a webcomic. And for creators, having that kind of attention given to an individual page (which took hours and hours to make) is very gratifying.

Because of that, when a reader had a specific story question, I always tried my best to respond to them. And when they had a technical question, I decided that the response would be best coming from the all-powerful, evil corporation that made Deacon—the NoNeCo Corporation! Using the voice of NoNeCo gave me a chance to have a bit of in-canon fun, the readers loved it and so it soon became a bit of a tradition. Below are collected some of my favorite exchanges.

The first time I used the NoNeCo voice was actually to praise another reader. Not surprisingly for a sci-fi story involving android romance, a common question readers had was about whether Deacon was "anatomically correct". Here is commenter Peter Van Splunter's answer for that:

Peter Van Splunter   page 17

The android manufactorers are smart guys - they have to make sure their product is still sold if there's no unrest/war. So... why not make them multifunctional? Make love if there's no war :)

(and they just have to attach a sizeable yet simple part. After all, the steam-powered hips are already in place for the battle-stuff. Hurray for efficiency!)

NONECO CORPORATION

Hello Peter!

I see a bright future for you in NoNeCo's marketing department! Please contact HR with your holo-resume and your government mandated DNA psych profile and someone will be in touch with you about setting up an interview within the following 72 hours.

Thank you very much for your interest in the career opportunities of NoNeCo. Together we can help manufacture a brighter tomorrow!

Soon I found that voice could also be useful for answering story logic questions in a light-hearted manner. Something on the page seem to defy the laws of physics? NoNeCo has an app for that!

Vincent Miller   page 23

I am surprised that watercooler remained intact through all of that, thats some sturdy plastic. That and the conviently placed Robo-Recharge station they inexplicably have on Da Vinci Four. I guess Homocidal Kill Bots come through there alot, and that was installed in case they needed a pick-me-up. "Low battery putting a dampener on your blood thirsty murderous rampage? Not anymore!"

NONECO RESPONDS

NONECO CORPORATION

Thank you for your interest in the NoNeCo Universal Charging Platform. Unlike other charging systems on the market which require proprietary connectors and offer limited yields, the NUCP will work with any device you need to recharge—even our competitors'!—at nearly unlimited throughput. So whether you are topping off your anti-grav tank or just want to listen to your favorite tune one last time, you'll always have power when you need it.

Worried about your neighbors syphoning your juice and running up your power tab? Sleep easy! Just because the connection is universal doesn't mean it's open to all comers. Our highly customizable security protocols allow you to make sure that only those who should have power, get to have power.

We at NoNeCo understand that with great power comes great responsibility—and awesome performance! So, what are you waiting for? Contact our Sales Team to get your NUCP system installed today!

Jessica M. | page 42

I, for one, want to know how Deacon's suit is apparently defying gravity and not simply falling to the ground. I call shenanigans! Not possible! I demand you reinstate gravity immediately!

NONECO CORPORATION

Hello Jessica!

Thank you for your interest in NoNeCo's system-renowned sportswear line with HipHugger™ technology. Yes, it really is true! If, after a long workout, you find yourself overheated and in need of a cool down, you can simply pull the zipper of our FullFlex Jumpsuit down to the 75% position without fear of any unwanted "wardrobe malfunctions." In fact, you can completely expose your upper torso and adonis belt without the slightest risk of further slippage—even if you choose to continue to engage in vigorous activity! I myself own three of these suits and I'm delighted to tell you, it works like a charm.

As you know, these jumpsuits are limited edition items so please be sure to get your order in soon because they won't last long! I'm sure you'll find they will support you in your personal workouts in ways you've never experienced before.

Because together, we really can manufacture a brighter tomorrow!

Sometimes it was just fun to speculate how a corporation like NoNeCo would take advantage of some of my story conceits, such as my suggestion that it was possible that something as complex as sexual orientation could be predicted by detecting a change in a single chromosome:

Rors Lam | page 25

I never knew I had a c37 pair in my x chromosome, great to finally know. really enjoying the strip

NONECO CORPORATION

Thank you for your interest in NoNeCo Home Genomics and for letting us know that you are pleased with our premiere consumer product, My 5 Minute Assay. While we are always eager to respond to concerns and questions from our customers, it is certainly a delight to hear back when they are happy!

Thus, as VP of Marketing and Sales for NHG, it is my pleasure to send you a 10% off coupon for our other best-selling premiere consumer product, My 24 Hour Genetic Engineer. As I'm sure you are aware, with this product you can make safe, fast and effective alterations to your genetic code with plug-and-play ease! Many of society's leading lights have already used our Genetic Engineer products to banish facial wrinkles, enhance mathematical aptitude, increase the frequency of their erections and eliminate male pattern baldness.

We of course understand that our premiere products can be out of the price range of even highly successful customers like yourself, but having taken the liberty to pull your credit-income report, I feel confident that (with this coupon!) the cost of My 24 Hour Genetic Engineer is within your means. When you think of the fantastic possibilities such a product affords to enhance your life, surely that's worth at least three to four years of wages, no? And remember we offer the best credit terms of any division of NoNeCo!

I want to thank you again for taking the time to write us. Nothing is more valuable to us than our customers, especially outstanding and productive citizens like yourself. I truly believe that together, we are manufacturing a brighter tomorrow. :)

As readers realized what I was doing, many chose to participate in the reality of being able to speak to NoNeCo representatives directly. Of course, a common request was the desire to order a Deacon of their own!

Lance Williford   page 35

Winona captured Deacon's nervousness perfectly and uniquely. WTB a Deacon, btw... ;)

NONECO CORPORATION

I agree, Lance!

And a NoNeCo representative will be in contact with you in the next 24 hours to discuss your pre-order of our Advanced Soldiering Operative. The ASO is the perfect solution for all your security and military needs—whether you are protecting the interests of a small nation or merely looking to keep over-excited fans off the stage for your last set. While we currently have no release date for the ASO, please know that we are working hard to dot all the i's and cross all the t's to get these premium operatives out to preferred customers like yourself as soon as possible. Placing a deposit down now ensures that you'll be one of the first in line to take part in this evolutionary leap in artificial intelligence and security solutions.

Thank you again for your interest in NoNeCo Defense. Together we will manufacture a brighter tomorrow.

This was especially fun as it gave me an opportunity to play up the, ahem, darker side of a corporation-ruled galaxy:

Tiffany Santiago   page 46

Do you think I could get a Deacon for Christmas? It would truly make me the worlds happiest woman! Perhaps there's a discount or something lol!!

NONECO CORPORATION

Hello Tiffany!

Alas the D-Class ASO Model isn't yet shipping, so I can't speak to any promotions we might be offering during the Holiday season at this time. I will, say, however, that our credit terms here at NoNeCo Artificial Life are very flexible, with easy payment plans and the option of exchanging terms of servitude from those within your immediate family to make up for late payments, etc. thus placing one of these advanced, premium models within the reach of nearly any full citizen! I am certain that no matter what the final retail price turns out to be for your "Deacon," with a few swipes of your Contractual IdentiCard, we could arrange to have one placed under your Christmas tree in short order and with minimum hassle on your part.

Because together, we truly can manufacture a brighter tomorrow. :)

Readers had questions about Jeff as well. On page 52, one reader exclaimed it was "impossible" for Jeff's hair to look so nice after sex. NoNeCo representatives were happy to respond:

NONECO CORPORATION

Thank you very much for your question about our legacy styling pomade, Frozen Cashmere. And it's not impossible, it's cosmetic history!

While NoNeCo Cosmeceuticals no longer makes this product, its soft, natural shine and supernatural hold (originally designed for lunar miners in full EnviroSuits!) keeps it a popular item on the secondary market more than a decade later. With nanotech structural agents, it's child's play to maintain a beautiful shape with a resilient, soft hold! In fact, Frozen Cashmere provided complete protection against sweat and other fluids (as well as ionizing radiation up to twenty times what is considered safe for humans.)

If you like what you're seeing with Jeff's hair, please don't hate him—instead, please check out our most popular styling pomade, Vibrant Silk. It has all the hold that Frozen Cashmere had, but now includes NoNeCo's patented StyleMemory which allows you to program in up to seven different hair styles and have them emerge based on keywords or time of day. Now, not only will you have the ability to look great after sex—you'll be able to customize your look based on the partner and afterglow!

I hope this answers your question. And I very much hope you'll consider giving Vibrant Silk a try!

By the time the comic was entering its final act, readers had gotten so into the game that they decided to post comments in the voice of one of the characters! This was my favorite exchange and I can't think of a better way to wrap up this section:

Ayella page 75

Dear madam/sir,

Thank you for your apt response to my complaint. However, I have not - as you helpfully suggested - put my D3763 to uses the D model was not intended for. The user guide enclosed with it clearly stated that the D was entirely modeled after biological human beings, and (I quote) 'designed to experience the full range of human emotions and sensations'.

Also, I do not wish to make use of either solution you proffered. I wish to KEEP my D3763, as I already stated in my former letter, so neither an upgraded replacement model, nor a complete refund will suffice.

I simply wish for you to return to me what is rightfully mine. Furthermore, I demand that no unrequested alterations will be made to my D3763. I wish to have it back in EXACTLY the physical and psychological state it was before you repossessed it.

Of course I am deeply sorry for the loss of NoNeCo employees it caused and send my sincerest condolences to their families. Yet in my humble opinion it was NoNeCo's programming in the first place that caused it to behave in such a manner since it was (I quote again) 'designed to experience the full range of human emotions and sensations'.

I hereby give you three more working days to comply to my request. If my D3763 has not been returned to me by next Wednesday February 5th, I will have to take matters to a more legal level. Since my lawyer informs me I have an airtight case, I urgently advice you to meet my ultimatum, to prevent matters becoming any more unpleasant than they already are for all parties involved.

Regards,

Jeff

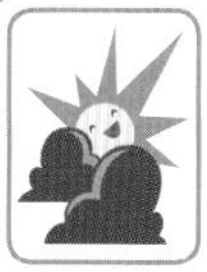

NONECO CORPORATION

Dear Jeff:

My name is Ben Tibble and I am the senior VP of customer relations here at NoNeCo Artificial Life. I am in receipt of your most recent correspondence to lower-level support and understand completely your distress and disappointment as the result of actions from our employees that can only be considered rash and ham-handed. Customer satisfaction is our utmost priority at NoNeCo and we have clearly failed you in this regard. Please accept my deepest apologies.

That said, I understand when you feel you've been wronged, an apology on its own rarely suffices. Of course, we both have legal options at our disposal. Your lawyer could involve the courts in an attempt to retrieve the property you feel is rightfully yours. We could instruct our own lawyers to sue you for breaching the terms of your non-disclosure agreement by involving this lawyer (an unauthorized third party) in this dispute.

(CONTINUED)

NONECO RESPONDS

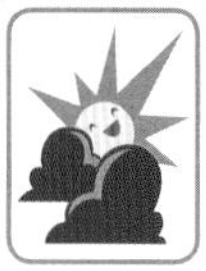

But really, I trust none of that will be necessary. And I believe we have a solution that will appeal to you.

Our testing of the D3763 prototype is nearly complete. Once I receive the go-ahead that our team has learned all we need to from these anomalies, we are perfectly comfortable with letting him go. But NoNeCo prides itself on outstanding customer service and after what you've been put through, I find merely replacing what was taken to be rather poor compensation.

Therefore, while you are waiting for us to finish our testing, I have authorized that an additional four C-model ASOs be dispatched immediately to your location in order to ensure that you get everything that you deserve. I have taken the liberty of using your HereIAM locator to pinpoint your position so you should see them arrive within moments after you finish reading this message. Noticing through your social listings that you are on retreat at a remote location, I can only imagine the relief and comfort that having four massively strong, nearly-human helpers can provide you and those with you.

And, as I am sure that after receiving this additional compensation you will no longer need the services of your lawyer, I would like to also provide your attorney and their office similar compensation as well for their trouble. After all, as a senior VP, I feel ultimately responsible for what's happened here. Would you mind sending their HereIAM code on to me? If you're too busy at the moment, no worries. I'm sure you can pass that code on to the C-models when they arrive. I think you'll find them to be even more diligent in fulfilling their orders than the D-model prototype you are acquainted with.

As always, thank you very much for your passionate support of the D-model project. I look forward to hearing that this solution has brought the entire matter to a satisfying conclusion.

Sincerely,

Ben Tibble
SVP, Customer Relations
NoNeCo Artificial Life

I'm just a regular guy with a regular day-job but I was able to raise money for printing this book through the very generous support of Kickstarter backers. Kickstarter is an online "crowd-funding" service that allows folks to donate money towards the completion of a creative project they believe in.

The printing of this book would not have happened without the amazingly generous support of the following awesome people. I am deeply grateful for what they have made possible. As far as I'm concerned, the Kickstarter backers and those who donated while the comic was running are the real heroes of *Artifice* and I thank them all from the bottom of my heart.

-Alex

Matthew Anthony

Janelle & Bob Billings

Emma Coats

Andrew D

Glenn Elliott

Danny Levitin

Martin Lochschmidt

George Luis

Justin Murdock

Daniel N.

R. Styles Randolph

Travis Riggs

Robyn Smith

Tom Armstrong & Vicino

Clidiane Aubourg

Sola Balisane

Lyndsey Bellamy

Stephen P. Berg

Pierre Blanchet

Nathan Blumberg

Frank Bramlett

M Briggs

Lydia Cannon

Anthony R. Cardno

Jennifer Cavenee

Thomas Dawkins

Brandon Eaker

Jami Eatmon

Thomas Felts

Ian Fox

Nathan Frazer

Joshua Glisson

Alison Hao

Joseph Hatfield

Johnathon Haywood

Ken Hollie

Robert Hulshof-Schmidt

Alexandra K.

Becky Kilfoyle

Ian Klein

Andy Lawson

James Massey

James Neill

Neil Patrick Harris

Paul Pedersen

Milena Popova

Sawyer Rankin

Victor S

Yve S.

Anne Schneider

Nicholas Sewell

Olivia Sexton

Cassandra Silvia

Cotina Spann

Eze Stryker

Aidan T

Chuck Taggart

John Tomlinson

Jeff Verona

Wayne Woods

Charles K. Alexander II
Sazz and Andy
Tanya Armstrong
Barbara B.
Bradley Baker
Amy Basnett Daughtry
Mark Baxter
Michele and Dustin Blue
Dan Boland
Gene Breshears
Peter R Brooks
Bobii Byers
Butch Charlebois
Ben Claycamp
Alicia Colón
Benoit Comanne
Randall & Anthony Cupp-Angelo
Mathieu Doublet
Kathryn E.
Linda E.
Claire Elliott
Christopher Enzi
Becky F
Patrick Fillion
Brandon Fox
Kerry Freeman
Ricky G
Alice G.

Ricky Gellissen
Jenn Green
Jon Harrison
Miranda Harvey
Frede Herstad
Denys Howard
Virginia Hull
Bee Hyde
Dannell Ivery
Autumn Jordan
Jenny K.
Daniel Kauwe
Sara Klitzke
Sheana Knight
Sabra Lovegrove
Jennifer M
gerG Maclaurin
Rowan McBride
Elanor McCaffery
W. Mo
Emily Morse
E. J. Murray
Kyrstin Myers
Sian Nelson
Jo Neri
Charles Nicolosi
J L Niehoff
E.K O
Dario Parente

Katie Parnell
Jacob Pauli
Kat R.
Wong Si-Lin Rebecca
Gabriel Rodriguez
Damian Rogan
Minia Roth
Edna Ann Rouse
Joe Ruhnke
Boris Sbarufatti
Michael Shumate
D. Simmons
Tom Stermer
Brynn Stott-Cohen
Jim Swarts
Andrew T.
Helen & Norm Taylor
Ziel Toft
Larisa VanWinkle
Jennifer Volintine
Brian W
Rachel Walker
Kirsten Wallace
Julian White
Dieter Wolfram
Cynthia Wood
Alexandra Z.
Kelli Zielinski

$60+ BACKERS

ABOUT THE CREATORS

Alex Woolfson
Writer/Publisher, AMW Comics

Alex Woolfson dictated his first action story, the as yet unpublished "Detective Dan and Super Detective Sandy," to his mother at the age of six. His mother was very impressed, thus inspiring in Alex a life-long love of making up bromance stories for women and other cool folk to enjoy. In his teens and twenties, he wrote and directed plays and films involving demons and first kisses. Then, in 2006, he launched the Yaoi 911 comics project with the goal of creating adventure stories for women and men featuring heroes who just happened to like other guys.

Alex currently lives in the Bay Area and hopes someday to own a sweet, cuddly dog the size of a small elephant.

Artifice is his first graphic novel.

Winona Nelson
Artist

Winona Nelson was created in Wisconsin in 1983 and raised in Duluth, Minnesota. The result of genetic experimentation combining an abstract painter mother and wildlife artist father, this specimen began drawing as a toddler.

As a juvenile, she was strategically exposed to science fiction and fantasy movies, books, and video games. By adolescence, successful influence implantation resulted in a decision to go into art for games and comics. Winona was then programmed in classical realism at the Safehouse Atelier in San Francisco and put to work as a concept artist and character designer in Bay Area game studios.

She has now morphed into freelance form and works in book covers, game and card art, and comics. ***Artifice*** is her first graphic novel. Winona lives and works in Philadelphia with fellow artist specimen Anthony Palumbo, under the scrutiny of their surveillance and control cat, Diego-tron.

To read more of Alex's comics for free, please visit amwcomics.com